AN INTRODUCTION TO
GREAT WESTERN

LOCOMOTIVE DEVELOPMENT

AN INTRODUCTION TO
GREAT WESTERN
LOCOMOTIVE DEVELOPMENT

JIM CHAMP

PEN & SWORD
TRANSPORT

To my grandfather, J.R. Cory, one time premium apprentice on the Metropolitan Railway, who grew up beside the Great Western Railway.

First published in Great Britain in 2018 by
PEN & SWORD TRANSPORT
An imprint of Pen & Sword Books Ltd
Yorkshire - Philadelphia

Copyright © Jim Champ, 2018

ISBN 978 1 47387 783 2

The right of Jim Champ to be identified as
Author of this work has been asserted by them in accordance
with the Copyright, Designs and Patents Act 1988.

A CIP catalogue record for this book is available from the British Library

Typeset in Sabon LT Std 11/14
Typeset by Aura Technology and Software Services, India
Pinted and bound in the UK by CPI Group (UK) Ltd., Croydon, CR0 4YY

Pen & Sword Books Ltd incorporates the Imprints of Aviation, Atlas, Family History, Fiction,
Maritime, Military, Discovery, Politics, History, Archaeology, Select, Wharncliffe Local
History, Wharncliffe True Crime, Military Classics, Wharncliffe Transport, Leo Cooper,
The Praetorian Press, Remember When, Seaforth Publishing and Frontline Publishing.

For a complete list of Pen & Sword titles please contact
PEN & SWORD BOOKS LTD
47 Church Street, Barnsley, South Yorkshire, S70 2AS, England
E-mail: enquiries@pen-and-sword.co.uk
Website: www.pen-and-sword.co.uk

Or
PEN AND SWORD BOOKS
1950 Lawrence Rd, Havertown, PA 19083, USA
E-mail: Uspen-and-sword@casematepublishers.com
Website: www.penandswordbooks.com

Contents

Acknowledgements

The root of this volume is in an article I wrote for the GWR modelling web site. I became fascinated by the complexities of the various pannier tank classes, and started writing them up to clarify my own understanding. When I had completed that, I felt there was enough to be worth sharing. In order to deal with the challenges of copyright, I redrafted various drawings, and learned a great deal from doing it. Some more articles followed. So I must pay tribute to Mikkel Kjartan and Russ Elliot, successive editors of GWR Modelling http://www.gwr.org.uk, who kindly gave me a platform, and also John Daniel's *Great Western Archive*, http://www.greatwestern.org.uk/, which first inspired me. I must also thank Les Summers, who suggested presenting the sketches with shading rather than as plain line drawings. In addition to that I must give credit to Don Ashton, who has helped me with understanding valve gears and other details, the various authors I've used as sources, and many contributors to the GWR E-list on Yahoo groups, who have answered various questions over the years.

Introduction

When I started becoming interested in modelling the Great Western Railway, I discovered that there seemed to be no single source which gave a general introduction to their locomotive fleet. So I started to acquire books. Some hundreds of pounds later, I have more detail than I ever believed I needed. So this volume is intended to provide the general introduction that I couldn't find.

The Text

There is no new research here, although there are occasions when I present my own interpretation on matters and I hope those instances are all made clear. I am strictly looking over the shoulders of giants, seeing nothing they have not seen more clearly. My key sources are:

- The Railway Correspondence and Travel Society Series, *The Locomotives of the Great Western Railway*. Fourteen small paperback/pamphlet volumes, published from 1951 to 1993. Essential for the serious student of the subject.
- J.H. Russell's *A Pictorial Record of Great Western Engines*, published in three coffee table sized volumes in various editions from 1975 to 1999 by OPC. Seed material for many of my sketches, plus many more. Many photos, and an important companion to the RCTS series.
- Harry Holcroft's *An Outline of Great Western Locomotive Practice*, published by Ian Allen in 1971. Holcroft trained on the GWR and worked for Churchward on the later standard locomotives. He later worked for the SECR and Southern Railways, and also collaborated with Gresley on valve gears.

- K J Cook's *Swindon Steam*, published by Ian Allen in 1974. Cook was assistant head and then head of the works through much of the Collett and Hawksworth eras and later succeeded Hawksworth as Western Region Chief Mechanical Engineer. He finished his career as North Eastern & Eastern Region CME, so was effectively a successor of both Churchward and Gresley.

The majority of material comes from the RCTS volumes.

I hope that I have made a satisfactory distillation of my predecessors' work into a useful introduction to the topic. From here – well, I don't believe you will be disappointed if you obtain the above volumes, but there are many more, most notably various monographs on individual classes and groups of classes.

The most limited part of this work is the coverage of nineteenth century and absorbed classes, in particular those that did not survive well into the twentieth century. I have taken the view that most enthusiasts will have the twentieth century as their primary interest. There was an enormous amount of complexity in the early classes, their rebuilds and renewals; I believe that a brief paragraph on most classes is sufficient for this volume. The list is not exhaustive either; some classes and especially individual locomotives have simply been omitted.

A quick note on tractive effort; this highly nominal and theoretically based figure may be given undue importance. Cylinders were rebored when worn, and, for example, nominal 18½in cylinders were not scrapped until they had been bored out to over 19in. Tractive effort figures recorded in this volume are rounded to the nearest 500lbs.

The Sketches

Every line drawing in this volume has been redrawn into a reasonably consistent format.

The originals came from a variety of sources, but the foundation of many were Great Western weight diagrams as, for example, reproduced in Russell's *A Pictorial Record of Great Western Engines*. Other sources include weight diagrams and general arrangement diagrams from the *Great Western Railway Journal*, the NRM archives, the RCTS volumes, and E.L. Ahrons drawings from various books.

The sketches are not simple tracings of the original drawings. In most cases, detail has been added from other sources, drawings have been combined and components copied from different drawings where they were suitable. I also checked details against my own and published photographs and there have been occasions when I've got on the bike and ridden over to Didcot or elsewhere to clarify details.

They are shaded to give a three dimensional effect. The shading is primarily for texture, but in most cases the shading should not be completely incompatible with the original paint colours. Cabside numbers shown are, in almost all cases, the number by which the class was known. The sketches are never intended to represent an individual locomotive on a particular date and there will be plenty of cases where the sketch shows a combination of features that was never found on the locomotive with the number shown. The reason for drawing numbers, and in some cases names, was simply that the sketches looked better with numbers rather than blank plates.

They are provided strictly for comparison, and to aid this the smaller types are reproduced to a larger size, although each wheel arrangement is drawn to a consistent scale. Accuracy varies considerably. Original drawings may have become damaged or distorted over the years and scanning and redrawing the drawings, be it from the pages of a book or by NRM facilities, introduces further distortion. I also have doubts about the accuracy of the original drawings. Weight diagrams especially were neither intended nor used for construction or maintenance. Thus, I don't think a sometimes hard-pressed drawing office would always have drawn them to the limits of accuracy. I sometimes see what seem to me to be clear errors. The actual accuracy is going to be variable from sketch to sketch, but it's certainly no better than the nearest scale inch and may sometimes be several inches out.

The amount of detail shown varies according to what was reliably available in the sources available for each locomotive. Weight diagrams tend to omit valve gear, ash pans, brake gear and sand boxes. Inside motion is largely omitted, which has the effect of making many of the earlier classes, especially double framed ones, look decidedly bald between the front pairs of wheels. If I am not confident in a fitting I have tended to omit it. Brake gear seems to be an especial problem since changes were not uncommon; some of the third party drawings show hangers that are not supported by photographic evidence. Wheel spokes are difficult too, but as far as possible at least the number of spokes is correct. Most of all I have not dared to include rivets!

This seems to have significant implications for the fine scale modeller. Weight diagrams are only of very limited use, and great care would need to be taken before scaling dimensions from them. Indeed, back in the day the drawing office staff were trained never to scale from any drawings, but only to use listed dimensions. Where possible the full engineering drawings, as used by the factory to manufacture the components, will always be a better option. One must also bear in mind that steam locomotives were not mass produced, but built in batches, often over a period of years. Minor fittings frequently varied in position. Details varied between lots, and might be updated later: what is shown on original GWR drawings is sometimes different from what can be seen on preserved locomotives now.

I must repeat the advice given by J H Russell in his introduction to his books. He quotes J N Maskeleyne who said in 1935:

'If a model or drawing is to be made, be careful to have at hand a photograph showing the particular engine concerned, and of the period in time desired, as every engine seemed to differ in some way ... watch out for the small details. Boiler fittings are always suspect, chimneys in particular, so always try and make the fittings please the eye and look like the photograph ... Also use the drawings with caution ... a drawn line does not prove authenticity.'

On the other hand, I can thoroughly recommend this exercise to new modellers. Redrawing the item you are planning to model is an excellent way to gain a much improved understanding of how the object is put together and how the parts relate to each other, and with modern IT facilities is a quicker exercise than you might think, certainly far faster than doing it with pen and paper as our grandfathers did. It is a continual surprise to me how much you learn from drawing something. Of course, you learn even more by making the model, but it can be a bit late by then! If you can look at these sketches and gain a greater understanding of how these locomotives evolved over the years then I will have achieved my aims, but if you use them as the main source for anything beyond simple representational modelling then I have done you a disfavour by creating them.

CHAPTER 1

Overview

Maintenance and Appearance

Many of the variations in the appearance of individual locomotives were related to maintenance practices. When a major overhaul was due, the Great Western would dismantle a locomotive virtually down to its component parts. The boiler would normally take longer to repair than the rest of the locomotive, so, by the beginning of the twentieth century, an alternative boiler (and, with saddle and pannier tanks, matching water tanks) would be fitted as soon as

Didcot Railway Centre. *Still very much a typical 20thC GWR running shed. (Photo: Jim Champ)*

the rest of the locomotive was ready, in order to bring the locomotive back into service. Because of the interchangeability of boilers, this boiler might well not be the same design (or even class) as the one that came off. A locomotive might be rebuilt with pannier tanks at one major overhaul, yet revert to saddle tanks at the next one, depending on what was available. Over the years, the earlier boiler classes went out of use – no new Standard Goods, Sir Daniel or Metro boilers were built after the 1920s for instance – and so the amount of variation tended to reduce. If enlarged coal bunkers or a better cab were required, especially on the older classes, then it appears that the works involved might simply construct something that fitted in their current style, rather than refer to Swindon for an official new design. This sort of variation is especially marked on the nineteenth century tank engine classes.

The Design Schools – Swindon and Wolverhampton

There is very little new in the world and internal politics and personalities had as much to do with the way things developed on the GWR in the nineteenth century as they do in companies and government today.

There was always something of a split between the Northern division and the Southern division of the GWR. The Southern Division could very simplistically be described as the lines built by Brunel and their extensions and amalgamations, and was originally mainly broad gauge. The Northern division was formed around the West Midland Railway, absorbed (or technically amalgamated) in 1854, which was in itself an amalgamation of several previous lines, and was principally standard gauge. With the West Midland came its works at Stafford Road, Wolverhampton, and its locomotive superintendent, Joseph Armstrong. Armstrong was from Newcastle, and had known Stephenson and Hackworth from his youth. He had already worked for a wide variety of lines, including the Liverpool & Manchester and London & Brighton. He became the deputy locomotive superintendent of the Northern section, reporting only to Gooch.

When Gooch resigned at Swindon, Joseph Armstrong was promoted to locomotive superintendent of the GWR at Swindon in 1864 and his younger brother George took the post of Northern Division locomotive superintendent. George's assistant was William Dean, who was moved to Swindon to be Joseph's assistant in 1868. Dean brought with him his own assistant, William H. Stanier, whose eldest son William Arthur was to have no mean railway career.

Joseph Armstrong died in 1887, and Dean was promoted, effectively over George Armstrong's head, to be Joseph's successor. George is recorded as having stated he had no intention of taking orders from anyone and Dean appears not to have attempted to give orders to his one-time boss. George eventually retired in 1897 at the age of seventy-five.

Thus, in the earlier days of the GWR Swindon built broad gauge and Wolverhampton standard gauge locomotives. As the broad gauge faded, Swindon took on standard gauge as well, and came to be run by Wolverhampton trained staff. However the two factories were very independent with their own design teams and practices until George Armstrong retired.

In the Armstrong era a locomotive rebuilt at Wolverhampton would be appreciably different to one rebuilt at Swindon. One particular detail was in the copper chimney cap. Wolverhampton favoured what is generally known as a rolled top, which was less flared than the Swindon style and had a lip with a more rounded profile. The majority of rolled chimney caps were replaced shortly after George Armstrong retired, but some may have survived as late as 1906. In minor details such as the shape of bunkers on tank engines, Wolverhampton styled features persisted as late as the 1920s.

When Dean retired in 1902, he was succeeded by Churchward, who had started his career with the South Devon Railway. Churchward brought all the design under the Swindon umbrella and the independence of Wolverhampton was greatly reduced. The last new locomotives built there were a batch of Swindon-designed small prairies in 1908.

Churchward was succeeded by Collett, who was recruited after serving an apprenticeship with the marine engineering firm of Maudslay, Sons and Field in London, so Hawksworth in 1941 was the first Swindon trained CME! It is important, though, not to get too focussed on the CME. The design of something as complex as a steam locomotive was a team effort; it was not a case of the chief mechanical engineer beavering away on his personal drawing board. The Chief Mechanical Engineer was a senior executive of a large concern, with many responsibilities, and some were notably much more hands-on than others. In 1935, the CME's department on the GWR employed over 30,000 men and women. The head of such an organisation simply could not spend much time bent over a drawing board, no matter how much he might like to.

Standard Locomotives

Gooch and Dean

Standardisation came early to the Great Western. Daniel Gooch ordered standard locomotives in 1840 and was known to reject them if they didn't adequately conform to the specified dimensions.

The use of standard components across multiple classes really started during the Dean era, even though locomotive design was going through rapid change at the end of the nineteenth century. There were a group of four classes built from 1884 to 1888 (3201 2-4-0, 3501 2-4-0T, 2361 0-6-0 and 1661 0-6-0T), which had many components in common, most notably motion. A little later on the larger outside frame 4-4-0s (Duke, Bulldog, Badminton and Atbara) also comprised a group with many standardised components, and the amount of standardisation increased over the course of their lives. The standard parts included cylinders, pistons, crossheads, connecting rods and their two sizes of wheel.

The Churchward Standard Classes

Churchward was the great apostle of standardisation. In January 1901, whilst Dean was still nominally in charge, he produced his well-known table of six proposed standard types.

Type	2-8-0	4-6-0	4-6-0	2-6-2T	4-4-2T	4-4-0
Engine No.	97	-	98	99	2221	3473
Date of first engine	June 1903	-	March 1903	Sept 1903	Dec 1905	May 1904
Boiler:-						
Length of Barrel	15 ft. 0 in.	15 ft. 0 in.	15 ft. 0 in.	11 ft. 2 in.	11 ft. 2 in.	11 ft. 2 in.
Diameter of Barrel	5 ft. 0 in.	5 ft. 0 in.	5 ft. 0 in.	5 ft. 0 in.	5 ft. 0 in.	5 ft. 0 in.
Length of Firebox	9 ft. 0 in.	9 ft. 0 in.	9 ft. 0 in.	8 ft. 0 in.	8 ft. 0 in.	8 ft. 0 in.
Length of connecting rods	10 ft. 8½ in.	10 ft. 8½ in.	10 ft. 8½ in.	6 ft. 10½ in.	6 ft. 10½ in.	6 ft. 10½ in.
Wheels:-						
Diameter of pony or bogie	3 ft. 3 in.	3 ft. 3 in.	3 ft. 3 in.	3 ft. 3 in.	3 ft. 3 in.	3 ft. 3 in.
Diameter of coupled	4 ft. 7½ in.	5 ft. 8 in.	6 ft. 8½ in.	5 ft. 8 in.	6 ft. 8½ in.	6 ft. 8½ in.
Diameter of Radial	-	-	-	3 ft. 3 in.	3 ft. 3 in.	-
Cylinders, one pattern for all types	18 in. diameter x 30 in. stroke with 8½ in. diameter piston valves					

In this original plan, a single boiler with an 8ft long firebox was envisaged for 8 wheel locomotives, but this would have been too heavy, especially for the tank engines. A 7ft firebox boiler, thinner and lighter than the proposed standard, was already being introduced on the later outside frame 4-4-0s and this boiler was developed as the Standard 2, whilst the same length firebox was matched to the new standard diameter barrel to produce the higher capacity but heavier Standard 4 on the Cities. Five of the six types were put into production, but the last, a 4-6-0 with 5ft 8in wheels was not immediately progressed with. Collett introduced the mixed traffic 4-6-0 Churchward had envisaged, first with 6ft diameter wheels as the Hall Class, and then, reusing standard components from Churchward 2-6-0s, the Granges.

Perhaps more important than standard wheel sizes and other headline dimensions was that what we would now call consumable parts, components that needed to be held at the running sheds and replaced regularly, were very standardised. This meant that the running sheds needed to keep a relatively small stock of such components, which brought savings in the value of spares stock held, the administrative complications of managing and supplying the spares stock, and even the storage required at the sheds. There were various components – fusible plugs and vacuum pump components were among them – which were standard across the entire fleet.

The key development work for the standard classes was done around 1902 to 1905, mainly with the 4-6-0 Saint class express locomotives and the 2-8-0 2800 class heavy freight class. The first outside cylinder 4-6-0, no. 100, was something of a prototype, and had significant differences from the eventual standard. No 100, as built in 1902, had a parallel boiler with a raised firebox, inside frames and outside cylinders. It was quite different to anything seen on the GWR before. Some of the design features, like the wheelbase, were to be perpetuated for over forty years, but valve gear, cylinders and other vital components were different to the later standard.

Churchward was an integrator rather than an inventor, and his locomotives took the best from many sources, both British and, unusually for his time, overseas. His standard locomotives contain ideas that are readily traced back to American, French and Prussian sources mixed with contemporary British and traditional Great Western practice. The result was a harmonious whole that was very much more than the sum of its parts, and was to influence design in the UK until the end of steam and beyond.

The first real standard locomotives were nos. 97 and 98, the first true Saint and the 2-8-0 prototype. They were built and developed together, and had many parts in common. The most obvious difference was the short cone tapered boiler with 200psi working pressure, but perhaps more important was the front end layout, which was quite different to No. 100. The cylinders consisted of a pair of identical castings, bolted back to back, which incorporated cylinders, piston valves and all the main steam passages together with the saddle that the boiler was mounted on. The main frames stopped short of the cylinders, and separate 'extension frames' were bolted on to carry on to the front of the locomotive. The extension frames were really bar frames, made from much thicker steel than normal plate frames, but of reduced depth. This reduced depth was driven by the cylinder layout.

Essentially the same front end was to be used on some thousands of other locomotives of getting on for a dozen different classes. This led to an important design detail – the cylinders had to be aligned an inch and a half above the centreline of the wheels in order to provide sufficient clearance for the 2-8-0 cylinders against the loading gauge. The locomotives had generously sized valves for the period and long travel valve gear.

In 1910, Churchward started to think about locomotives for secondary lines, as the new standards were filling all requirements for main line services. We know from Holcroft's memoirs that he was thinking on the lines of inside cylinder inside frame types with large diameter piston valves above the cylinders, but that this concept turned out to be impractical. Holcroft had recently visited Canada, and had been struck by how the 2-6-0 type was used as a maid of all work on secondary lines, and on his return suggested that something of the sort should be considered on the GWR.

Holcroft wrote that after some thought Churchward came into the drawing office and 'on reaching my board he said: "Very well then; get me out a 2-6-0 with 5ft 8in wheels, outside cylinders, the No. 4 boiler and bring in all the standard features you can." With that he departed, and it was the end of the matter as far as he was concerned.' This was the genesis of the 4300 class 2-6-0.

Another aspect of standardisation was in maintenance. By the 1930s, Swindon works had very sophisticated equipment for measuring and aligning locomotive frames, and made extensive use of jigs to ensure components were truly interchangeable. On the two cylinder standard classes this permitted the factory to pre-assemble complete units of cylinders and extension frames. When a locomotive requiring new cylinders came into the works the old extension frames were unbolted and the new unit, called by the factory a new front end, installed in its place. The result was much reduced time out of service in the works, with only a marginal increase in repair costs.

Churchward's Successors

Churchward's designs were essentially found satisfactory for their designated roles by his successors. But requirements changed and traffic changed. Most new designs were associated with a need to provide more powerful locomotives, coupled with the requirement to adhere to the varying weight restrictions on different parts of the route network.

To meet these restrictions not all locomotives were allowed in all locations. A basic system was formalised in the Churchward era, and the GWR lines and locomotives were divided into four groups, uncoloured (axle load up to 14 tons), Yellow (max 16 tons), Blue (max 17tons 12cwt), and Red (max 20 tons). To this was later added Double Red (max 22½ tons, which in practice was just the King class). The track was similarly categorised, with a couple of intermediate classes in which heavier axle loads were permitted at reduced speed. There was much more to route restrictions, with all sorts of local restrictions for factors like physical clearance.

The locomotive stock was also divided into power classes, and every section of line had permitted maximum loads for locomotives of different power classes. There were eventually seven power classes which roughly corresponded to tractive effort, Ungrouped (up to 16,500lbs) being the lowest, going through A (18,500), B (20,500), C (25,000) D (33,000), E (38,000) and special (>38,000 and again just the King class).

These weight limits were a particular problem for the more powerful locomotives produced in the Collett and Hawksworth regimes. Various new and modified classes were strongly influenced by weight restrictions, notably the King, Manor and 1600 classes.

Boilers

'The modern Locomotive Question is principally a matter of boiler'.

G.J. Churchward, 1906.

Boilers were the subject of continuous development, especially until the end of the Churchward era. It's surely a mistake to think that a Dean Goods (P class) boiler constructed in 1884, pressed to 140psi with a round top firebox and 268 1½in diameter tubes, had much in common with the last of the type, pressed to 200psi with Belpaire firebox, 219 1⅝in and 2 5⅛in tubes, which were still being built as late as 1950.

This volume uses the GWR classification system for boilers, originated under Churchward, which divided boilers into classes based on the physical size of the boiler and thus which locomotives it would fit. This system consisted of a two letter code but for the purposes of this volume only the first letter, or an associated name, is used. The first letter is normally regarded as the boiler class, and indicated the principle dimensions of the boiler. The second letter can be regarded as a subclass, and in some cases there were twenty or more of these. Differences between subclasses could include superheat (presence and degree), firebox type, and water feed type and location. Subtler details like minor variations in dimensions and the presence or absence of brackets to locate the boiler or tanks (influencing on exactly which classes a boiler could be fitted to) were also reflected in subclasses. Most of the classes also had names, usually either a standard number, or else that of a class associated with the boiler. There were nearly 30 of these classes, and some letters were reused after the original type became extinct.

Another system which will be encountered is that used in the RCTS volumes. This complex system enables classification of the appearance of boilers, and is usually one or more letters followed by a number, which describe firebox type and dome location (or absence). The RCTS volumes further allocate boilers to over 100 'Groups', which are boilers of substantially similar type. The two systems have very little overlap. RCTS classifies boilers from several different classes as being R3 or D4 and in groups some contain boilers of more than one GWR sub class and vice versa.

Boiler Development: Gooch, Armstrongs and Dean

Broad gauge boilers were typically domeless with raised dome topped and later round topped fireboxes.

On the narrow (standard) gauge, boilers with domes and without raised fireboxes appeared with Joseph Armstrong's 360 class goods type of 1866. Under the Armstrongs and William Dean these parallel boilers without raised fireboxes were the dominant type. The 0-6-0 Standard Goods and the Sir Daniel class 2-2-2 classes, built the same year, introduced what turned out to be the first of the standard boiler classes – boilers based on those for these classes were in use seventy years later.

The general trend of things on the GWR was that, by the 1860s and 1870s, domes were mainly fitted towards the front of the boiler, with a round top firebox flush with the boiler. The next trend was for the dome to move towards the rear of the boiler barrel, appearing to be central between cab and funnel. There was also a period around 1880 when domeless parallel boilers were favoured. This was followed by raised round top fireboxes – a broad gauge feature – on a few classes. Another trend was smokebox length. Early smokeboxes were very short, but over time they grew longer, often with the chimney position unaltered so it appeared to be set back on the smokebox.

The style of smokebox also changed. Earlier smokeboxes were complex fabrications which incorporated boiler supports which met the frames. They might incorporate wing plates – lateral plates extending out towards the side of the frames – but these went out of use towards the end of the nineteenth century.

A subtle change was the position of the water feed into the boiler. This appears in all sorts of places, on the back of the firebox, at the side of the boiler, and finally, under Churchward, top feed. This apparently small detail has a big influence on the life and maintenance requirements of the boiler.

Boiler pressures increased throughout the history of the GWR. In the 1870s around 140psi was typical, increasing to 180psi by the turn of the century. Under Churchward 200psi or 225psi was most common, whilst Collett introduced 250psi boilers in the King Class, and Hawksworth, less successfully, 280psi boilers on the 10xx County Class.

Churchward

Churchward was the major innovator when it came to boilers and is considered to have taken charge of boiler development towards the end of the Dean era. Soon after he was appointed chief assistant to Dean, Belpaire fireboxes appeared on a few classes. Next, the Belpaire fireboxes were raised, some by as much as eight inches above the boiler. In many cases the dome was eliminated and the steam feed taken from the corners of the firebox. Finally, the barrel was tapered up to the raised firebox, still without the dome, strongly influenced, it is believed, by the Brooks Locomotive Works of the USA.

This was definitely a series of trends, not a fixed cycle. The raised Belpaire firebox with parallel boiler in particular seems to have been an intermediate stage, not found on classes that retained parallel boilers by the mid twentieth century. There were also classes that moved 'backwards' in the cycle; the final design of M class boiler on the Dean Single regained a dome alongside a raised Belpaire firebox. The design progression appears to have been worked out mainly with the 4-4-0s and then the early 4-6-0s.

At the same time, there was also much development of the earlier parallel boiler types. The development of these is much less obvious to the casual eye, but it is clear that there was a great deal of design work carried out with all sorts of variations in tube layout and, perhaps even more important, subtleties like the width of the water space in the firebox, which profoundly affected water circulation. Although various domeless types were tried, it seems clear that the designers concluded that on locomotives where there was room to make them of generous size, the increase in steam space and freedom from priming provided by the dome justified the moderate cost in weight. Thus, by the end of the GWR, all standard parallel boilers were low set and had large domes, and all taper boilers were tall, without domes and collected steam from the corners of the firebox.

By the start of the twentieth century, most boiler barrels were constructed in two sections – presumably reflecting the practicalities of manufacturing the plates. Standard No 1 boilers were constructed in two roughly equal length pieces. Initially – short cone boilers – these had a tapered portion against the firebox and a parallel portion against the smokebox. Fairly soon, however, they were made from two tapered portions of equal length. Later, large boilers followed the same pattern. Shorter boilers, such as the Standard 4, had a longer tapered section and a shorter parallel section at the front. *The Great Bear*'s freakishly long boiler barrel was made from three sections – a coned section between larger and smaller diameter parallel ones.

Other Churchward developments included top feed and superheating. Top feed meant that boiler water was introduced through the top of the boiler and delivered onto trays. These trays sloped down to the front of the boiler barrel where they had notched ends so that the water fell onto the main body of water in the barrel in a series of fine streams. This led to increased boiler life because air in the feed water was released into the steam space, reducing corrosion of boiler components, scale and sludge was deposited in the trays, and the water was delivered into the coolest part of the boiler, minimising cooling of firebox and tubes.

In the early twentieth century, the major development was superheating. A 'saturated' boiler normally has all the fire tubes of around the same size, on the GWR typically between 1⅝in and 2in. In a superheated boiler, a number of rows of the small tubes are replaced by fewer rows of fewer large tubes, on the GWR typically a bit over 5in. Superheater 'elements' are inserted into these large diameter tubes. These are normally tubes in a U shaped arrangement, about the length of the barrel, and on the GWR there were usually four or six of them in each large tube. After the steam leaves the main boiler space, it passes through the regulator and then these tubes on the way to the cylinders. Steam in the main boiler will not heat to above the boiling point of water because of the presence of liquid water, but there is no liquid water in the superheater and the temperature of the steam may be considerably increased, which increases both the power and efficiency of the locomotive.

The primary drawback to the increased steam temperature is lubrication. The high temperatures tend to carbonise the oil, and so more oil is required to maintain adequate lubrication and the steam passages, valves and pistons become coated with carbon. After early experiments with a higher degree of superheat, Churchward opted to use only moderate superheat, and as a result his locomotives experienced less carbonisation than was seen on other lines. Churchward's superheater design permitted no more than two row of tubes and this was the arrangement on larger boilers, whilst smaller boilers such as those fitted to Dean Goods had only one row. The two row restriction made maintenance much easier, since any element could be removed without disturbing any other.

Churchward is often criticised over the relatively low degree of superheat he used, but he was one of, if not *the* first to introduce it in the United Kingdom and by 1914 the GWR had many more superheated locomotives than any other British railway. The eventual steam temperature is related to both steam pressure and degree of superheat. Other lines reduced steam pressure with their early superheated boilers with a view to reducing costs, whilst the GWR was increasing their boiler pressure and with it the boiler efficiency. Churchward was using 225psi on Standard 1 boilers, which was well above that used on other lines. We can be certain that Churchward's team did extensive testing before the degree of superheat was decided on. It is hard to believe that what they did was not optimal at that time.

Superheating also affected the smokebox size. The ends of the superheater elements and the connecting pipework meant that chimneys had to move forward to accommodate this equipment, sometimes with a further lengthening of the smokebox. Churchward also introduced the drum type smokebox. The complex fabrications of earlier smokeboxes could be difficult to keep airtight. The drum smokebox was a simple cylinder which was much easier to maintain. It did require a fabricated saddle underneath to support the boiler, but in the case of the standard two cylinder locomotives this saddle was cast as part of the cylinder casting, which further reduced the number of joints to keep air and steam tight. A few very long smokeboxes could be observed which were constructed to enable a short boiler to fit on the locomotive. The prototype 4700, which had to run with the much shorter Standard 1 boiler until the Standard 7 was available, was an example.

Another significant design factor is weight. The use of the Standard 2 and Standard 4 boilers to keep the weight – and thus axle loading and route availability – within bounds on some classes has already been mentioned, but in general his locomotives were within the available limits. However, after the First World War, schemes were drafted for uprating 2800, 2900 and 4000 classes with the Standard 7 boiler. These would have been very potent locomotives, but the enlarged Saint and Star designs could not be managed within the required weight limits.

Collett

Collett immediately ran into the problems with weight that had prevented Churchward from upgrading Stars and Saints with Standard 7 boilers. The Castle's Standard 8 boiler was effectively a Standard 7 with a smaller diameter barrel, intermediate between the Standard 1 and the Standard 7, and brought the locomotive right up to the weight limit. The King's Standard 12 was an enlarged Standard 7 with longer barrel and firebox built up to a new weight limit. The Manor brought another problem, since it required a higher capacity boiler (and especially a larger firebox and grate area) than the Standard 4 of the 4300 it was replacing. However, the locos needed to be significantly lighter than their sisters, the Granges with Standard 1 boilers, so the all new Standard 14 had to be designed. It came between a Standard 2 and a Standard 1 in all the main dimensions. Collett also introduced high tensile strength nickel alloy steel to build some boilers, mainly Standard 2 for 2-6-2 tanks, of higher pressure but no extra weight.

Collett's other problem was several hundred absorbed locomotives with what must have seemed like several hundred designs of boiler. GWR maintenance practice required a stock of spare boilers, and it would have been impractical to hold spares of so many different types. So three of the standard boiler designs were modified, producing Standard boilers 9, 10 and 11, which were based on the older types but with shorter and longer fireboxes. The Standard 10 was later used on a number of new GWR classes.

Hawksworth

Hawksworth's team must have had similar difficulties in keeping weight within limits when designing the 10xx County 4-6-0s. A Standard 8 Castle boiler would presumably have been a possibility, especially if Hawksworth could have accepted the lower boiler pressure, but tooling was available from building LMS 8F (hence William Arthur Stanier-designed) boilers for the Ministry of Defence and this was used to build a noticeably shorter and fatter boiler than the GWR designs, the Standard 15.

Collett had followed Churchward's lead in using only moderate superheat even when better lubricants were available. With the good quality coal available to the GWR in the 1930s this brought no steaming problems and reduced usage of lubricating oil. Oil consumption was a significant expense, enough to be listed separately in the company's annual accounts.

During and after the Second World War, however, the quality of coal available diminished significantly and higher degrees of superheat were introduced, together with changes to the lubrication systems which increased oil consumption. Standard 1 boilers with three rows of superheater tubes were introduced on the modified Hall class in 1944. These had about 20% extra superheater heating surface and 5% less surface area in the fire tubes. All 10xx Counties had three row superheaters. New Castles had three row superheaters from 1946 and four row superheaters were introduced on Castles in 1947 and Kings in 1948. Some three row superheated Standard 4 boilers were built in 1958-60. Superheated Standard 2 boilers had originally been built with two rows of elements, but changed to one row from 1917. 2 row superheater Standard 2 boilers were re-introduced in 1948.

Wheels and Hammer Blow

Railway wheels are constructed with steel tyres. In service the tyres wear, and wheels must be put on a lathe and turned to restore the correct profile until they wear beyond safe limits and must be replaced. Tyres were not replaced until there had been an inch or more loss of thickness through re-turning and wear. Thus actual wheel diameters could be up to two inches less than the nominal size.

Early tyres were relatively thin, but during the 1890s the thickness of new tyres was increased twice, increasing wheel diameter since the wheel centres were left unchanged. Nominal 4ft 6in wheels went to 4ft 7in and then 4ft 7½in, and nominal 5ft 0in wheels to 5ft 1in and then 5ft 2in, with similar changes for other standard sizes. During the 1890s some classes were built new with the intermediate thickness tyres. All replacement tyres had the new standard thickness, so all locomotives received the increased wheel diameter in the course of routine maintenance. In the tables of dimensions for each class wheel diameters that were later increased are marked with a † symbol.

Hammer-blow is an inevitable result of conventional steam locomotive design. The various reciprocating and rotating components of the drive system all produce forces. The rotating components produce a vertical load on the track in a cycle with each revolution, whereas the reciprocating forces produce a lengthwise oscillation which is transmitted to the train. Unfortunately, the more that the rotating forces on the wheels are balanced out then the worse the reciprocating balance is, and vice versa. A two cylinder locomotive is the worst case – in 4 cylinder locomotives pairs of cylinders are moving in opposite directions and balance each other out to an appreciable extent. So the design must achieve a compromise between the two. One is transmitted to the train, shakes up passengers and goods and increases wear, whilst the other – hammer blow – is transmitted to the track, ballast, and worst of all bridges. It's been calculated that a Saint at 120mph (see the Saint section) would be generating sufficient hammer blow that the wheels would be lifted off the rail by the out of balance forces. Effectively at that speed 60 tons weight is being hammered onto the track more than 8 times a second so this is not a small concern.

Frames

There were two general types of frame construction used; plate and sandwich. Plate frames consisted of a single thickness of steel, normally an inch or more thick. Sandwich frames, by contrast, consisted of two much thinner plates of steel separated by thick planks of oak, all through bolted. Sandwich frames were more flexible than plate frames, which had both advantages and disadvantages. A third type, bar frames, made from thicker steel, was rarely used in the UK, although the extensions used to carry the outside cylinders and front buffer beams on Churchward's standard two cylinder classes could be said to be bar frames.

GWR frames were normally either double – both inside and outside the wheels – or single – inside – frames. The GWR quite often favoured inside frames for driving wheels and double frames for carrying wheels on six wheeled locomotives. Single outside frames were unusual on the GWR.

Double frames had various advantages over inside frames, most notably in providing greater width for bearing surfaces, not only for the wheel bearings but also inside connecting rods and other hardware, but on the other hand they were heavier, more expensive to construct and brought a greater maintenance overhead.

There was a considerable locomotive shortage towards the end of the broad gauge, and new locomotives had to be constructed which would only have a short life before the gauge conversion. Double frames had a particular advantage, since a locomotive could be built with the wheels located outside both sets of frames for use on the broad gauge and then readily altered to have the wheels between the frames for the standard gauge. These were the 'convertibles'.

Renewal

The word 'renew' in a current British dictionary has a number of shades of meaning, mostly with a sense of repair. But in an eighteenth or nineteenth century edition, amongst the definitions that have the sense of renovate or repair, there are also definitions that literally mean make new again. Additionally business may use a word as a technical term with a sense that is different to normal speech. Renewal was a significant term in the company accounts, since new engines to expand the fleet, renewals/replacements of life expired locomotives in the existing fleet and repairs and rebuilding of locomotives capable of further life were financed from three separate funds, or budgets in modern parlance.

In the Armstrong and Dean era renewal was the process of literally making a locomotive new again. The old no 57 was scrapped and replaced with a new no 57 of roughly the same type, but of basically current design. So although the identity was nominally preserved, and some parts might be reused, it was essentially a new build, but, crucially in financial terms, not an expansion to the fleet. This worked in the late nineteenth century when just about all classes were 6 wheeled and old 0-6-0s were replaced with new 0-6-0s and old 2-2-2s with new 2-2-2s, but by the 1920s the GWR directors were being asked to approve renewals that weren't remotely like for like – 14 Bulldogs with 10 Halls for example.

Whilst most renewals were erected principally from new components, there are grounds to suspect that on occasion there could be a very high percentage of a locomotive's predecessor included in a renewal. This was the case with Swindon lot 309, the supposedly new King to replace the one 'written off' at Shrivenham in 1936.

Maintenance, renewal and capital funds may not all be healthy at the same time: after the first world war the GWR had a healthy maintenance fund, since maintenance had been put off in order to do war work. They also had a lot of maintenance work to catch up with, so the money needed to be spent. In the 1930s depression the GWR had low revenue and economies were required from the maintenance fund, but there was a good amount of money in the renewals fund. Thus there were times when a bit of juggling might be helpful, and this explains some oddities in locomotive classes.

For example the first batch the first of conversions of the Star class into Castles were rebuilds of the existing locomotives from the maintenance fund, and kept their original numbers. The later ones, the Abbeys, were new locomotives from the renewals fund, albeit using a lot of second hand parts. Rebuild versus renewal was not simply budget manipulation though, because these renewals appear, sometimes at least, more thorough than a rebuild. An example is the life span of the 8100 class 2-6-2Ts, which were based on 5111s, but lasted much longer than the rebuilt 5111s. One wonders how much of the original 99 was in 8100 when scrapped in 1962...

Some of the things that Collett is criticised for: the Dukedogs and the variations in large wheel 2-6-2 rebuilds for instance, seem much more logical when looked at in this light. The maintenance funds must also have been healthy at the end of the 19th century when Swindon was doing some quite astonishing rebuilds like the conversion of the 3521 class from rather unsatisfactory 0-4-2/0-4-4T tanks to 4-4-0 tender engines.

Most sources, most notably RCTS, take the approach of treating a class and its renewals as a single entity. This succeeds in preserving the identity of a class as it was seen by the organisation, but, because renewals were essentially new locomotives of a design contemporary with their renewal date, this approach doesn't clearly show the evolution of design and appearance.

In this volume a renewal is treated as a new class; for example, 439 class 1868 and 439 class 1885. This helps with tracing design themes: the various 439 class 2-4-0s are a good example. The 1868 Swindon built 439 class was a transition between the appearance of Gooch's broad gauge locomotives and Joseph Armstrong's later Swindon design theme, but the 1885 Wolverhampton locomotives were pure George Armstrong/Wolverhampton in appearance. Renewals were not built in a batch like 'all-new' classes, so tended to be rather more variable in details of construction.

When dealing with the early locomotives it can be very difficult to trace classes and their development. A line absorbed by the GWR in 1863 might have itself been formed from the amalgamation of several other lines. Each of those lines would have had its own locomotive policy – or possibly just a random selection of locomotives bought because they were available, cheaply or otherwise. The combined line might then have commissioned further locomotives, but rarely in classes running into double figures. All those locomotives would be absorbed into the GWR stock and probably later renewed, sometimes as whole classes, sometimes merging different classes, and sometimes as single locomotives

The 182 class 2-4-0, for instance, was built by EB Wilson in 1853 for the Oxford, Worcester and Wolverhampton Railway. Members of the class were rebuilt in every decade between then and the end of the century, usually with new boilers, often with new frames, sometimes with different wheel sizes and the last were scrapped in the 1900s. About the only thing that remained common was that they were always double framed. By the time they were scrapped, photos and drawings make it clear that all major components must have been changed from the originals. Yet this class does not appear to have been officially renewed, just rebuilt at various times and places.

Weather Protection

Very early locomotives had no crew protection other than waist high side panels to reduce the chances of falling off a locomotive in motion. A weatherboard with windows was soon found to be desirable, at first a rather vestigial 'spectacle plate' and later a larger panel. This was followed by narrow open cabs with short roofs, then longer roofs and wider cabs with forward facing windows both alongside and over the firebox. It is recorded that in the early days of cab roofs the drivers objected to them because of the increased noise. The widest cabs of all were on the Hawksworth County Class, which necessitated wider than standard tenders.

Much the same process happened over the bunker of tank locomotives, although spectacle plates survived much longer, with even the early batches of Collett 5700 pannier tanks having a spectacle plate over the bunker rather than a fully enclosed cab. There is some evidence that Churchward's decidedly minimal cabs were at least partly to the liking of the crews, since on at least two occasions, larger cabs and roofs were fitted on experimental locomotives and later cut back.

Auto Fitting & Condensing Gear

Some equipment, notably autofitting gear and condensing apparatus, was only required on some members of some classes and could be readily removed or added. In the nineteenth and early twentieth centuries it is evident that locomotives were given such equipment as required and might come into the works with the equipment and go out without. This policy appears to have changed with Collett as CME. In his era, specialist subclasses were maintained; 4800/5800 and 6400/7400 with and without autofitting are examples, as are the 9700 sub class of condensing equipped 8750 large panniers, the steam brake only 6700 and 6750 sub classes and the renumbering of oil burning locos in 1948.

Auto gear for push pull operation started being fitted as early as 1906, but became more widely installed as the steam railcars started to go out of service. Available records suggest locomotives fitted with auto gear at one major overhaul might have it removed at a subsequent one. It seems likely that, when an autofitted locomotive came into the shops for repair, the gear could be removed and fitted on a newly repaired one in order to maintain the desired number of auto fitted locomotives in service.

Reversing Gear

There were three styles of reversing control fitted to GWR locomotives; lever, screw and steam. Each had advantages and disadvantages.

The earlier classes typically had lever reverse (normally called pole reverse by the GWR), where a substantial lever in the cab was used to control the valve gear. Lever reverse was mechanically simple and cheap to manufacture and maintain, and a locomotive could be changed from full forward to full reverse with a single heave on the lever. On the other hand, it offered less precise control of the valve gear settings. On locomotives with slide valves, it was generally impractical to change reverser settings with the regulator open because of the effects of steam pressure. The full weight of the valve gear, albeit countered by a spring to a certain extent, acted directly on the lever, so the driver had to maintain a firm grip on the lever when making adjustments, otherwise the locomotive could drop into full forward gear. Churchward's first standard classes were fitted with lever reverse, and this was continued on freight and shunting classes right up to the end of steam.

Screw reverse was introduced on some classes towards the end of the nineteenth century. The lever was replaced with a wheel with a couple of knobs, turned to change the valve settings. This gave finer control of the valve gear settings and a great mechanical advantage. On the other hand, it required many turns of the wheel to change from full forward to full reverse, which was a particular disadvantage when shunting.

Screw reverse replaced lever reverse on the Saints and was fitted to all subsequent passenger classes. Under Collett, it also tended to be fitted to mixed traffic classes. It was almost essential on autofitted locomotives, which were mostly slide valve fitted, since the fireman controlled the reversing settings and the driver the regulator.

Steam reverse was a powered system. The valve gear was operated by a pair of small cylinders, and controlled remotely from the cab. This offered, in theory, both fine control and easy transition from forward to reverse. In practice, however, steam reverse systems had a tendency to drift away from the desired settings, and all the extra apparatus was expensive to fabricate and maintain. Steam reverse was only used on a few of the late Dean classes, and retained only on the Aberdares.

Oil Firing

There was a small trial of oil firing with the experimental 0-4-0 locomotive 101 at the turn of the century, but this was not followed up.

Starting in 1945 the GWR ran a limited trial of oil firing on 2800 and Castle class locomotives. This was primarily due to coal shortages. The trial was initially promising, and was extended greatly by the UK Government to include over 1,200 locomotives across all the major Railway Companies. However it was abandoned in 1948, when it was realised that there was insufficient foreign exchange currency available to buy large quantities of oil; the converted locomotives were returned to coal firing between 1948 and 1950.

Finally, in 1958, a single 8750 class pannier tank was converted by Robert Stephenson and Hawthorns.

Chapter 2

Six Wheeled Tender Engines

Six wheeled locomotives were already more or less standard by the time the Great Western narrow (standard) gauge lines were being built. Even though it had much larger locomotives on the broad gauge, all narrow gauge locomotives were six wheeled right up to 1894, with the exception of a handful of 0-4-0 shunting tanks. There appears to have been a policy, whether deliberate or not, not to outshine the broad gauge. The broad gauge was finally abolished in 1892, and the first ten wheeled locomotive, no 36, appeared as early as 1896.

Single Driver Classes

All GWR narrow gauge singles were 2-2-2s until the 3001 class were rebuilt as 4-2-2s from 1894.

378 Sir Daniel. *Named after Sir Daniel Gooch, this Joseph Armstrong design was the first standard gauge locomotive built at Swindon. (Photo: Brian Stephenson Collection)*

Boilers

These were all nineteenth century classes and predated Churchward's standardisation work. At the end of the nineteenth century there was a great deal of boiler development done, with many variations in dome position – or absence of dome, styles of fireboxes and Belpaire fireboxes coming in at the end of that period. There was also a certain amount of early standardisation work being done and some boiler types were used across multiple classes. Most of the boiler types listed here started out with smaller diameters. Classes O and Q were to a certain extent interchangeable.

Boiler Class	Name	Barrel		Firebox Length
		length	diameter	
N	Duke	11ft 0in	4ft 5in	5ft 1in
O	Standard Goods	11ft 0in	4ft 5in	5ft 4in
Q	Sir Daniel	11ft 0in	4ft 3in	5ft 4in
M	Bogie Single	11ft 6in	4ft 2in	6ft 4in
B	Standard 2	11ft 0in	4ft 5in	7ft 0in

The large driving wheels used by single driver classes, especially coupled with the loading gauge – and even the GWR loading gauge was very small by world standards – limited boiler diameter; it simply had to fit in between the wheels, not above them. However, it doesn't seem to have been a major limitation of design until the Dean single, as, up to that point, the same boilers were being used for both single driver and 0-6-0 classes. The Standard 4 and tapered Standard 2 boilers were the first that could not have been fitted to the 8 foot singles.

Early Absorbed Classes

There were many more locomotives, and even classes, than are listed here. These are the most significant in one way or another.

110 Class

Builders	Benjamin Hick & Sons
Line	Birkenhead Railway
Dates Built	1849-1851
Number Built	6
Driving Wheel Size	6ft 0in
Cylinder Dimensions	15in x 22in
Dates Withdrawn	1862/3

The Birkenhead Railway was divided between the GWR and the LNWR in 1860, and only four of the six came to the GWR. As is obvious, they didn't survive very long in their new ownership and neither did those that went to the LNWR. This was the case with many others unlisted here.

209 class

Builder	Beyer, Peacock & Co
Line	West Midland Railway
Dates Built	1861
Number Built	6
Driving Wheel Size	6ft 6in
Cylinder Dimensions	16in x 20in
Dates Withdrawn	1883 (renewed as 2-4-0s into the 196 class)

A class built for the West Midland Railway to a Beyer Peacock design. The renewal is supposed to have reused nothing but a small part of the frames.

215 class

Builder	Vulcan Foundry
Line	Shrewsbury & Hereford
Dates Built	1853/4
Number Built	6
Driving Wheel Size	5ft 6in
Cylinder Dimensions	14in x 20in (most)
Dates Withdrawn	1875/6

A class of small locomotives which had a reasonable life on the GWR.

GWR Classes
Early classes – Gooch Designs and Contractor built.
69 class (1855)

Builder	Beyer, Peacock & Co
Dates Built	1855-56
Number Built	8
Driving Wheel Size	6ft 6in
Cylinder Dimensions	15½in x 22in
Dates Withdrawn	1872-1875

69 class as built, 1855. From a Beyer Peacock drawing.

Built by Beyer Peacock to a Gooch specification. They had outside frames and 6'6 driving wheels. They were numbered 69-76 and were renewed between 1872 and 1875.

157 class (1862)

Builder	Sharp, Stewart & Co
Dates Built	1862
Number Built	10
Driving Wheel Size	7ft 0in
Cylinder Dimensions	16in x24in
Dates Withdrawn	1879-1881

These were built by Sharp Stewarts in 1862 to Gooch specifications, and were not unlike the 69 class, but with larger driving wheels. They were numbered 157-166. They were little altered in their lives, with only one receiving a new boiler, from an Armstrong Goods. They did receive weatherboards and it is possible that some may have been given open cabs.

Most were scrapped in 1878/9 when the new 157 class took over their numbers in what was originally planned to be a renewal exercise. The last three stayed in service until 1881; these survivors were renumbered 172-4 for their declining years.

Joseph Armstrong Designs
Early Wolverhampton Singles, 7, 8, 30, 32, 110

Builder	GWR/Wolverhampton
Dates Built	1855-1856
Number Built	5
Driving Wheel Size	Variously 6ft 0in, 6ft 2in & 6ft 6in
Dates Withdrawn	1872-1875

These were Joseph Armstrong designs built at Wolverhampton between 1859 and 1862. In no sense were they a class, although most sources give 7, 8 and 110 the same wheelbase. They had varying driving wheel diameters between 6ft and 6ft 6in. 30 and 32 were officially renewals of absorbed locomotives, and 32 may have included its parent's boiler. They were scrapped between 1873 and 1887.

378 (Sir Daniel) class

Builder	GWR/Swindon
Dates Built	1866-1869
Number Built	30
Tractive Effort	9,500lbs
Driving Wheel Size	7ft 0in[†]
Cylinder Dimensions	18in x 24in
Boiler Class	Special, N
Dates Withdrawn	1898-1904

These were the first standard gauge locomotives built at Swindon, and were a Joseph Armstrong design. Ten, 378-387, were built in 1866 and the rest, which were numbered 471-480 and 577-586, in 1869. They had double frames. Like all these early engines, they were built with just weatherboards. Open cabs arrived in the 1880s, as did various boiler changes as with all the early classes. The basic boiler dimensions remained unchanged despite all the variations in dome position (or absence), tubing arrangements and everything else. The 'Sir Daniel' boiler became a standard type, class Q under Churchward, and long outlived the locomotives that gave it its name. In spite of that a few Sir Daniels, at some time in their careers, were fitted with O class (Standard Goods) boilers.

[†] During the lifetime of classes marked [†] the wheel diameter increased due to the use of thicker tyres on the wheels. The wheel centres were not changed.

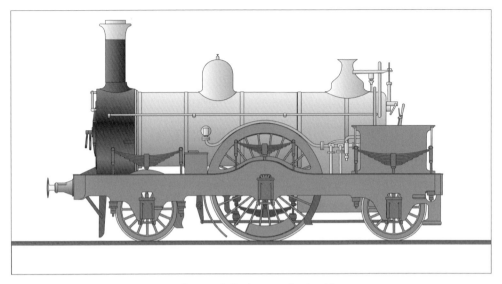

378 (Sir Daniel) class *as built, 1866.*

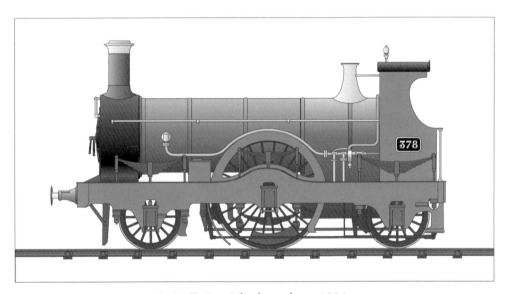

378 (Sir Daniel) class *about 1881.*

One Sir Daniel was scrapped in 1898 and two more in 1900. Dean then elected to rebuild the class as 0-6-0s. Although this seems a startling conversion it was much simpler than it might appear. The Sir Daniels were very similar to the Armstrong Standard Goods, with an appreciable number of common parts, and the biggest part of the work was probably extending the frames downward for the smaller centre driving wheels. These conversions could always be distinguished because they retained a curved rise of the frames above the driving wheels. Twenty-three conversions had been made when Churchward took charge in 1902, but thereafter the remaining four were scrapped, unaltered, in 1903/4.

Queen class

Builder	GWR/Swindon
Dates Built	1873-1875
Number Built	21
Tractive Effort	11,000-14,000lbs
Driving Wheel Size	7ft 0in[†]
Cylinder Dimensions	18in x 24in
Boiler Class	Special, N
Dates Withdrawn	1904-1914

These were similar to, but slightly larger than the Sir Daniels, still with 7ft driving wheels but a longer wheelbase and larger boilers. The first, No. 55 Queen herself, was built in 1873 and was often used on royal trains. Twenty more followed in 1875 and were numbered 999, 1000 and 1116-1133. Again, they were built without cabs and acquired them later.

The Queen class was one of the major classes of their era and they changed quite radically over their lives. Number 55 started off with open splashers, smoke box wing plates and a weatherboard, and finished up

55 (Queen) class *about 1885.*

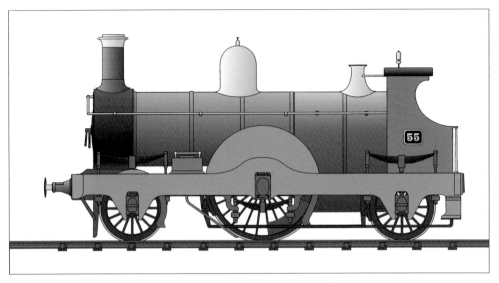

55 (Queen) class. *Diagram A around 1905.*

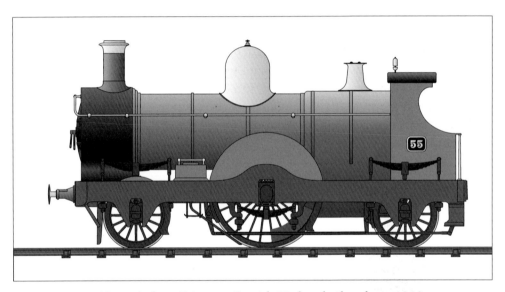

55 (Queen) class. *Diagram D with N class boiler about 1910.*

with enclosed splashers, no wing plates and a cab – quite different in appearance.

They received the usual nineteenth century variations in boilers, both Swindon and Wolverhampton-built, going from forward located domes, rearward domes and domeless boilers, flush and raised round topped and Belpaire fireboxes. The last survivors eventually received N class boilers, which were slightly larger than the originals, with longer barrels but a shorter firebox.

They were mostly withdrawn between 1904 and 1906, although one survived as late as 1914.

157 class (1878)

Builder	GWR/Swindon
Dates Built	1878-1879
Number Built	10
Tractive Effort	11,000lbs
Driving Wheel Size	7ft 0in[†]
Cylinder Dimensions	18in x 24in
Boiler Class	Special, N
Dates Withdrawn	1903-1914

They were numbered 157-166 and were substantially similar to the Queens, the most obvious difference being slotted design frames with cut-outs. The original boilers were somewhat intermediate between Sir Daniels and those used on the Queens. They had originally been planned to be renewals of the Sharp Stewart 157 class, but, in the end, were considered as new locomotives, the difference being primarily administrative. They had all the usual nineteenth century variations in boiler type, and, like the Queens, ended up with N class boilers. Most were withdrawn between 1903 and 1906, with one surviving until 1914.

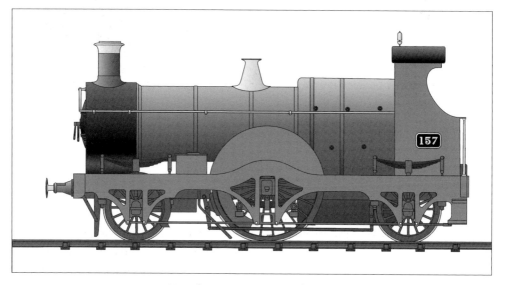

157 class (1878) *around 1900.*

George Armstrong (Wolverhampton) Design
69 class (1872)

Builder	GWR/Wolverhampton
Dates Built	1872-75
Number Built	8
Driving Wheel Size	6ft 6in
Cylinder Dimensions	17in x24in
Dates Withdrawn	1872-1875

They were renewals of the 1855 69 class and so were given the same numbers. They were somewhat longer than their progenitors, with larger cylinders but the same driving wheel size. By 1885 they had acquired cabs. Between 1895 and 1897 all were rebuilt as 2-4-0s of the 'River' class.

Dean Designs
No. 9 and No. 10
These were Dean prototypes, and not especially successful ones. No. 9 started life in 1881 as a rather absurd express 4-2-4 tank engine with 7ft 8in driving wheels and was so prone to derailment it probably never went into service at all: at times the GWR denied it had ever existed. In 1884 substantial parts of this locomotive were included in a new no. 9, which was a more conventional 2-2-2, still with the 7ft 8in driving wheels. No. 10 followed in 1886 and was generally similar to No. 9. Both were reconstructed in 1890 with 7ft driving wheels. They were scrapped in 1905 and 1906.

3001 (Dean Single) class

Builder	GWR/Swindon
Dates Built	1891-1892
Number Built	30
Tractive Effort	14,000lbs
Driving Wheel Size	7ft 8½in
Cylinder Dimensions	19in x 24in
Boiler Class	M
Dates Withdrawn	1894 (rebuilt as 4-2-2s)

Arguably the most elegant of the Victorian steam locomotives, the Dean Single started its life as something of an ugly duckling. The first members of what became the Dean Single class were 3021-8, broad gauge convertible 2-2-2s

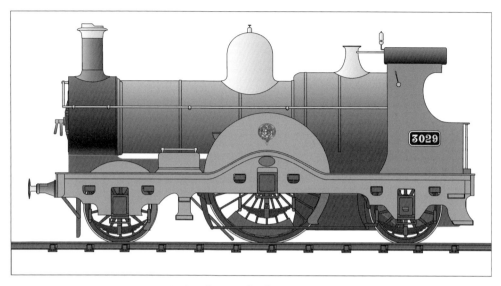

3001 class *as built as a 2-2-2.*

built in 1891 for a very short life on the broad gauge, being converted to the narrow gauge the next year.

3029-3030 were built new as standard gauge at the end of 1891, and 3001-3020, also standard gauge, followed in 1892. All these were 2-2-2s with 7ft 8½in driving wheels and 4ft 7in leading and railing wheels on a 9ft 6in-9ft wheelbase. The 165psi boiler was a new design, restricted to 4ft 3in diameter by the large driving wheels but with an 11ft 6in barrel, very long for a 2-2-2. The firebox was approx. 5ft 8in by 3ft 8in, but dimensions varied, even on the first lot. The firebox was round topped, but raised appreciably above the barrel – an old feature revived – and there was a generous sized dome. All springs were under the frames.

The 2-2-2s were built without names and they were given them in 1893. There was no especial pattern to the names, but many of the names from the big Gooch broad gauge 4-2-2s were reused.

Those locomotives built to the broad gauge were rebuilt to narrow gauge between May and August 1892. Between March and December 1894, all thirty 2-2-2s were rebuilt as 4-2-2s following a derailment in Box Tunnel in September 1893. The broad gauge engines had received two significant rebuilds in three and a half years.

2-4-0 and 0-4-2 Classes

The 2-4-0s make the Swindon/Wolverhampton design divide particularly obvious. Whereas, for example, with 0-6-0 tanks one looks at features like the

108 Class. *One of a pair of renewals of absorbed locomotives. Very typical 19thC Wolverhampton above the footplate, but below the footplate they were the only two inside framed 2-4-0s built by the GWR. (Photo: Brian Stephenson Collection)*

depth of the foot plate valances to distinguish Swindon and Wolverhampton, with the 2-4-0s they used very different styles of framing and much else.

Boilers

As with the singles, the early four coupled locomotives rarely had standardised boilers, but the later classes received them.

Boiler Class	Name	Barrel		Firebox Length
		length	diameter	
N	Duke	11ft 0in	4ft 5in	5ft 1in
O	Standard Goods	11ft 0in	4ft 5in	5ft 4in
P	2301	10ft 3in	4ft 5in	5ft 4in
Q	Sir Daniel	11ft 0in	4ft 3in	5ft 4in
T	Metro	10ft 6in	4ft 3in	5ft 1in

Locomotives
Early Absorbed Classes

As mentioned in the introduction the early locomotive stock was highly varied and built by many manufacturers. The following are perhaps the nearest to being usefully considered as classes. There were a considerable number of others, both 2-4-0 and 0-4-2.

171 class 2-4-0

Builders	R & W Hawthorn
Line	Oxford, Worcester and Wolverhampton Railway
Dates Built	1852/3
Number Built	12
Driving Wheel Size	5ft 9in
Cylinder Dimensions	16in x 20in
Dates Withdrawn	1871-1899

These were among the first OWW locomotives, and were double framed. One did not survive to be taken over by the GWR in 1863! Several of them had major rebuilds, some twice, ending up with T class boilers.

182 class 1853

Builders	E.B. Wilson & Co
Line	Oxford, Worcester and Wolverhampton Railway
Dates Built	1853
Number Built	6
Driving Wheel Size	5ft 8in†
Cylinder Dimensions	16in x 20in
Dates Withdrawn	1886-1904

The double framed 182s were built in 1853 by EB Wilson for the Oxford, Worcester and Wolverhampton Railway, and absorbed when the West Midland became part of the GWR in 1863. They were frequently rebuilt over the years, but were never officially renewed. As well as boiler changes, they also acquired new frames and in some cases at least different wheel sizes beyond the general expansion of tyre thickness. The first was withdrawn in 1886 and most were finally scrapped in the 1890s, with the last going in 1904. It seems likely that all original components were long gone by the time they were eventually withdrawn.

190 class

Builders	E.B. Wilson & Co
Line	Newport Abergavenny & Hereford Railway
Dates Built	1855/6
Number Built	4
Driving Wheel Size	6ft 0in[†]
Cylinder Dimensions	16in x 22in
Dates Withdrawn	1886-1904

The members of the 190 class were very similar to the 182s, and like them were much rebuilt over a long service.

196 class 1862

Builders	Beyer Peacock
Line	West Midland Railway
Dates Built	1862
Number Built	6
Driving Wheel Size	6ft 6in
Cylinder Dimensions	16in x 24in
Dates Withdrawn	Renewed 1879-1883

A class built by Beyer Peacock in 1862 for the West Midland Railway. Two had substantial rebuilds in 1877 in which they had weatherboards added. They were renewed in 1879-1883. When renewed, three were initially reconstructed as 2-4-0T before being rebuilt again as 2-4-0s.

202 class (0-4-2)

Builders	Vulcan Foundry
Line	Shrewsbury & Chester
Dates Built	1842/4
Number Built	4
Driving Wheel Size	5ft
Cylinder Dimensions	15in x 24in
Dates Withdrawn	1870-5

A class of double framed locomotives built by the Vulcan Foundry for the Shrewsbury & Chester in 1852/4. One was destroyed in a boiler explosion in 1859 and a new one, most likely incorporating the usable parts from the old, was built the next year. They were never renewed or received major rebuilds and scrapped from 1870-5.

GWR Classes
Gooch Design
149 (England) class 1862

Builders	George England
Dates Built	1862
Number Built	8
Tractive Effort	8,500lbs
Driving Wheel Size	6ft 6in
Cylinder Dimensions	16in x 24in
Dates Withdrawn	1878-1883 (renewed)

Built by George England and Co in 1862, to a Gooch design, this was an express passenger locomotive, unusual at a time when most passenger work was done by singles. They were numbered 149-156. They had slotted outside frames with the footplate rising in curves to clear the coupling rods, and open splashers with the spokes visible behind the springs. The boiler was domeless with a slightly raised round top firebox, and was substantially similar, if not identical to, that on the 157 class 2-2-2s. The general appearance was similar to the Gooch 69 class singles.

   Little altered over their lives, they were withdrawn between 1878 and 1883 and renewed as the 1878 149 class.

320 class
These two were conversions of Gooch 2-4-0Ts which had been built with outside cylinders, well tanks and condensing gear. They were converted in 1867 and 1873 respectively, and withdrawn in 1881. The boilers were used as stationary boilers at Wolverhampton, but little else is recorded.

Joseph Armstrong Designs
111 class 1863

Builders	GWR/Wolverhampton
Dates Built	1863-1867, 1886-1887

Number Built	20
Driving Wheel Size	6ft 0in[†]
Cylinder Dimensions	16in x 24in, 17in x 24in
Wheel Spacing	7ft 5in½in + 8ft 0½in
Boiler Class	special, O, T
Dates Withdrawn	1903-1914

These were Joseph Armstrong designs, which continued to be built at Wolverhampton when George Armstrong was in charge from 1864. They had plain outside frames with the footplate rising in curves to clear the coupling rods. In the eccentric numbering of the GWR early days, the first batch of six in 1863/4 was numbered 111-114, 115A and 116A.

Four more followed in 1886, numbered 5A, 6A, 7A, 8A. That same year, 115A/116A, 5A-8A were renumbered 1004-1009. In 1886/7 1010/11, 372-377, 30 and 110 followed, 30 and 110 being considered renewals of earlier locomotives.

The first batch had raised round top fireboxes and no domes, but the rest, which could be considered to be George Armstrong designs, were built with domed boilers. Initially they all had open splashers and weatherboards.

Cabs and enclosed splashers appeared by the late 1880s, along with larger cylinders and thicker tyres, bringing the wheels up to 6ft 2in. The 1886 locomotives were built with these features. A considerable variety of boilers

111 class. *The first batch as built under Joseph Armstrong.*

were fitted over the years, encompassing not only varying dome positions, but also boilers as small as the Metro and as large as the Standard Goods.

Most were withdrawn between 1903 and 1906, but a few lingered on longer, the last being scrapped in 1914.

No 108 and 109

Builders	GWR/Wolverhampton
Dates Built	1866/7
Number Built	2
Tractive Effort	10,000lbs
Driving Wheel Size	5ft 0in
Cylinder Dimensions	15in x 24in
Dates Withdrawn	1887

These two anomalies were renewals of Birkenhead Railway absorbed engines and were the only GWR 2-4-0s built with inside frames. However the upper works were typical Wolverhampton practice.

439 (Bicycle) class 1868

Builders	GWR/Swindon
Dates Built	1868
Number Built	6
Tractive Effort	10,000lbs
Driving Wheel Size	6ft 1in
Cylinder Dimensions	16in x 24in
Wheelbase	7ft 3in+ 8ft
Dates Withdrawn	Renewed 1885/1886

The first 439 class was built at Swindon in 1868. They were numbered 439-444 and presented a unusual appearance for the standard gauge. Looking very much like broad gauge locomotives – the earlier Hawthorn class 2-4-0 for instance – they had wholly inside frames, and there were no conventional splashers; instead the 'footplate' arched over each 6ft 1in driving wheel in much the same manner as several contemporary broad gauge classes. The two big wheels with all spokes visible led to the nickname. Other than the addition of weatherboards, and then cabs, they were little changed until renewed.

481 class 1869

Builders	GWR/Swindon
Dates Built	1869
Number Built	20
Driving Wheel Size	6ft 1in[†]
Cylinder Dimensions	16in x 24in
Wheelbase	7ft 6in + 8ft
Boiler Class	special, T
Dates Withdrawn	1887-1890

Although in some respects these were similar to the 439 class, these engines looked entirely different. The framing and footplate rose and fell in a series of double curves. Starting at the front buffer beam, it then dropped down over the leading wheels, rose again to clear the coupling rods, then dropped again at the rear. The leading splashers were open, but the trailing ones were closed in by a plate that extended back to form a low side sheet for the crew. There was just a spectacle plate as weather protection.

They started life as 481-490 and 1122-1131, but in 1870 1122-1131 were renumbered 587-592, 12, 19, 20 and 54. The class was divided into two during their working lives, with three, nos. 12, 19 and 20, maintained and modified in Wolverhampton style and the rest in Swindon fashion. Apart from various boiler changes, no. 12 received a substantial rebuild with straight frames above the leading wheels, but otherwise they only received normal replacements, gaining cabs and thicker tyres. No. 20 was renewed in 1895 as one of the 439 class, whilst the other two were scrapped in 1903 and 1906. The rest of the class were renewed at Swindon between 1887 and 1890, reusing perhaps some parts of the frames and motion.

56 or 717 class 1871

Builders	GWR/Swindon
Dates Built	1871/1872
Number Built	11
Tractive Effort	11,000-13,000lbs
Driving Wheel Size	6ft 0in[†]
Cylinder Dimensions	17in x 24in
Wheelbase	8ft 6in + 8ft 6in
Boiler Class	O, Q
Dates Withdrawn	1903-1919

Numbered 56 and 717-726, they were larger and more powerful than the 439s and 481, having a longer wheelbase and a Standard Goods sized boiler. They had inside frames and the extended footplate valance at the front giving double frames, something that was to be found on quite a number of the 2-4-0s towards the end of the century.

They went through the normal nineteenth century changes of weatherboards to cabs, varying boilers and so on, and a couple eventually received Belpaire boilers. The class was never renewed.

806 class 1873

Builders	GWR/Swindon
Dates Built	1873
Number Built	20
Route Colour	yellow/uncoloured
Power Class	Ungrouped
Tractive Effort	10,000-12,000lbs
Driving Wheel Size	6ft 6½in†
Cylinder Dimensions	17in x 24in
Wheelbase	8ft 3in + 8ft 6in
Boiler Class	O, Q
Dates Withdrawn	1903-1919

This class was rather similar to the 717s, but with a slightly shorter wheelbase. Again, they had inside frames for the driving wheels and the footplate valance was brought down to make outside frames for the leading wheels. The footplate rose over the wheel cranks and dipped between them to an intermediate level, not to the original height. See 439 (1885) below for an illustration of a similar design. They were built with weatherboards, and acquired cabs in the usual way of things.

481 class 1887

Builders	GWR/Swindon
Dates Built	1887-1890
Number Built	18
Route Colour	Uncoloured
Power Class	Ungrouped
Tractive Effort	11,000-13,000lbs
Driving Wheel Size	6ft 2in

Cylinder Dimensions	16in x 24in
Wheelbase	8ft 3in + 8ft
Boiler Class	T
Dates Withdrawn	1904-1921

These were Swindon renewals of the earlier 481 class, numbered 481-490, 587-592, 28 and 54. 28 was officially not a renewal but a new build, but of course the difference was mainly on the books of the accountants. They had a straight footplate, conventional splashers with a small cut out to access the connecting rods, inside frames for the driving wheels but the foot plate valances extended down to make outside frames for the leading wheels.

Boilers fitted were T or Metro class, with, over their lifetimes, various dome position and firebox types. Most were scrapped between 1904 and the Great War, but the last of all lasted until 1921 and is said to have acted as pilot to *The Great Bear* bringing an express into Paddington on one occasion. The combination must have looked more than a little ludicrous.

George Armstrong Wolverhampton Designs
149 (Chancellor) class 1878

Builders	GWR/Wolverhampton
Dates Built	1878-1883
Number Built	8
Route Colour	Yellow
Power Class	Ungrouped
Tractive Effort	9,000-12,000lbs
Driving Wheel Size	6ft 6in[†]
Cylinder Dimensions	17in x 24in
Boiler Class	O
Dates Withdrawn	1903-1920

These were renewals of the original 149 class locomotives at Wolverhampton, with slightly larger boilers and cylinders. They were built new with cabs and had slotted outside sandwich frames, curving up over the driving wheels. They retained numbers 149-156.

The splashers may have been open when first built, but they were certainly soon closed in. They received a variety of boilers over the years, ending up with Belpaire firebox Sir Daniel class boilers.

Two were withdrawn early, in 1903 and 1907, but the others went from 1918 to 1920. They had lasted long enough to be given diagram L.

149 (Chancellor) class *1878. Diagram L around 1903.*

196 class 1882

Builders	GWR/Wolverhampton
Dates Built	1879-1887
Number Built	12
Driving Wheel Size	6ft 0in†
Cylinder Dimensions	17in x 24in
Wheelbase	8ft + 8ft 6in (varied)
Boiler Class	O, Q
Dates Withdrawn	1903-1927

This George Armstrong class was considered – at least partially - a renewal of locomotives absorbed from the West Midland Railway, 196 class 2-4-0s and 209 class 2-2-2s. The numbers were 196-201 and 209-214. They varied appreciably in detail, with even differing wheelbases on some locomotives in their earlier years. There were various changes and minor rebuilds – indeed three of the old 196s had been renewed as 2-4-0T and spent three years in that configuration before re-joining their sisters. They had a mixture of class O and class Q boilers, with all the usual variations of boilers of the period: fireboxes, dome position and the like.

They had inside frames for the driving wheels, but the footplate valance was brought down to make outside frames for the leading wheels. The general footplate design was similar to the 439 class as illustrated below. They were mostly withdrawn between 1911 and 1920, but there was another chapter to be written: two were sold off in 1911 and passed through various hands before ending up with the Cambrian Railway and thence back into GWR hands as 1328 and 1329, finally being withdrawn again in 1926/7.

439 class 1885

Builders	GWR/Wolverhampton
Dates Built	1885/6 & 1895
Number Built	7
Tractive Effort	11,000lbs
Driving Wheel Size	6ft 2in
Cylinder Dimensions	17in x 24in
Boiler Class	O, Q
Dates Withdrawn	1907-1918

More renewals of an earlier class with the same numbers. This was an example of a Swindon style class transformed into Wolverhampton style, but the whole appearance was much more conventional than their parents. The frames were very similar in general treatment to the 1879 version of the 196 class.

439-444 were built in 1885, and there was a surprise expansion to the class in 1895, when another, no. 20 was built. This loco was nominally a renewal of one of the smaller 481 class.

439 class (1885). *Diagram A about 1905.*

111 class 1886

See 111 class 1863 above. Two locomotives numbered out of series as renewals of early singles, these were new members of a rather older class. There is a subtle but important detail here when considering the nineteenth century classes. Wolverhampton was not building an 1863 design. They were building new locomotives to the specification that the older locomotives had been upgraded to during their lives to date.

3226 class 1889

Builders	GWR/Wolverhampton
Dates Built	1889
Number Built	6
Route Colour	Uncoloured
Power Class	Ungrouped
Tractive Effort	9,000-12,000lbs
Driving Wheel Size	6ft 1in†
Cylinder Dimensions	17in x 24in
Boiler Class	Q
Dates Withdrawn	1914-1922

3226 Class. *This shows one of the class in a late 19thC configuration with a Wolverhampton style chimney.*

Nos. 3226-3231 were built in 1889 at Wolverhampton under George Armstrong. They were effectively an updated version come continuation of the 111 class. As built, they had similar framing and other detail to the 111s in their updated form, with enclosed splashers and cabs. They acquired a number of boiler designs over their lives, finishing up with the Sir Daniel type, one with a Belpaire firebox and another with top feed.

Dean (Swindon) Designs
2201 class 1881

Builders	GWR/Swindon
Dates Built	1881/2
Number Built	20
Route Colour	yellow/uncoloured
Power Class	Ungrouped
Tractive Effort	10,000-12,000lbs
Driving Wheel Size	6ft 7in[†]
Cylinder Dimensions	17in x 24in
Boiler Class	O, Q
Dates Withdrawn	1904-1921

This was effectively a Dean version of the 806, with the same size wheel centres, and were one of the classes built with an intermediate tyre size. They were all built in 1881 and 1882 but the twenty locomotives can be divided into two groups with different framing arrangements. 2201-2210 resembled the 806s with complex footplate curves, but they were built new with cabs and both sets of splashers were open. 2211-2220 had different framing with a straight footplate and secondary small splashers over the cranks. All were later rebuilt to have the straight footplate.

There were considerable variations in the boilers carried and they received the other normal upgrades. There were Churchward diagrams for Belpaire and round top fireboxes, but none appear to have been superheated. Towards the end of their lives, some received top feed and those fitted with Belpaire fireboxes came into the yellow route restriction.

Nos. 7 and 8, 1886
These were experimental 2-4-0s with 7ft drivers and an unusual 'tandem' compound cylinder arrangement in which the cylinders were located one in front of the other with a common piston rod. No. 7 was standard gauge and No. 8 broad gauge. They met with little success and were eventually dismantled

in 1890. In 1894, some components were used in Armstrong class 4-4-0s, which were regarded as renewals of these engines.

Nos. 14 and 16, 1886/8
These were broad gauge convertibles which somewhat resembled the Barnum class. They too were renewed, forming the other two members of the Armstrong class

3201 and 3501 (Stella) class 1885

Builders	GWR/Swindon
Dates Built	1884/5
Number Built	25
Route Colour	Uncoloured
Power Class	ungrouped/A
Tractive Effort	14,500-18,500lbs
Driving Wheel Size	5ft 1in†
Cylinder Dimensions	17in x 26in
Boiler Class	P
Dates Withdrawn	1904-1921

The 3201 class was part of an interesting exercise in standardisation, being one of four classes with identical cylinders and motion – two 2-4-0 passenger classes, tender and tank, and two 0-6-0 freight classes, again tender and tank.

3201 (Stella) class. *Diagram Y with superheated boiler. 1916.*

To ring the changes even further, some of the tank engines were built as broad gauge convertibles. Unfortunately, none of the results appear to have been especially well thought of.

3201 to 3205 were the original tender 2-4-0s, with boilers of roughly P class dimensions. 3501-3510 were built as broad gauge tank engines and 3511-3520 standard gauge. The broad gauge locos had short lives as such, some being converted to tenders whilst still on the broad gauge and the rest were given tenders when they became standard gauge in 1892. The rest of the 2-4-0T were converted to tender engines in 1894/5, giving a single class of twenty-five.

They then proceeded to receive a very wide variety of boilers on the P class theme, superheated and not, domeless and not, top feed and not. An oddity was the fitment of a parallel Standard 3 boiler to one locomotive in 1901. A few were withdrawn in 1919, but seven survived as long as the 30s, the last going in 1933.

3206 (Barnum) class 1889

Builders	GWR/Swindon
Dates Built	1889
Number Built	20
Route Colour	Yellow
Power Class	A
Tractive Effort	13,500-17,500lbs
Driving Wheel Size	6ft 2in
Cylinder Dimensions	18in x 24in – later 18in x 26in
Wheelbase	9ft + 8ft 6in
Boiler Class	special, N
Dates Withdrawn	1926-1937

The Barnums had slotted outside sandwich frames. They had a new boiler design with an unusually long round top firebox for the period. The original design boilers were replaced with variations on class N, which was of similar dimensions, but a slightly wider diameter. As one would expect for a class that lasted into the 1930s, the changes were rung with the boilers, with domed and domeless, Belpaire and round topped fireboxes, saturated and superheated, with and without top feed.

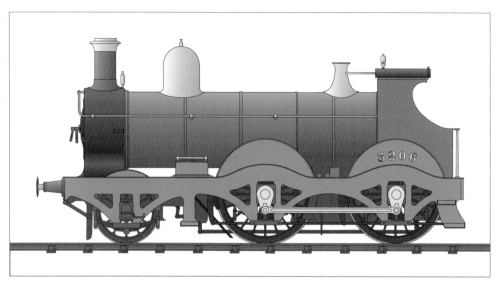

3206 (Barnum) class. *Diagram F with 1889 boiler.*

3206 (Barnum) class. *Diagram A1 with superheated class N boiler and showing top feed apparatus, which most of the class received.*

They also received some significant cylinder changes. They started out with 24in stroke cylinders, but from 1905 they started being fitted with 26in stroke cylinders, which must have necessitated new crank axles and possibly valve gear changes. The last change, to two engines only in 1924, was to lengthen the frames at the leading end and fit Bulldog piston valve cylinders. The first was withdrawn in 1926, but the majority survived into the 1930s, the last two being withdrawn in 1937.

3232 class 1892

Builders	GWR/Swindon
Dates Built	1892/1893
Number Built	20
Route Colour	Yellow/Ungrouped
Power Class	Ungrouped
Tractive Effort	11,500-13,000lbs
Driving Wheel Size	6ft 7in[†]
Cylinder Dimensions	17½in x 24in
Boiler Class	Q, O
Dates Withdrawn	1918-1930

This class had frames similar to the 439 or 886 classes, inside for the drivers but outside for the leading wheels, but instead of rising over the wheels the footplate was level, and there were small additional splashers over the con rods which were open not closed, presumably to aid access for lubrication.

They were the last all-new class of 2-4-0 and were a development of the 2201 class. As built, they had Sir Daniel boilers. Later on, Standard Goods boilers were fairly widely used, and towards the end of their lives several had top feed and a few superheated boilers. One was withdrawn in 1918, but the rest went from 1923 – 1930.

3232 class. *Diagram G. As built with Sir Daniel boiler.*

3232 class. *Diagram A10. Superheated Standard Goods boiler with Belpaire firebox around 1915.*

69 (River) class 1895

Builders	GWR/Swindon
Dates Built	1895-1897
Number Built	8
Tractive Effort	10,500-12,000lbs
Driving Wheel Size	6ft 8in[†]
Cylinder Dimensions	17in x 24in
Boiler Class	Q
Dates Withdrawn	1907-1918

The Rivers were nominal rebuilds of the 1872 69 class 2-2-2s. As 2-4-0s, they retained slotted outside frames, curving over each wheel to clear the coupling rods. Driving wheels were originally 6ft 8in, later 6ft 8½in. Some sources suggest the frames were all new, others that the front part of the frames were re-used. They had Sir Daniel class boilers right through their lives. Some of the boilers were reused from the 69 class, but two had new boilers when built. Some had Belpaire boilers fitted towards the end of their lives. Boiler pressures used varied with different boilers, and thus so did tractive effort.

They were all given short river names – *Thames* was apparently considered but rejected because it didn't fit the available space! One was destroyed in a collision in 1907 and another withdrawn that year. The rest were withdrawn between 1913 and 1918.

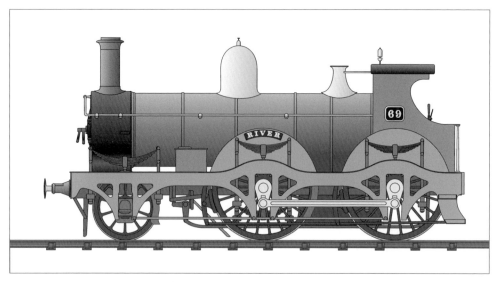

69 (River) class *2-4-0. Diagram H. Boiler with forward dome and round top firebox.*

Absorbed Classes at the Grouping
Midland and South Western Junction Railway
Dubs 2-4-0

Builders	Dubs & Co
Dates Built	1894
Number Built	3
Route Colour	Uncoloured
Power Class	Unclassed/A
Tractive Effort	13,500 – 15,000lbs
Driving Wheel Size	5ft 6in
Cylinder Dimensions	17in x 24in
Boiler Class	Own/Std. 11
Dates Withdrawn	1952/4

Three lightweight 2-4-0s designed and built by Dubs and Co. At the grouping, they were allocated 1334-6 and diagram A7. In 1924, they were all rebuilt with Standard 11 boilers at rather higher pressure than the originals, increasing the tractive effort. They survived until 1952/4 and British Railways, outlasting much newer MSWJR locomotives, and were also the last 2-4-0s on the GWR, having been kept on especially to run the Newbury to Lambourne line.

0-6-0 Classes

The typical freight locomotive of the Great Western during the nineteenth century was, like most other lines, an 0-6-0 with wheels around 5ft diameter. Freight was the major part of the business, and these were, together with the 0-6-0 tanks, the most numerous locomotives.

945 (927 class). *One of the Coal Engines - a smaller wheeled version of the Standard Goods. A late nineteenth century photo. (Photo: Brian Stephenson Collection)*

Preserved 2251 Class 3205 *in the sunshine at the Bluebell Railway. (Photo: Jim Champ)*

Boilers

Boiler Class	Name	Barrel			Firebox length
		length	diameter		
B	Standard 2	11ft 0in	4ft 5in	5ft 0in	7ft 0in
K	Standard 10	10ft 3in	4ft 5in	5ft 0in	6ft 0in
O	Standard Goods	11ft 0in	4ft 5in		5ft 4in
P	2301	10ft 3in	4ft 5in		5ft 4in
Q	Sir Daniel	11ft 0in	4ft 3in		5ft 4in
U	2021	10ft 0in	3ft 9in		5ft 0in

Early Absorbed Classes
46 class

Builders	Longridge
Line	Shrewsbury & Birmingham
Dates Built	1849-52
Number Built	5
Driving Wheel Size	4ft 9in
Cylinder Dimensions	15in x 24in
Boiler Class	Long boiler type
Dates Withdrawn	1868-1889

One of the five came to the GWR via the Shrewsbury & Chester and was numbered out of sequence. Another was converted to a saddle tank during its life.

50 class

Builders	Stephenson's
Line	Shrewsbury & Birmingham
Dates Built	1849-51
Number Built	5
Driving Wheel Size	4ft 9in
Cylinder Dimensions	15in x 24in
Boiler Class	Long boiler type
Dates Withdrawn	1869-1877

Again all five were built for the S&B, but one came to the GWR via the Shrewsbury & Chester and was numbered out of sequence.

239 class

Builders	R & W Hawthorn
Line	Oxford, Worcester and Wolverhampton Railway
Dates Built	1852/3
Number Built	6
Driving Wheel Size	5ft 0in
Cylinder Dimensions	17in x 24in
Dates Withdrawn	1872-1902.

These were similar to the 171 Class 2-4-0s. Two did not survive to the GWR. Only one had a significant rebuild, receiving an O class boiler. The others were all gone by 1885.

248 and 253 classes

Builders	E.B. Wilson & Co
Line	Oxford, Worcester & Wolverhampton Railway, Newport, Abergavenny and Hereford Railway
Dates Built	1854/5
Number Built	5, 7
Driving Wheel Size	5ft 3in
Cylinder Dimensions	16in x 24in
Boiler Class	Special, O, Q
Dates Withdrawn	1877-1907

Five of this standard EB Wilson design were bought by the OWW and seven by the Newport, Abergavenny and Hereford Railway. All were absorbed with the West Midland. They were much rebuilt over their lives, acquiring larger cylinders and other changes – even in some cases new frames – but don't seem to have been officially renewed. The NAHR locos (253 on) had different framing to those of the OWW.

Astonishingly, substantial parts of the frames, motion and wheels of no 252 have survived, having been cut down into an instructional model of locomotive motion after the rest of the engine was scrapped. These parts are currently in store with the Leeds Industrial Museum.

264 class

Builders	E.B. Wilson & Co
Line	Oxford, Worcester & Wolverhampton Railway,
Dates Built	1856
Number Built	4
Driving Wheel Size	5ft
Cylinder Dimensions	16in x 24in
Dates Withdrawn	1878-9, 1921

The 264s were slightly smaller than the 248 class. No 264 had a major rebuild in 1875, with new larger cylinders and at least partially new frames, at which time it was substantially similar to contemporary members of the 248 class. This engine was reboilered time and again, ending up with a Belpaire firebox O class boiler and running over one million miles.

240 and 260 classes (1861)

Builders	West Midland Railway
Dates Built	1861/2
Number Built	8
Driving Wheel Size	5ft 0in
Cylinder Dimensions	16in x 24in
Dates Withdrawn	1886-7

GWR 240/4/6 had started out as Hawthorn built locomotives for the OWW that had been renewed, probably using few original parts, at the West Midland works at Worcester in 1861. 260-264 were erected at Worcester as all new locomotives, but all were very similar. In GWR ownership, they received larger cylinders and lengthened frames. Apart from the frame construction they were also similar to the 280 class.

280 class

Builders	Midland Railway/W Fairbairn & Sons
Dates Built	1861/2
Number Built	14

Driving Wheel Size	5ft 3in
Cylinder Dimensions	16in x 24in
Boiler Class	Special, O, Q
Dates Withdrawn	1882-6

These were to a design by Matthew Kirtley for the Midland Railway. Two had been bought by the OWW from the Midland, new or nearly so. The rest were built by Fairbairn for the West Midland after the OWW had been amalgamated into it. They were later fitted with 5ft wheels and larger cylinders, but apart from cabs and boiler fittings they had few other changes before they were scrapped.

298 class

Builder	Vulcan Foundry
Line	Shrewsbury & Hereford
Dates Built	1855
Number Built	4
Driving Wheel Size	5ft 0in
Cylinder Dimensions	16in x 24in
Dates Withdrawn	1870/8

This class was similar in design to the 202 class 0-4-2s from the same manufacturer.

913 class

Builder	Beyer Peacock
Line	Llanelly Docks Railway
Dates Built	1868/70
Number Built	6
Driving Wheel Size	4ft 9in
Cylinder Dimensions	16in x 24in
Dates Withdrawn	1877-1886

This class was built in two batches, the first two being somewhat smaller than the other four.

GWR Classes
Early GWR Classes
57 class 1855

57 class (1855) *in original condition.*

Builders	GWR Swindon
Dates Built	1855/6
Number Built	12
Tractive Effort	9000lbs
Driving Wheel Size	5ft 0in
Cylinder Dimensions	15½in x 22in
Dates Withdrawn	Renewed 1870-1890

57-68 were the first standard gauge locomotives built for the GWR at Swindon. They were pure Gooch designs, and had slotted outside sandwich frames and partial inside frames. They looked very much like scaled down versions of broad gauge locomotives with domeless boilers. They were all renewed, mostly in the 1870s, and in this case nearly all components of the old locomotives were scrapped.

77 class 1857

Builders	Beyer Peacock
Dates Built	1857, 1861
Number Built	6

Tractive Effort	12,000lbs
Driving Wheel Size	5ft 0in†
Cylinder Dimensions	16in x 24in, 17in x 24in
Dates Withdrawn	1902-4

This class started with two Beyer Peacock built locomotives, 77 & 78, having plate frames rather than sandwich. The first two were essentially Gooch boilers on a Beyer designed chassis. 167-170, which had originally been built for another line, followed in 1861 and had Beyer design boilers when new. They received the normal Victorian miscellany of boilers and cabs in the late 1870s. They were never renewed as such.

79 class 1857

Builders	GWR Swindon
Dates Built	1857-1862
Number Built	24
Driving Wheel Size	4ft 6in
Cylinder Dimensions	16in x 25in, 17in x 24in
Dates Withdrawn	Renewed 1878-83

These were built in four lots from 1857-1862 at Swindon, numbered 79-90 and 119-130. They were essentially similar to the 57s, but had smaller wheels and larger cylinders. They were little altered until renewed from 1878-1883. The 1878 renewals were partly as tender locomotives and partly as tank engines. The whole of the 3rd and 4th lots, 119-130 became the 119 class of 0-6-0ST.

131 class 1862

Builders	GWR Swindon, Slaughter, Gruning & Co
Dates Built	1862-5
Number Built	28
Driving Wheel Size	5ft 0in
Cylinder Dimensions	16in x 24in
Dates Withdrawn	1877-1887 (16 renewed)

These were an updated version of the 57 class, fitted with Stephenson link motion. Two batches were built in 1862, 131-136 at Swindon, while 137-148 were built for the GWR by Slaughter, Gruning & Co. The rest, 310-319, were built at Swindon in 1864/5. They mostly received larger cylinders and cabs in the 1870s. Twelve were scrapped between 1879 and 1883, three more were renewed, in 1877/8, as locomotives substantially similar to the 1873 57 class and the rest were renewed as the 136 class between 1877 and 1887.

57 class 1873-90

Builders	GWR Wolverhampton
Dates Built	1873/5, 1890/1
Number Built	18 (see notes)
Tractive Effort	13,000-15,500lbs
Driving Wheel Size	5ft 0in[†]
Cylinder Dimensions	17in x 24in, 18in x 24in
Dates Withdrawn	1908-1927

The second 57 class was built in Wolverhampton from 1873 to 1875. They had double frames throughout with sandwich frames on the outside. They retained nominal 5ft wheel diameter. Two of the original 57s were renewed as saddle tank engines (60 and 67) but were later converted back to tender locomotives.

Three of the 1862 131 class were renewed into substantially the form of this class, and three brand new locomotives to essentially this design were constructed in 1890/91, 316-318. As was typical of these early classes at the end of the nineteenth century, they received a bewildering variety of boilers of differing shapes and dimensions, including boilers of the Standard Goods and Sir Daniel types, and even towards the end of their lives boilers with Belpaire fireboxes.

One was scrapped as early as 1908, but the majority went from 1911-1913. The 316 series lasted a little longer, all surviving the First World War and the last not being withdrawn until 1927. Of the renewed 131 class, two went in 1894 and 1906, but the third lasted until 1924 after a second renewal in 1896.

79 class 1877

Builders	GWR Swindon
Dates Built	1877-1880
Number Built	13
Driving Wheel Size	4ft 6in[†]
Cylinder Dimensions	17in x 24in
Dates Withdrawn	1905-1918

In general, the first two lots of the 79 class were renewed as tender locomotives, and the second two lots as tank engines – the 119 class. The exception was no 122, which was renewed as a tender engine of this class. These new locomotives were generally similar in appearance to the contemporary renewed 57 class, but retained smaller wheels. They received a similar variety of boilers to the 57 class cousins. One went in 1905; the rest between 1912 and 1918.

136 class

Builders	GWR Wolverhampton
Dates Built	1884-7
Number Built	13
Tractive Effort	14,000-16,000lbs
Driving Wheel Size	5ft 2in
Cylinder Dimensions	17in x 24in
Dates Withdrawn	1905-1925

The Wolverhampton renewals of the 1862 131 class were particularly complicated. As noted above, twelve were scrapped rather than being renewed. Three effectively joined the 1872 57 class, and the rest were treated as a separate class, one which, most likely, included no components at all from the old locos. The class boundaries appear to be particularly hazy and indistinct for this group.

136 class (renewed 131) *in turn of the century condition.*

Over the years, they mainly acquired Standard Goods or Sir Daniel class boilers with the usual variety of dome position etc. During the Great War, five were loaned to the LNWR. One went in 1905, and the majority in 1919. The last was withdrawn in 1925.

322 (Beyer) class 1864

Builders	Beyer Peacock & Co
Dates Built	1864, 1866
Number Built	30
Tractive Effort	13,000lbs
Driving Wheel Size	5ft 0in
Cylinder Dimensions	17in x 24in
Dates Withdrawn	Rebuilt 1878-1885

This class of thirty, twenty ordered under the Gooch regime (322-341) and the rest (350-359) by Joseph Armstrong, was entirely of Beyer Peacock design. They had plate (not sandwich) double frames with the running plate rising over each wheel to clear the cranks. They were rebuilt quite heavily from 1878 (see 328 class below), but not officially renewed. In six cases, these rebuilds consisted of a conversion to saddle tank, and some numbers were swapped between locomotives so the tank locomotives took numbers 322-327, and the remaining locos 328 on.

322 (Beyer) Class *as built.*

Joseph Armstrong Designs
360 class 1866

Builders	GWR Swindon
Dates Built	1866
Number Built	12
Route Colour	uncoloured
Power Class	ungrouped
Tractive Effort	13,000-14,000lbs
Driving Wheel Size	5ft 0in[†]
Cylinder Dimensions	17in x 24in
Dates Withdrawn	1918-1933

They were similar to their successors, the very numerous Standard Goods, but had double frames with the outside frames slotted out. They were built at Swindon as 360-371, but 370 and 371 were renumbered to 1000/1001 in 1866; 1000 was renumbered 1015 in 1867. Over their lives, they tended to receive Sir Daniel type boilers rather than Standard Goods, but in their last days no more Sir Daniel boilers were being constructed, so in 1923 a couple received 2301 (P class) boilers, and later even received superheated versions. Most were withdrawn in 1918/19, three were withdrawn in the 1920s, the last outliving its sisters by several years and not being withdrawn until 1933.

360 Class *as built.*

328 Beyer class 1878

Builders	GWR Wolverhampton
Dates Built	1878-1885
Number Built	24
Route Colour	Uncoloured
Power Class	Ungrouped/A
Tractive Effort	15,000-18,000lbs
Driving Wheel Size	5ft 0in[†]
Cylinder Dimensions	17 or 17½in x 24 or 26in
Boiler Class	O, Q
Dates Withdrawn	1912-1934

These were rebuilds, but officially renewals, of the earlier Beyer 322 class, less six that had been converted to tank engines. The rebuilds included new cylinders, and in many cases they were rebuilt with 26in stroke cylinders, which must have required new crank axles and presumably other changes to the motion. Curiously these changes were not static; it is recorded that some were converted back from 26in stroke to 24in stroke. There are also recorded changes between 17in and 17½in cylinders. They received the usual variety of boilers, but these tended to condense down into the Standard Goods type. When they received Belpaire fireboxes, these were all on Standard Goods boilers. Top feed was used on some boilers towards the end of their lives and

322 (Beyer) Class *in a post World War One configuration.*

three received superheating. One went in 1912, but the rest all lasted into the 1920s, the last survivor not being withdrawn until 1934, outliving most of the Armstrong Standard Goods and running over 1.5 million miles.

388 (Armstrong) Standard Goods 1866

Builders	GWR/Swindon
Dates Built	1866-1876
Number Built	310
Route Colour	Ungrouped
Power Class	Uncoloured
Tractive Effort	13,000-16,000lbs
Driving Wheel Size	5ft 0in[†]
Cylinder Dimensions	17in x 24in
Wheelbase	7ft 4in + 8ft 4in
Front Overhang	4ft 10in
Rear Overhang	2ft 10in
Boiler Class	O, Q
Dates Withdrawn	1904-1934

This was the largest class of 0-6-0 tender engine on the GWR, more numerous than the later Dean Goods. They were normally referred to as Standard

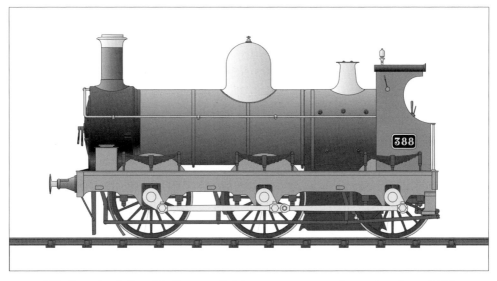

388 (Standard Goods) *diagram F. Most common configuration from 1889.*

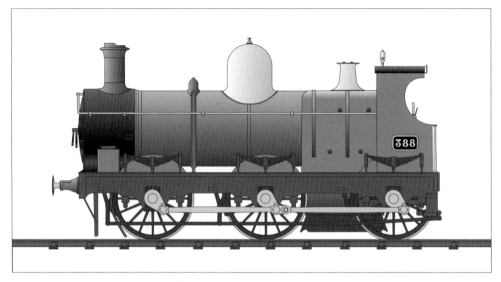

388 (**Standard Goods**) *diagram A9. 1919 on, drawn with top feed.*

Goods, not Armstrong Goods, at least whilst the majority were in service. 310 were built between 1866 and 1876, and typically for this period there were appreciable changes in the specification between batches, especially with boilers and cabs.

They were similar to the 360 class, but were slightly longer and had solid plate frames without slots. The wheelbase and front overhang were identical with the slightly later 1076 class 0-6-0ST, built from 1870.

The majority were built with just spectacle plates and no cab. The last two batches had deeper frames at the spring brackets, the last batch having side sheets as a first step towards a cab. Boilers varied considerably and there were also changes to domes, safety valve covers and chimneys over the course of the run.

They had perhaps the most unstructured numbering allocation of any GWR class. They were built late enough that many were built as renewals of earlier locomotives, but early enough that the fleet was still expanding rapidly. This was also before any kind of class numbering was introduced: a time when the numbering was based on how a locomotive was held on the company books.

Thus, there were three groups of numbers a Standard Goods could receive:

- Numbers from 388 upwards were additions to the railway's fleet bought from capital.
- Numbers from 1000 upwards were additions to the fleet paid for by revenue
- Numbers below 200 were renewals of withdrawn locos in the capital stock.

There was also an admixture of renumberings for administrative purposes.
A highly-simplified list would be:

1866-1869 (seven lots)	388-406, 407-412,419-425, 26, 42, 38, 1012-4, 238, 37, 429-438, 445-454, 370-1, 426-8, 41, 43, 44, 46, 50.
1870-1872 (six lots)	41-6, 1082,498-500,1083-5,497,501-516, 1086-1105,593-602, 1106-1115, 603-612, 657-676, 24,31,48,51,52, 677-716
1873-4 (two lots)	776-805,874-893
1875-6 (three lots)	21,-3, 25, 27, 29, 32, 39, 53, 117, 1186-1195, 1196-1215

There were no large scale renumberings of the class, but until 1870 there
were a good number of renumberings between the three groups of numbers,
presumably for accounting purposes. The most extreme case was No. 38,
which received that number in 1870, having carried 428, 1066 and 1090
during its first three years of existence.

There were very many minor variations of boiler carried by the class. In the
end, they settled down with a boiler with 5ft 5in diameter and 11ft long
barrel – the O or Standard Goods type. A few carried the slightly smaller
Sir Daniel (Q) boilers at one stage or another, and around 1899 there was a
trial of Dean Goods (P class) boilers which was not continued with.

Open cabs came from 1879, with Swindon fitting a slightly narrower cab
which left the rear splasher exposed whereas Wolverhampton cabs were flush
with its outer face.

In 1884, ten were converted to broad gauge, having the wheels outside both
sets of frames; ten more followed in 1187/8. They were of course converted back
in 1892. Belpaire fireboxes started to appear from 1901, superheating (only ever
on a minority of the class) from 1911 and a very few acquired top feed.

There were six diagrams in the Churchward era, the principal ones being
for round top and Belpaire boxes, with boiler pressure listed as 150psi for the
round top boxes and 165psi for the Belpaire boxes. The other four diagrams
were mostly concerned with superheater options.

A number were sold to the ROD (Railway Operating Division of the Royal
Engineers) for service during the First World War. All were sent to Serbia
rather than France, but eight of them were lost when their ship was sunk in
the English Channel.

Withdrawals started from around 1904, but the majority survived the First
World War. Large scale scrapping went on in 1910-1921 and from then they
went steadily, with only a very few making the 1930s. The last went in 1934.
None have survived – unless you wish to count the eight that are somewhere
on the bottom of the English Channel!

927 (Coal Engines)

Builders	GWR/Swindon
Dates Built	1874
Number Built	20
Route Colour	ungrouped
Power Class	Uncoloured/A
Tractive Effort	15,000-17,500lbs
Driving Wheel Size	4ft 6in†
Cylinder Dimensions	17in x 24in
Boiler Class	O
Dates Withdrawn	1905-1928

This was to all intents and purposes a version of the Standard Goods. A single batch, 927-946, was built in 1874. They were used principally on coal traffic between S. Wales and Birkenhead, hence the name.

They received much the same sorts of modifications over time as their larger wheeled sisters. Most received Belpaire boilers, but only one is known to have been superheated and two had top feed. Power class varied; some were ungrouped and others class A. All were route availability uncoloured without weight restrictions.

One was withdrawn as early as 1905, but the majority were withdrawn 1919-1923 with the last one going in 1928. None have survived.

William Dean Designs
2301 (Dean Goods) class

Builders	GWR Swindon
Dates Built	1883-1899
Number Built	260
Route Colour	Uncoloured
Power Class	Ungrouped/A
Tractive Effort	13,000-18,000lbs
Driving Wheel Size	5ft 0in†
Cylinder Dimensions	17in x 24in, 17½in x 24in
Wheelbase	7ft 3in + 8ft 3in
Front Overhang	4ft 10in
Rear Overhang	4ft 0in
Boiler Class	P
Dates Withdrawn	1907-1910 (rebuilds as 3901), 1921-1955

2301 (Dean Goods). *Diagram A10, superheated boiler from 1915.*

The Dean Goods is surely one of the classic steam locomotives, and perhaps the quintessential pre-Churchward GWR class with a long life and much war service. Oddly, then, they were less numerous than the Standard Goods class.

260 Dean Goods were built in twelve lots between 1883 and 1899. By this time, Dean's block system of numbering was in place and they were numbered 2301-2360 and 2381-2580. They were simple inside framed 0-6-0s. The front overhang and wheelbase were also the dimensions of the 1813 class, built from 1882, the first of the main line of inside frame pannier tanks. Although some records suggest the first batch were built with 5ft diameter wheels, the actual diameter was probably 5ft 1in on the earlier batches, as this was the period where tyre thicknesses were increasing. They eventually settled down at 5ft 2in.

They were a little shorter than the Standard Goods in front of the trailing wheels, but had a longer rear overhang. This was matched with the boilers, which had shorter barrels than the Armstrong goods, but the same length fireboxes. The first twenty had domeless boilers when new and, unusually, smokeboxes flush with the boiler barrel. Subsequent boilers were all domed, although the last of the domeless boilers lasted until 1905. Dome position varied of course in the normal way at this period. They all had cabs from new.

Boilers were subject to the normal nineteenth century permutations. Belpaire fireboxes appeared from 1901 and superheating from 1911. The vast majority of the class were eventually fitted with superheated boilers. They acquired 17½in cylinders from 1908.

In 1907-10, 2491-2510 were heavily reconstructed as 2-6-2 tanks for suburban service and renumbered 3901-3920. These conversions used the same wheels and motion, but new Standard 5 boilers.

There were six diagrams in all, but two of these are for the First and Second World War pannier tank conversions. The others were the two varieties of firebox plus two superheater variants. In their original form of 150psi boilers and 17in cylinders, they were ungrouped for power, whilst in the ultimate form with 180psi boilers and 17½in cylinders they were in power class A. In either case weight was in the uncoloured group.

The first withdrawal was an accident loss in 1907, followed by the twenty conversions to 3901 class. Apart from those, and war losses, the class remained intact until 1929. From then on, the earlier locomotives were withdrawn steadily until the war came. The MOD requisitioned 100 for war service, so several recently withdrawn locomotives had to be reinstated. Withdrawals did not start again until 1945. The GWR was loaned LNER J25 and LMS Johnson class 2 engines to help fill the ranks, but they were not liked.

Fifty-four survived to British Railways and these mostly lasted until British Railways standard classes arrived in the early '50s. There was a notable swansong for the class since the new Standard class proved to be incapable of the work of the Dean Goods until they had significant front end changes. This went down very well at Swindon! The last of the class went in the late 1950s. One is preserved in ex Swindon Works but non-running condition and is at the Steam Museum in Swindon.

In 1917, sixty-two were taken over by the ROD and sent to France. Sixteen of these later went to Salonika. Most were returned in 1919 and a few in 1921, but seven were never returned. One of them was fitted with condensing gear and pannier tanks while retaining its tender.

In 1939, 100 were sold into MOD service, ten of which were fitted with pannier tanks and condensing gear. Seventy-nine were captured or destroyed when France fell in 1940. Eight more were taken into MOD service at the end of 1940. The captured locomotives were used by the Axis during the war, and although most stayed in France at least one travelled as far as Austria and another to Russia.

After the war, twenty-two of the survivors were sent to China. A few of the remaining engines served in Tunisia and Africa and six ended up owned by the Italian State Railways. None returned to service with the GWR (or BR) although many eventually returned from France and were scrapped in the UK in the late '40s and early '50s.

2361 class

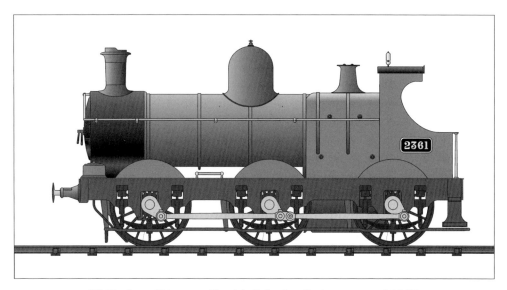

2361 class. *Diagram U with Belpaire firebox around 1910.*

Builders	GWR Swindon
Dates Built	1885/6
Number Built	20
Power Class	Ungrouped/B
Route Colour	Uncoloured
Tractive Effort	14,000-18,500lbs
Driving Wheel Size	5ft 0in†
Cylinder Dimensions	17in x 26in
Boiler Class	special or P
Dates Withdrawn	1930-1946

These, 2361-2380, represent the gap in the Dean Goods numbering sequence. They were more closely related to the Stella 2-4-0s and the 1661 tank class, with many components standardised between them. They were thus outside framed and had 17in x 26in cylinders, rather than the 24in stroke of the Dean Goods. A second batch was started, but were completed as 0-6-0ST, the 1661 class. The 2361s were built with a longer boiler than the Dean Goods.

From 1899, all new replacement boilers fitted were P class (Dean Goods) type, but the longer boilers continued in use until they were no longer economical to repair.

They started to receive Belpaire boilers from 1901 and, with one exception, received superheating after the war. The working pressure on some of the Belpaire firebox boilers was as high as 180psi, which put engines thus equipped engines into power group B, but the route availability was always uncoloured.

There were three diagrams, one with the original boiler, and two with Belpaire fireboxes, one superheated and one not. Withdrawals started in 1930, with three left in 1939. Two of these were withdrawn that year but reinstated in the absence of so many Dean Goods on war service. The last went in 1946, and none have survived.

379 Sir Daniel 0-6-0 rebuilds

Builders	GWR Swindon
Dates Built	1900-1902
Number Built	23
Route Colour	Ungrouped
Power Class	Uncoloured
Tractive Effort	14,000-15,000lbs
Driving Wheel Size	5ft 2in
Cylinder Dimensions	17in x 24in
Boiler Class	Q, O
Dates Withdrawn	1903-1920

These conversions were turned out as an alternative to constructing another batch of Dean Goods. There were twenty-three conversions in all. Although rebuilding a 2-2-2 into an 0-6-0 would seem to be a major conversion, in this case it was a fairly simple task. The Sir Daniels had many components in common with the standard (Armstrong) goods, most notably cylinders and motion, so the conversion consisted mainly of reworking the frames to suit 5ft 2in drivers instead of the 4ft 2in carrying wheels and 7ft 2in drivers of the 2-2-2. This gave them a distinctive appearance with an apparently unnecessary rise in the footplate over the centre driving wheels plus higher mounted springs on those wheels.

They mostly kept Sir Daniel boilers at first, although Standard Goods boilers, both with round and Belpaire fireboxes, were also widely fitted. The first was withdrawn as early as 1903 after only three years life as an 0-6-0. The majority had gone by the end of 1914, although the last survived until 1920. None have survived.

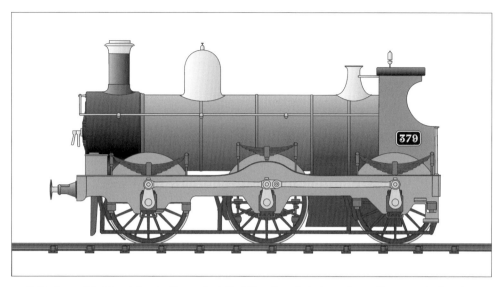

379 class *(Sir Daniel rebuilt as 0-6-0). The sketch is based on diagram A, but has been drawn with a front dome boiler.*

Collett Designs
2251 class

Builders	GWR Swindon & BR(W) Swindon
Dates Built	1930-1948
Number Built	120
Route Colour	Yellow
Power Class	B
Tractive Effort	20,000lbs
Driving Wheel Size	5ft 2in
Cylinder Dimensions	17½in x 24in
Boiler Class	Standard 10
Dates Withdrawn	1958-1965

With the exception of the 1361 class of 0-6-0ST, Churchward built no new locomotives without leading wheels, but by the 1930s many old 0-6-0 classes had been withdrawn and there was a need for new locomotives that could be used on lighter routes than the 4300 class. Accordingly, the 2251 class was designed, which had many components in common with the 5700 pannier tanks but used a larger boiler, the Standard 10. This had originally been developed for absorbed classes. It was effectively a Standard 3 boiler with a

2251 class. *Diagram A27.*

shorter firebox – the Standard 3 being a Standard 2 with a shorter barrel. It had an 8in longer firebox than the P class, as well as a rather larger barrel, so was a higher capacity but heavier unit. Consequently, they were route class yellow, so could not replace the Dean Goods on all duties.

They had a full modern cab with side windows – quite a contrast from the rather minimal crew protection on Standard and Dean Goods classes, although 2211-2240 were built without side windows during the war.

The class was not built in numerical order. 2251-2299 were built in order between 1930 and 1938, followed by 2200-2250 between 1938 and 1945, the previous occupants of the 2200-2250 region having become extinct in the meantime. 3200-3219 followed in 1946-48, using a number series which had been vacated by renumbering the surviving members of the Duke class.

As with other Collett classes, cab side windows were plated over during the war, and restored or fitted for the first time afterwards. The majority of the first twenty were built with lever reverse. Thereafter, all were built with screw reverse and screw reverse was fitted to the remainder as they visited the shops for major repairs.

Various members of the class were fitted with 4,000 gallon ex-ROD tenders, which were available from withdrawn Aberdares. The majority, however, had 3,000 gallon GWR tenders of various types.

Withdrawals started in 1958, and the last went in 1965. One has been preserved; it was bought direct from BR in running condition and so was never in a scrapyard. It is currently owned by the South Devon Railway.

Absorbed Classes (Nineteenth and early Twentieth century)
Bristol and Exeter
Sharp Stewart 0-6-0
This was a class of ten, which were delivered in 1875. They had 5ft drivers and 17in x 24in cylinders. They were extensively rebuilt at Swindon from 1892-1896, with the conversion including lengthening the wheelbase. They were withdrawn from 1906 to 1911.

Absorbed Classes at the Grouping
Cambrian Railways
Small Goods class 0-6-0

Builders	Cambrian/Sharp Stewart
Dates Built	1861-5, 1872-5
Number Built	9
Route Colour	Uncoloured
Power Class	Ungrouped
Tractive Effort	11,500lbs
Driving Wheel Size	4ft 6in
Cylinder Dimensions	16in x 24in
Boiler Class	Own, U
Dates Withdrawn	1899-1947

These were Sharp Stewart-built 0-6-0 tender engines dating back to the early 1860s. Most had been scrapped by the grouping, but nine were left to come into GWR ownership. Of these, five were scrapped immediately, not even wearing the GWR number they were allocated. The remainder were allocated diagram A16. Surprisingly, the others all survived for some years. One was reboiled with a U class (2021) boiler but the other three were left largely unchanged. Two even survived the Second World War to be scrapped in 1945 and 1947 respectively.

Large Goods (73 class 0-6-0s).

Builders	Cambrian/Neilson & Co Vulcan Foundry Neilson, Reid & Co
Dates Built	1894/5, 1899
Number Built	10
Route Colour	Yellow
Power Class	A

Tractive Effort	18,500lbs
Driving Wheel Size	5ft 1½in
Cylinder Dimensions	18in x 26in
Boiler Class	Own, P (when rebuilt)
Dates Withdrawn	1926-1947

This class of inside frame 0-6-0s was the first on the Cambrian not to come from Sharp Stewart. Of the ten, five came from Neilson & Co in 1994, three from the Vulcan Foundry in 1895 and two from Neilson, Reid & Co in 1899. They joined the GWR with two varieties of boiler. Between 1924 and 1933 seven were fitted with superheated P class boilers while the others were withdrawn in 1926 and 1932. Three of the rebuilt locos were withdrawn in 1935 and 1938, whilst the remaining three were scheduled to be withdrawn in 1939. However the war – and presumably in particular the sale of Dean Goods to the War Department – intervened and they were reprieved until 1944, 1946 and 1947.

Large Belpaire Goods (15 class)

Builders	Robert Stephenson & Co Beyer, Peacock & Co
Dates Built	1903-1919
Number Built	15
Route Colour	Yellow
Power Class	A
Tractive Effort	18,500lbs
Driving Wheel Size	5ft 1½in
Cylinder Dimensions	18in x 26in
Boiler Class	Own, Standard 9 (when rebuilt)
Dates Withdrawn	1922, 1952-4

They were built in three batches between 1903, 1908 and 1918. The first five were from Stephenson's, and the second two batches from Beyer Peacock. When they reached the GWR three were immediately scrapped. Two of the remaining ones, which had had new boilers fitted fairly recently, were given superheaters, together with new smokeboxes and other details. They kept these modified boilers until the 1930s. No more were modified in this way however, as the new Standard 9 boiler, developed to replace the standard Barry boiler, was suitable; this boiler, superheated, was fitted to almost all of the class. Subsequently, unsuperheated Standard 9 boilers were also used on the class, and they tended to swap between the two specifications.

One was destroyed in an accident in 1933, but the rest survived to British Railways. They were withdrawn from 1952-54, and none have survived into preservation.

Midland and South Western Junction Railway
Beyer Peacock 0-6-0

Builders	Beyer, Peacock & Co
Dates Built	1899, 1902
Number Built	10
Route Colour	Yellow
Power Class	B
Tractive Effort	17,000-19,000lbs
Driving Wheel Size	5ft 2½in
Cylinder Dimensions	18in x 26in
Boiler Class	Own, Standard 10 (when rebuilt)
Dates Withdrawn	1934-38

1003 Class (ex MSWJR) *as rebuilt to diagram A24.*

Six were built in 1899, and four more, almost the same, in 1902. They had inside frames and inside cylinders. They were numbered 1003-11 and 1113 on joining the GWR. All were rebuilt between 1925 and 1927 with Standard 10 boilers and in this form looked very like the later GWR 2251 class. They were withdrawn between 1934 and 1938.

Taff Vale Railway
K and L class 0-6-0s

Builders	Kitsons TVR
Dates Built	1874-1889
Number Built	85 (41 to GWR)
Route Colour	Uncoloured
Power Class	A
Tractive Effort	17,000 – 18,500lbs
Driving Wheel Size	4ft 6.5in
Cylinder Dimensions	18in x 26in
Boiler Class	Own
Dates Withdrawn	1907-1930

This was once a class of eighty-five. They were mostly built by Kitsons between 1874 and 1889, with the rest being built in the TVR's own factory. They were a typical late Victorian inside framed and inside cylinder 0-6-0, used mainly for mineral traffic. The differences between K and L class had become largely notional after years of modifications. About half of the survivors were withdrawn in 1923 and only one remained in service by 1928, this being withdrawn in 1930. Some of their tenders were reused for other purposes – some, as water tanks, survived into the 1960s.

CHAPTER 3

Eight Wheeled Tender Engines

The GWR was very late in adopting eight wheel locomotives for the standard gauge, but it was also very early in introducing ten wheeled classes. The 4-4-0s had a very short reign as the premier locomotive type. All the four-coupled express locomotives were scrapped by the mid 1930s and even the eight wheel mixed traffic classes were being replaced by new classes of 4-6-0.

Tenders and Turntables

The longer eight wheel locomotives brought a new infrastructure requirement. The six wheeled locomotives were all much the same length, and could be turned on a 42ft turntable, the largest standard size at that time. A 4-2-2 single with one of the larger tenders had a wheelbase of around 50ft, and a new 55ft standard turntable was introduced and soon installed at larger sheds and stations.

Once the Duke class (medium wheel 4-4-0s) were being planned, it must have been obvious that longer locomotives were going to spread round the system faster than the directors wanted to authorise new turntables. A range of short wheelbase tenders were constructed with the Dukes, and later also used on the 3521 class and some other classes.

4-2-2 Class

3001 (Dean Single) class)

Builder	GWR/Swindon
Dates Built	1891-1899
Number Built	80
Tractive Effort	12,500-14,500lbs

Driving Wheel Size	7ft 8½in
Cylinder Dimensions	19in x 24in
Boiler Class	M, Standard 2
Dates Withdrawn	1908-1915

Arguably the most elegant of the Victorian steam locomotives, the Dean Single was amongst the last of the breed. They also existed in many variations. Sometimes it seems as if no two were quite the same and it could almost be said that few stayed the same for very long. They retained the class M boilers that had been designed for the 2-2-2, but with numerous variations.

3001 to 3030 were built as 2-2-2s and are covered in that section. 3031 was the first to be built as a 4-2-2 in 1894 and the 2-2-2s were converted to

3031 (Dean Single) class. *Diagram B as built with round top firebox.*

3031 (Dean Single) class. *Diagram C. Parallel Standard 2 boiler and drumhead smokebox.*

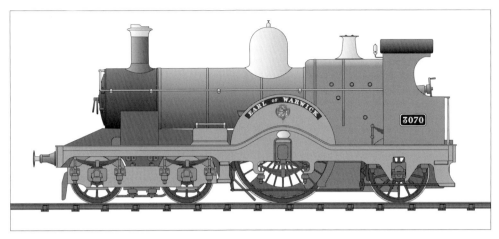

3031 (Dean Single) class. *Diagram F. Class M boiler with raised Belpaire firebox.*

4-2-2 that year. 3032-42 were built later in 1894, then 3043-60 in 1895, and 3061-3080 in 1897/9.

Those built as 4-2-2s had the trailing wheel springs over the footplate and outside a narrow cab. At this stage, the class presented a largely uniform appearance. It did not last.

The 4-2-2s carried names right from the factory. There was no especial pattern to the names, but many of the names from the big Gooch broad gauge 4-2-2s were reused. Quite a number were renamed at some stage in their lives, and towards the end several names that clashed with Saints and Stars were removed.

Rebuilt 2-2-2s retained underhung springs on the trailing wheels at first, but the springs were moved to over the footplate between 1895 and 1899. Former 2-2-2s always retained a slightly deeper section of frame by the trailing wheels.

In 1898, in common with other classes, thicker tyres were fitted to the wheels, increasing the drivers to 7ft 9in.

One locomotive was rebuilt to diagram C with an untapered Standard 2 boiler in 1900. This was a domeless boiler with Belpaire firebox – shorter in the barrel and longer in the Firebox than the M class. It had a 4ft 5in barrel so had to be pitched rather high – 8ft 6in – to clear the driving wheels. Twelve more were rebuilt to diagram C in 1905/6. Only parallel Standard 2 boilers were used, since the tapered ones could not have been fitted between the wheels without an impractically high boiler pitch. A wide cab was fitted which covered the majority of the trailing wheel springs. With the high boiler came a shorter funnel, so this rebuild was quite distinctive with a much less 'Victorian' appearance. The drumhead smokebox had a door of Churchward style and lacked the prominent polished ring of the Dean type.

Two locomotives were given 180psi domeless raised Belpaire firebox boilers of otherwise similar dimensions and pitch as the original boilers in 1901/2. This was diagram D.

Six locomotives received domed, 180psi, round top firebox boilers in 1909. These boilers were otherwise similar to the original ones. This was diagram E.

The last major boiler change for the 4-2-2s was diagram F, rebuilt from 1910. This 180psi boiler, still class M, was similar in basic dimensions to the originals, but had a raised Belpaire firebox, a large dome and a drumhead smokebox. Some thirty locomotives received this style of boiler, with some of the later ones being given top feed as well. None were ever superheated. This rebuild tended to have the tallest chimneys of all, but there was much variation.

Cabs varied considerably, in length as well as width. As a general principle round top fireboxes were matched with narrow cabs with large circular front windows while Belpaire fireboxes were associated with wider cabs which had quadrilateral windows at the side of the firebox, and small round windows above it. The size of the cut-out on the side of the cab also varied, being smallest on the locos with Standard 2 boilers. There were also variations in the front bogie, and several experimental designs were tried.

It highlights how great a revolution Churchward wrought that in March 1899, 3080 Windsor Castle, the last Dean single, went into service, and just four years later, in March 1903, the same factory turned out 98, the first true Saint and the model for the twentieth century British steam locomotive.

The singles had short lives, some as little as twelve years. Train weights were increasing rapidly at the turn of the century and they started to be withdrawn from 1908. They were withdrawn steadily from then on, the last went in 1915. The design office investigated the possibility of converting them into 4-4-0s, but it turned out to be too expensive to be worthwhile. None were preserved, although a strictly non-functional replica is in existence at Windsor station.

4-4-0 Classes

The 4-4-0 classes were amongst the more confusing of GWR types. Under Dean and Churchward, a kind of mix and match approach was adopted and classes merged and separated. Locomotives were rebuilt and changed class, but not necessarily number, with different designs of boiler. 2-4-0s and 0-6-0s seemed to stay in class and many 0-6-0T classes appeared to merge into a single configuration, but nothing of the sort happened with the 4-4-0s.The variations shouldn't be exaggerated: larger Dean era 4-4-0s had a good number of common components, and only the 3521 class of 0-4-4T rebuilds was an exception.

Within classes, sub classes and the like the 4-4-0s can be arranged by wheel size and boiler size.

3295, one of the Badminton class. *Dare we guess that the group standing right front of the locomotive are the cleaners responsible for the intricate patterns on the paintwork? (Photo: Brian Stephenson Collection)*

City of Truro *at the Bluebell Railway. (Photo: Jim Champ)*

| Wheel Size | Boilers | | | | |
| | Largest | | | | Smallest |
	Standard 4	Standard 2	Standard 3	Duke	P class
6ft 8½in	City, County	41xx			
5ft 8in		Bulldog	Bulldog	Duke	
5ft 2in			3521		3521

There were five sizes of boiler, and large (6ft 8½in) medium (5ft 8in) and small (5ft 2in) wheels and different classes had different combinations. There were also variations in frame design, not to mention a good deal of reinforcement over the years.

Boilers

| Boiler Class | Name | Barrel | | | Firebox Length |
		length	diameter		
N	Duke	11ft 0in	4ft 5in		5ft 1in
P	Dean Goods	10ft 3in	4ft 5in		5ft 4in
W	Badminton	11ft 0in	4ft 5in		6ft 4in
B	Standard 2	11ft 0in	4ft 5in	5ft 0in	7ft 0in
C	Standard 3	10ft 3in	4ft 5in	5ft 0in	7ft 0in
D	Standard 4	11ft 0in	4ft 11in	5ft 6in	7ft 0in

The 4-4-0 boilers were among the types that Churchward worked on most while he was creating his standard boiler style. The early standard boilers about the turn of the century had parallel barrels, not tapered; the taper boilers were introduced as part of this development work. Boiler pressures increased over the years too, from 150psi on the early Dukes to 200psi on the later standard boilers.

Frames

Frames always seemed to be a source of problems with the double framed 4-4-0s and were frequently strengthened during the course of their careers. One could make a sweeping generalisation that very few of them were ever really strong enough and that patching frames was something of a Swindon custom! The 'normal' footplate height was too low to clear the outside cranks, so had to be raised. Locomotives built under the Dean regime had 'curved' frames, rising in an elegant curve up and down over each wheel hub, whereas in the Churchward era they were straight, with a single arc taking the footplate up to a higher level over the driving wheels.

GWR Classes
3521 class

Dates Built	1899 (rebuilt from tank engines)
Number Built	26 with P Class boiler, 14 with Standard 3
Route Colour	Yellow
Power Class	A
Tractive Effort	17,000lbs
Driving Wheel Size	5ft 2in
Cylinder Dimensions	17in x 24in
Wheelbase	5ft 6in + 7ft 0in + 8ft 6in
Boiler Class	P or Standard 3
Dates Withdrawn	1913 - 1934

The 3521 class had perhaps the most convoluted modification history of any GWR class, and in their original form were arguably the worst locomotives ever built in any numbers in Great Britain! They were built as 0-4-2 tank engines and had a short 7ft 6in coupled wheelbase, and then a 10ft 6in gap to a trailing wheel. All sources suggest this made them rather reluctant to stay on the track. A further twenty were built as convertible broad gauge saddle tanks.

They were later rebuilt with the trailing wheels replaced with bogies and an even shorter coupled wheelbase to become 0-4-4Ts, and the broad gauge locos converted to the narrow gauge. Even in this form they were rather

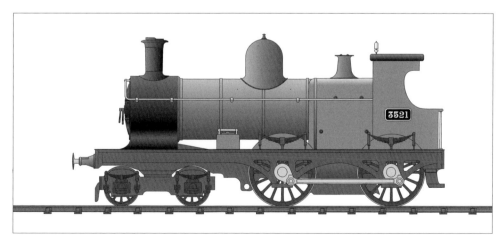

3521 class. *Diagram A13. This diagram, from about 1915, shows the smaller P class boiler in superheated form and with a Belpaire firebox.*

3521 class. *Diagram A27. Standard 3 boiler in superheated form around 1924. This was the last diagram issued for the class.*

unsatisfactory, so from 1899 to 1902 these hapless machines were taken in hand and rebuilt to a quite astonishing extent. They were turned into 4-4-0 tender engines with revised frames, bogies and in many cases boilers too. The standard sources state that the outside frames were reversed and shortened, and the inside frames truncated at the rear with a new piece welded on the front. There must also have been a piece inserted between the driving wheels on both sets of frames, since the coupled wheelbase was lengthened. The smaller boilered engines started with round top fireboxes, but development of boilers was in full swing during their lifetime. They all received Belpaire fireboxes, most were given superheaters and a couple received top feed. This all reflected the changes seen on Dean Goods and large 0-6-0 tanks with the same class boilers.

The large boilered variety were (re)built with early Standard 3 boilers which had domeless parallel barrels and a high raised Belpaire firebox. They also followed the normal line of boiler development, gaining tapered boilers with top feed, and in most cases superheating.

There was no pattern to the numbers of the locomotives rebuilt with small and larger boilers. Curiously, they were not renumbered in 1908 – one would have expected the two sub classes to be separated as happened with the rebuilt Dukes. They were usually coupled with very short wheelbase 2,000 and 2,400 gallon tenders or medium wheelbase 2,500 gallon units. In August 1921 two were sold to the Cambrian Railway, only to return to GWR stock in January 1922.

These locomotives attract a good deal of criticism, but they did run a normal lifetime – over 1 million miles in some cases – so they must have been considered worthwhile in their final guise. They were withdrawn in the late 1920s and early 1930s.

The Main Group

The 3521 class was something of an odd man out whereas there were many common features across the large and medium wheel classes.

Small Boiler, Medium Wheels

These classes all had the same chassis dimensions. There were three basic frame designs used across the medium wheel classes, but as we shall see, these were interchangeable.

Express 4-4-0s were withdrawn in the 1930s, but these mixed traffic 4-4-0s lasted until into the 1950s and it may be that the Western never really worked out what they wanted to replace them with. A lightweight 4-4-0 was sketched out under Hawksworth, using the Standard 10 boiler, but it never came to anything.

3252 (Duke) class

Dates Built	1895-1899
Number Built	59/60 (see notes)
Route Colour	Yellow
Power Class	B
Tractive Effort	17,000-19,000lbs
Driving Wheel Size	5ft 8in
Cylinder Dimensions	18in x 26in
Wheelbase	6ft 6in + 7ft 3in + 8ft 6in
Boiler Class	N
Dates Withdrawn	1902-9 (Bulldog conversions) 1936-39 (Dukedog conversions) 1949-1951 (the survivors)

The Dukes were pure Dean Locomotives and had curved frames. 3252-3291 were built between 1895 and 1897, and 3313-3331 in 1899.

Nineteen (or twenty if you count 3312 Bulldog herself, which was never really a Duke), apparently selected more or less randomly, were rebuilt as Bulldogs between 1902 and 1909. In the 1908 renumbering those not converted were given 3252-3291, and the gaps in the sequence were closed up. In the early days, some Dukes had straight nameplates on cab or boiler sides, but later on standard plates on the splashers were fitted. A good number lost their names over the years, some because the names clashed with the themed names of new classes and some, apparently, because the locomotive names were being mistaken by passengers for train destinations.

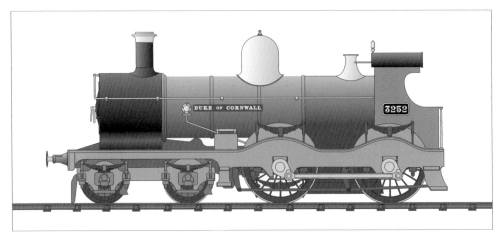

3252 class. *Diagram E. The Dukes as built with a straight name plate on the side of the boiler.*

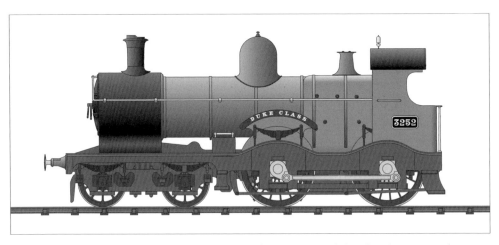

3252 class. *Diagram A39. This was the last diagram issued for the class around 1921, when the boiler was raised slightly for a revised cylinder design. Note the Belpaire firebox and wider cab. The sketch includes the tie bar and frame patches as used on the last survivors.*

They were given boilers with Belpaire fireboxes from 1903 to about 1917. A very few had domeless boilers with raised fireboxes in the early days; the last of these was removed in 1929. Most, but not all, acquired wider cabs when they were fitted with Belpaire boilers. These concealed the rear wheel springs. Superheated boilers started to be fitted from 1911 and top feed from 1913. They acquired piston valve cylinders in place of slide valves from 1915 on. Frame reinforcements were a constant theme, and the last survivors carried large patches round the horn guides and solid ties between them.

In 1946, the survivors were renumbered into the 90xx series to make space for 2251s in the 32xx range.

In their early days, the majority were coupled with very short 2,000 gallon tenders. The last few were turned out with equally short but larger capacity 2,600 gallon tenders. Later on, they were often coupled to medium wheelbase 2,500 gallon tenders. From 1930, some were coupled with standard 3,500 gallon tenders, but these were wider than the cabs, which set up unacceptable draughts. To resolve this the cabs on many of the survivors were flared outwards right at the rear.

Rebuilds into Dukedogs (see below) started from 1936, but the programme was halted in 1939, when twenty-nine had been converted. Scrapping of the remaining eleven commenced in 1949 and all were gone by 1952. Even without considering the Dukedog rebuilds, the Dukes were longer lived than their successors, the Bulldogs. No real replacement for the Dukes/Dukedogs with their wide route availability was ever built. The heavier 4300s and Manors took over much of their work, but when it came to yellow restricted routes only the 2251 0-6-0s and some of the lighter tank engines were alternatives.

3200 (9000, Dukedog, Earl) class

Dates Built	1936-9
Number Built	30
Route Colour	Yellow
Power Class	B
Tractive Effort	17,000-19,000lbs
Driving Wheel Size	5ft 8in
Cylinder Dimensions	18in x 26in
Wheelbase	6ft 6in + 7ft 3in + 8ft 6in
Boiler Class	N
Dates Withdrawn	1948-1960

In 1929 Duke no. 3265 was in the Swindon Factory for a major overhaul with rather sorry looking frames. The works, at Cook's suggestion, elected to replace the frames with a set of Churchward design straight frames from Bulldog no. 3365. The object of the exercise was to keep the Duke in traffic, rather than the Bulldog. Keeping the identity of the Duke rather than retaining the number that went with the frames avoided the sort of numerical confusion that attended the Duke to Bulldog conversions.

Twenty-nine more followed in 1936-9. They were designated as a new class and numbered from 3200. This was primarily a bookkeeping exercise to pay for the conversions from the renewal fund, but Collett elected to give the 'new' class new names and picked Earls as the series type. It is said that some of the noble Lords had made it known that they would like to see their names used

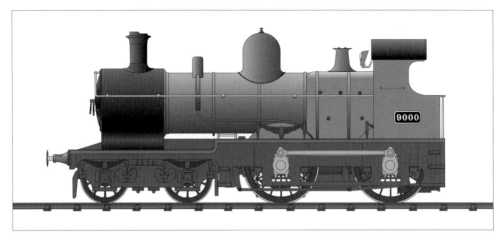

3200 or 9000 class. *This sketch is based on diagram A43, which was the first for the class, but it has been amended to show a post war configuration including the later top feed installation.*

on new locomotives, but that when they saw their names on these Victorian survivors they were unimpressed and the names were soon transferred to Castles. Cook gives the impression that this was Collett indulging in a little quiet humour at the Peers' expense.

There was considerable variation in the class, with two alternate top feed arrangements, various different chimneys, sand box arrangements and the like, but all had screw reverse.

They were partnered with the same variety of tender sizes as the Dukes, including, in a few cases, the surviving short wheelbase tenders. In 1946 they were, like the remaining Dukes, renumbered into the 90xx series to make room for new 2251s.

The Dukedogs all survived to British Railways. A few were withdrawn in 1948, a few more in 1954/5, and the rest between 1958 and 1960. 9017 went straight from service to the Bluebell Railway, where from time to time it bears the old number 3217 and/or the name *Earl of Berkeley*. There is no current Earl of Berkeley to object!

Medium Boiler, Medium Wheels
3300 (Bulldog) class

Dates Built	1899-1906
Number Built	121 (plus 20 converted from the Duke Class)
Route Colour	Blue
Power Class	B
Tractive Effort	19,000lbs
Driving Wheel Size	5ft 8in

Cylinder Dimensions	18in x 26in
Wheelbase	6ft 6in + 7ft 3in + 8ft 6in
Boiler Class	Standard 2
Dates Withdrawn	1931-1951

'Bulldog', no 3312, was built amongst a batch of Dukes, but given a slightly larger boiler as well as a few other experimental features. At the end of 1899 the first batch of Bulldogs, 3332-3352, was turned out, and no more Dukes were built. Unlike the Dukes, which had screw operated reverse, the Bulldogs were built with steam reverse.

3200 (Curved frame Bulldog) class. *This sketch is of the class in the 1920s with a Standard 2 boiler.*

3241 (Straight frame Bulldog) class. *This sketch is based on diagram A23, of around 1923, which shows the later Bird series. The 3241 and 3441 were not distinguished in weight diagrams by this date.*

3241 Series Bulldog *redrawn with Standard 3 boiler. Note the smokebox extended backwards to allow for the shorter boiler barrel. This would be diagram A41.*

After the first twenty, the remaining Bulldogs were built with straight frames. Batches built were 3353-72, 3413-32 and 3443-72. The earlier Bulldogs, rather than having nameplates over the splashers, had oval combined number and name plates on the cab sides, although some conversions retained their straight Duke nameplates for a while.

The first eighty were all built with parallel barrel Standard 2 boilers, and some of these continued in use, swapping between engines in the normal GWR style, until about 1913. However it was unusual for an engine to be refitted with a parallel boiler after receiving a tapered one. In the end, no less than 156 – including the twenty rebuilt Dukes and the fifteen members of the Bird series listed below – were constructed, making it one of the larger classes on the GWR.

In the 1912 renumbering they were given 3300-3319 for the converted Dukes, 3320-3340 for locomotives with curved frames built as Bulldogs, and 3341-3440 for those with straight frames. In the 1946 scheme, it was envisaged that the last survivors would be renumbered out of the 34xx series to provide space for 9400 pannier tanks, but in the event they were withdrawn before this became necessary.

As with the Dukes they were upgraded with top feed, superheaters and piston valve cylinders between 1910 and 1925. Not all received the piston valves before scrapping though. Like all the outside frame 4-4-0s, they received much frame strengthening over the years including tie bars like those added to the Dukes.

During the 1920s some Bulldogs, both straight and curved frame, were fitted with the smaller and shorter Standard 3 boiler as there were a good supply of these after the 36xx 2-4-2Ts were withdrawn, but Standard 2s were in great demand.

At first, the most commonly fitted tenders were medium wheelbase 2,500 gallon units. From about 1930, they started to use standard 3,500 gallon tenders, but, like the Dukes, the rear of the cabs had to be flared outward to reduce draughts. Some, especially those withdrawn to provide frames for Dukedogs, were never altered.

The class started to become redundant as early as the 1930s. The very successful and more versatile 4300 class had taken over much of their work, especially after the Hall class was introduced which released the 43xxs for lighter duties. Withdrawals started in the early 1930s, some being for Dukedog conversions, and only twenty-nine survived to British Railways. All but two were gone by 1949, the last surviving until 1951. In their last years they did little work, often being stored out of service.

3441 (Bird) class

Dates Built	1909/10
Number Built	15
Route Colour	Blue
Power Class	B
Tractive Effort	19,000lbs
Driving Wheel Size	5ft 8in
Cylinder Dimensions	18in x 26in
Wheelbase	6ft 6in + 7ft 3in + 8ft 6in
Boiler Class	Standard 2
Dates Withdrawn	1948-1951

This was to all intents and purposes a last batch of fifteen Bulldogs built in 1909 with deeper and stronger frames, although they did revert to screw reverse. They were numbered 3731-3745. They were also fitted with a new design of front bogie, which was based on those fitted to the 'Frenchmen' - deGlehn 4-4-2s.

3441 (Bird) series Bulldog. *Diagram A23 about 1923.*

They were renumbered 3441-3455 in 1912. For most purposes, they were considered part of the Bulldog class, tenders, changes and modifications were on the same lines, and from 1931 the same diagrams covered both Bulldogs and Birds. All survived to British Railways, none were converted to Dukedogs, and the last few were withdrawn in 1951.

Medium Boiler, Large Wheels

A curious feature of their large engine policy was that the GWR scrapped its express 4-4-0s very early – most went in the late 1920s and early 1930s, including the only modern inside frame 4-4-0 class, the Counties. At the same time the Southern and LNER were still building more.

Unlike the medium wheeled engines, there were some variations in wheelbase, which will be covered under the individual classes. There was still enough scope for engines to swap class from time to time.

Nos. 7, 8, 14, 16 (Armstrong class, 4100)

Dates Built	Rebuilt 1894 and again 1915-1923
Number Built	4
Route Colour	Red
Power Class	A
Tractive Effort	16,500-18,000lbs
Driving Wheel Size	7ft 1in, later 6ft 8½in
Cylinder Dimensions	20in x 26in, later 18in x 26in
Wheelbase	7ft + 7ft 6in + 9ft
Boiler Class	Special, later Standard 2
Dates Withdrawn	1928-30

7 (Armstrong) Class. *As built condition with the same boiler as the Dean Singles.*

4169 (Armstrong) Class. *As rebuilt post 1915 with Standard 2 boiler and 6ft 8½in wheels.*

These four engines had a very complex career. The four Armstrongs started out as nominal rebuilds of earlier prototypes, but probably very little of the original engines was used. At this stage, they were numbered 7,8,14 and 16 and were virtually 4-4-0 versions of the Dean Singles, with the same boilers and cylinders, smaller 7ft diameter wheels, and very handsome with it. Despite being amongst the earliest 4-4-0s, their deep curved frames are reputed to have been the strongest of the outside frame 4-4-0s.

They had the longest wheelbase of all the 4-4-0s, three inches longer than the Badmintons.

Rebuilding, Renumbering and Withdrawal
In 1905-10 they were rebuilt with Standard 2 boilers and wider cabs, and then superheated. Between 1915 and 1923 they were rebuilt again and given standard 6ft 8½in wheels, superheated Standard 2 boilers with top feed, and were renumbered from 4169-4172, having effectively merged with the other express Standard 2 classes into what was now the 4101 class. Once elegant Victorians, they were now transformed, looking very similar in appearance to the other Edwardian classes. They were scrapped from 1928-30.

4100 (Badminton, 3292) class

Dates Built	1897-9
Number Built	20
Route Colour	Red
Power Class	A
Tractive Effort	16,000-18,500lbs
Driving Wheel Size	6ft 8½in

Cylinder Dimensions	18in x 26in
Wheelbase	7ft + 7ft 3in + 9ft
Boiler Class	W, Standard 2, Standard 4
Dates Withdrawn	1927-1931

The Badmintons, like the Dukes, were built under Dean and as built looked very much like a large wheeled Duke. The twenty engines started life with domed boilers similar to the Dukes, but with a longer and Belpaire firebox (Class W). By 1913, all these class W boilers had been replaced by Standard 2s. They had Dean-style curved frames and were numbered 3292 to 3311.

In 1903 one Badminton, 3297 Earl Cawdor, was used for a quite extraordinary looking experiment, championed by Churchward's assistant F.G. Wright. Influenced

3292 (Badminton) class. *Diagram J. This sketch shows the class as first built.*

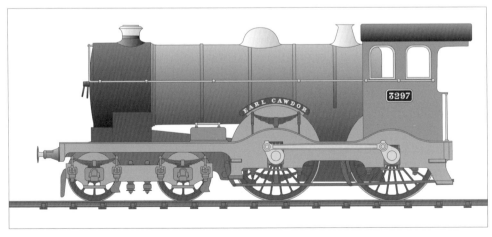

3297 (Badminton, Earl Cawdor). *Diagram O of 1903 showing the experimental boiler and cab fitted to 3297.*

4100 (Badminton) class. *Diagram A24 of about 1923. The sketch has been amended to show a style of frame reinforcement found on some of the class.*

particularly by NER practice this engine had a huge (5ft 5in diameter) parallel boiler with a round top firebox and was the very antithesis of Churchward's ideas. It even had a NER style cab with double side windows. The cab must have been unpopular with the Western enginemen, because it was speedily cut down and then replaced with a skimpier western cab in 1904. The large boiler was given an extended trial, in use until 1906, but the results must have been negative since it was cut up the following year and no change in GWR design practice ensued.

At the same time, another Badminton, Waterford, was being fitted with one of the large Standard 4 boilers. This must have been more successful, since between 1905 and 1910 sixteen more of the class were fitted with these boilers, making them equivalent to the Cities. In 1911/13, however, the Standard 4 boilers came off again and were replaced with Standard 2s, heavier duties now being undertaken by the new 4-6-0s.

Having been renumbered from 4100-4119 in 1908, they now formed the foundation of the 4100 class of medium boilered 4-4-0s. From this time, they received various frame strengthening exercises, superheating, top feed, and a little later piston valves. They were withdrawn in 1927-31. At least one was stored and offered for sale before being broken up. The number of potential customers for a 6ft 8in wheel outside framed 4-4-0 must have been distinctly limited.

4120 (Atbara, 3372) class

Dates Built	1900/01
Number Built	40
Route Colour	Red
Power Class	A

Tractive Effort	16,000-18,000lbs
Driving Wheel Size	6ft 8½in
Cylinder Dimensions	18in x 26in
Boiler Class	Standard 2
Wheelbase	6ft 6in + 7ft 6in + 8ft 6in
Dates Withdrawn	1902, 1907/8 (City rebuilds) 1927-31

The Atbaras were almost straight framed Badmintons, but the length and wheelbase were changed and the engines were a foot shorter overall. They were turned out from new with parallel Standard 2 boilers. Forty were built in 1900/01 and numbered 3373-3412. In their early days, many had the sort of combined name/number plates described under Bulldogs. Like the Bulldogs they had steam powered reversing gear. Sixteen were built with piston valves, but this early implementation was not very successful and they reverted to slide valves.

In 1902 No. 3405 was rebuilt with a Standard 4 boiler, effectively the prototype of the City Class.

Tapered Standard 2 boilers came in from 1904 and all the parallel boilers had gone by 1910. In 1907-9 3400-3409 were converted to City specification by being reboilered with Standard 4 boilers, and from then on were members of the City class. In the 1912 renumbering, the remaining Atbaras were allocated 4120-4148 (the Standard 4 conversions were renumbered in the 3700 series and one other Atbara had been scrapped after an accident). From this point, they were treated as members of the 4100 class and withdrawn with the others from 1927-1931.

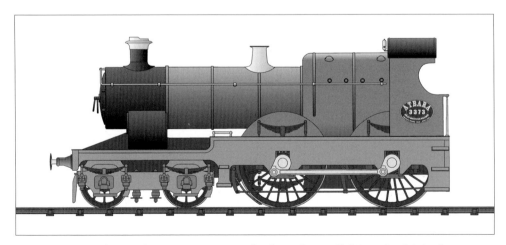

3272 (Atbara) class. *Diagram L as built with parallel Standard 2 boiler.*

4149 (Flower, 4101) class

Dates Built	1908
Number Built	20
Route Colour	Red
Power Class	A
Tractive Effort	17,500lbs
Driving Wheel Size	6ft 8½in
Cylinder Dimensions	18in x 26in
Wheelbase	6ft 6in + 7ft 6in + 8ft 6in
Boiler Class	Standard 2
Dates Withdrawn	1927-31

These were the deep, straight framed variety of the large wheel 4-4-0s, built in 1908 with screw reverse. They were numbered 4101-4120. Like their medium wheel counterparts, the Birds, they had the new deGlehn style bogie. They also had a different design of brake gear to their predecessors, with the brake rods inside the wheels - similar to the standard classes.

They were renumbered 4149-4168 in 1912, from which time all the Standard 2 boiler 4-4-0s from 4100 to 4172 were treated as one class. The combined class received superheating from 1909-13, top feed from 1911 and a new and successful design of piston valves from 1915.

As with their relatives, they rapidly became redundant as the 4-6-0 express engines came into service, and all were scrapped between 1927 and 1931.

4100 (Flower) class. *Diagram A19, around 1919.*

Large Boiler, Large Wheels
3700 (City, 3400) class

Dates Built	1902 (rebuilt Atbara), 1903, 1907/9 (rebuilt Atbaras)
Number Built	10 new, 10 rebuilt Atbaras
Route Colour	Red
Power Class	A
Tractive Effort	18,000lbs
Driving Wheel Size	6ft 8½in
Cylinder Dimensions	18in x 26in
Wheelbase	6ft 6in + 7ft 6in + 8ft 6in
Boiler Class	Standard 4
Dates Withdrawn	1927-31

Following on from the prototype, no. 3405, as mentioned in the Atbara section, these were the Standard 4 boiler version of the large wheeled 4-4-0s. The ten Cities proper were built in 1903. In 1904 *City of Truro* achieved enduring fame and unending controversy when it was timed at 102 mph at the hands of driver Moses Clement.

They were joined in 1907/8 by 9 more rebuilt Atbaras, and the combined class was renumbered as 3700-3719 in 1912. Superheating was fitted in 1910/2, top feed from 1911 and piston valve cylinders from 1915. They were essentially rendered redundant by the 4-6-0s and were, with the exception of *City of Truro*, scrapped between 1928 and 1931. 3717/3440 *City of Truro* survives, of course and has run in preservation.

3700 (City) class. *Diagram A13. This was the final configuration about 1916 on.*

3292 (Rebuilt Badminton) class

As noted above, seventeen Badmintons temporarily joined the large boiler class between 1905 and 1913. It is surprising that these were not renumbered into the 37xx series in the renumbering – perhaps their reversion to Standard 2 boilers was long planned. Some were superheated whilst carrying the large boilers, but none received piston valves in that configuration.

3800 (County) class

Dates Built	1904-1912
Number Built	40
Route Colour	Red
Power Class	C
Tractive Effort	20,500lbs
Driving Wheel Size	6ft 8½in
Cylinder Dimensions	18in x 30in
Wheelbase	7ft + 8ft 6in + 8ft 6in
Boiler Class	Standard 4
Dates Withdrawn	1930-33

The Counties were the last new 4-4-0s constructed for the GWR. They were pure Churchward standard engines with the Standard 4 boiler, inside frames and outside cylinders. In many ways, they resembled a truncated Saint, but the wheel spacing was similar to the Atbaras and Cities.

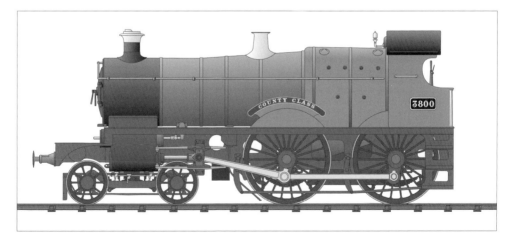

3800 (Churchward County) class. *Diagram N. The first batch as built with straight frames and without superheating.*

3800 (Churchward County) class. *Diagram A28. The last diagram for the class showing curved frames.*

They could be said to have been compromised by excess standardisation and no-one has ever seriously argued with the footplate crews' description of them as 'Churchward's Rough Riders'. The outside cylinders were a foot further forward than the inside cylinders on the Cities and the stroke was four inches longer, so the rocking moment from out of balance longitudinal forces must have been considerably greater than on their predecessors.

The first batch of Counties, 3473-3482 in the old scheme, came out in 1904, after the Cities, but before the last batches of Standard 2 boilered outside framed engines. They had straight frames, no top feed or superheaters at that date, and lever reverse. The cylinder centre line was offset 2½in above the wheel centreline like the early Saints.

They were followed in 1906 by 3801-3820. The main difference was that this batch had vacuum brakes, which meant the brake cylinder moved from between the cab steps to near the cylinders. The brake assemblies themselves moved too; from in front of the driving wheels with rigging outside the wheels, to behind the wheels with the rigging inside. They also had revised sanding arrangements.

The last batch, 3821-3830, had all the changes that the last batches of Saints had: curved ends, screw reverse and no offset between cylinder and wheel centres, as well as further changes to the braking arrangements.

3473 became 3800 in the 1912 renumbering, with 3474-3482 becoming 3831-3839. Thus, like the Saints, their numbers were quite out of sequence with build dates.

They were little altered over their lives – no new cylinders and curved frame front ends for the earlier locos for instance. One was turned out with a Standard 2 boiler in 1907. The success of this option may be judged by the appearance of the Flowers in 1908: it did not keep the small boiler very long! They were all withdrawn between 1930 and 1933 in the grand bonfire of the 4-4-0s, although one lingered on at Old Oak Common for a few years in the menial task of carriage heating.

Absorbed Classes at the Grouping
Cambrian Railway
Small Bogie Passenger class

Builders	Sharp Stewart & Co
Dates Built	1878-1891
Number Built	6
Route Colour	Ungrouped
Power Class	Unclassed
Tractive Effort	12,500-13,500lbs
Driving Wheel Size	5ft 6½in
Cylinder Dimensions	17in x 24in
Boiler Class	Own
Dates Withdrawn	1922-1930

These were six 4-4-0 tender engines with 5ft 6½in driving wheels, built by Sharp Stewart between 1878 and 1891. They all lasted to the GWR, but one was scrapped immediately and all were gone by the end of 1930.

Large Bogie Passenger class

Builders	Sharp Stewart & Co R. Stephenson & Co Cambrian Railway/Oswestry
Dates Built	1893-1904
Number Built	22 (21 to GWR)
Route Colour	Ungrouped
Power Class	Yellow
Tractive Effort	14,000lbs
Driving Wheel Size	6ft 0in
Cylinder Dimensions	18in x 24in
Boiler Class	Own
Dates Withdrawn	1922-1931

These were Sharp Stewart designed 4-4-0s with 6ft driving wheels. Sixteen were built by Sharps between 1893 and 1895, four by Stephenson's in 1897/8, and two in the Cambrian's own works in 1901 and 1904. One was destroyed in the Abermule disaster in 1921, but the others all came to the GWR. Five were scrapped on sight and four more in 1924. They received GWR safety valve covers (and presumably valves) but the last was withdrawn in 1931.

Midland and South Western Junction Railway
Dubs 4-4-0
The first 4-4-0 on the line. Built in 1893, and a fairly typical locomotive of the time. 6ft driving wheels, inside frames and cylinders and a flush round top firebox. Allocated 1127, it never carried the number and was scrapped in 1924.

North British 4-4-0s.

Builders	North British Locomotive Co
Dates Built	1905-1914
Number Built	9
Route Colour	Yellow
Power Class	A
Tractive Effort	16,500-18,500lbs
Driving Wheel Size	5ft 9in
Cylinder Dimensions	18in x 26in
Boiler Class	Own/Standard 2
Dates Withdrawn	1931-1938

They were built in ones and twos between 1905 and 1914. The design was fairly typical of the time, with inside frames and cylinders. There were some variations in boilers, most notably that a couple had two 'domes', the second carrying a top feed apparatus and safety valves.

They came to the GWR as diagram A35 and numbers 1119-1126. Thereafter there were more variations. Standard 2 boilers and GWR cabs were fitted to six of the class between 1924 and 1929, and several of the MSWJR boilers were superheated. By the time they were withdrawn, between 1931 and 1938, all had received either GWR Standard 2s or superheated MSWJR boilers, and some had received both at some stage.

2-6-0 Classes
Boilers

5322 (4300 class) *one of the classic Churchward 2 cylinder locomotives, here running at Didcot Railway Centre. (Photo: Jim Champ)*

Boiler Class	Name	Barrel		Firebox Length
		length	diameter	
K	Standard 10	10ft 3in	4ft 5in	5ft 0in	6ft 0in
B	Standard 2	11ft 0in	4ft 5in	5ft 0in	7ft 0in
D	Standard 4	11ft 0in	4ft 11in	5ft 6in	7ft 0in
O	Standard Goods	11ft 0in	4ft 5in		5ft 4in
P	2301	10ft 3in	4ft 5in		5ft 4in
Q	Sir Daniel	11ft 0in	4ft 3in		5ft 4in

GWR Classes
Inside Cylinder classes
2600 (Aberdare) class

Builders	GWR Swindon
Dates Built	1900-1907
Number Built	80

Route Colour	Blue
Power Class	D
Tractive Effort	23,000-26,000lbs
Driving Wheel Size	4ft 7½in
Cylinder Dimensions	18in x 26in
Wheelbase	7ft 6in + 7ft 6in + 7ft 6in
Boiler Class	Standard 2 or Standard 4
Dates Withdrawn	1934-1949

This class was effectively a goods version of the successful mixed traffic Bulldog and express Atbara classes, which put them firmly in the middle of the Churchward boiler development era. It is worthwhile to look at the development of this class alongside that of the 4-4-0s.

The first, no. 33, was turned out in 1900, so after the first 4-6-0 Kruger (see below) but before any of the 2-6-0 Krugers. It had a parallel Standard 2 boiler with a considerably raised Belpaire firebox and double frames. There was also a prominent compensation lever between pony track and leading driving wheels. It was fitted with steam reversing gear like some of the contemporary 4-4-0s.

2621-60 followed in 1901, suggesting that twenty numbers had been reserved for further Krugers. These had parallel Standard 2 boilers with raised fireboxes, some, indeed with steel fireboxes, and an early design of piston valves. They did not have the compensation gear on the leading bogie.

2661-2680 were built in 1902. 2661 had the one and only parallel Standard 4 boiler ever built, while the rest had tapered Standard 4 boilers. They were also constructed with slide valves. 2611-20 followed in 1903, and 2601-10 were built in 1906/7 after the demise of the Krugers.

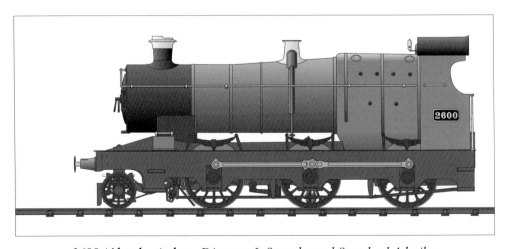

2600 (Aberdare) class. *Diagram I. Superheated Standard 4 boiler.*

The early piston valves created problems and locos built with piston valves received slide valves in 1904-9. The first batch, built with parallel Standard 2 boilers, received Standard 4 boilers between 1903 and 1910, but a handful did run with tapered No 2 boilers in the meantime.

Superheating was introduced from 1909-16, and in common with other contemporary classes there were a number of variations in the early days. Top feed was introduced in 1911; the first had the feed separate from and forward of the safety valve cover.

No. 33 was renumbered 2600 in the 1912 renumbering.

By 1915 all the problems with piston valves had been cured, and the class received them again, but the installation program was slow, with some locomotives not having them fitted until the 1930s.

They were initially fitted with 3,000 gallon tenders with coal rails, but solid fenders appeared from 1904. In 1929 the GWR had a plentiful supply of 4,000 gallon ex-ROD tenders, and fifty of these were fitted to Aberdares.

There were seven diagrams in all, covering various permutations of slide valves, piston valves, Standard 2 and Standard 4 boilers and the ROD tenders.

Scrapping started in 1934, twenty having been made redundant by new 7200 long range tank engines. The war interrupted the program, but they started to be scrapped again from 1944. One of them had an intervening spell as a gunnery target for USAF aircrews, who apparently did not do a great deal of damage, as it was repaired and returned to service, being withdrawn in 1945. Twelve made it to British Railways, but all were gone by the end of 1949; none have been preserved.

2602 (Kruger) Class

Builders	GWR Swindon
Dates Built	1901,1903
Number Built	9
Tractive Effort	25,000-30,000lbs
Driving Wheel Size	4ft 7½in
Cylinder Dimensions	19in x 28in
Wheelbase	8ft 6in + 7ft 6in + 7ft 6in
Boiler Class	Special
Dates Withdrawn	1906/7

The first of the remarkably ugly Kruger class was a 4-6-0 and is dealt with under that section. It came out in 1899. The chassis was very much of the Dean style, with outside frames. The rest of the class were all 2-6-0s, otherwise fairly similar. 2602 was built in 1901 and rather inevitably nicknamed Mrs Kruger. Eight more followed in 1903. They gave considerable trouble with boilers and

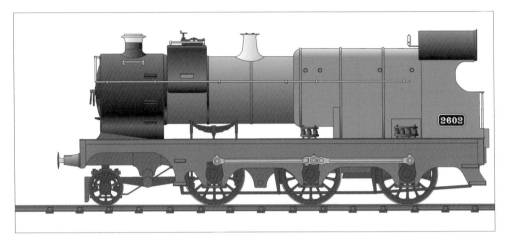

2602 (Kruger). *The first 2-6-0 as built with a saddle sandbox on the boiler. It was removed fairly soon. The rest of the class didn't have it and didn't look quite so ugly.*

motion components. The working pressure of the boiler was reduced to 165psi, but this does not seem to have made things better.

Officially, they were withdrawn between January 1906 and January 1907, but RCTS records that, in practice, the locomotives had been laid up for a year or more, some with the boilers removed. They did not run a great many miles in their short lives. The boilers continued to give service in Swindon works at lower pressure; indeed the last were not cut up until the 1960s. There was one diagram, A, for the 2-6-0 Kruger.

There were quite a number of features of the Krugers, especially the wide firebox boilers, which were ahead of their time – perhaps rather too ahead of their time – and a number of these were never again used by Churchward. It is ironic that one of these, the combustion chamber, probably should have been. A combustion chamber is effectively an extension of the upper part of the firebox into the boiler barrel. It brings the surface area of a wide firebox to about the same proportion to grate size as that of a narrow firebox and was exactly what Stanier had to introduce in order to make his GWR derived Pacific the success that Churchward's was not.

Churchward and Collett
4300 and 8300 classes

Builders	GWR Swindon, Robert Stephenson & Co
Number Built	322 (65 converted to 8300)
Dates Built	1911-1925
Route Colour	Blue (4300), Red (8300)
Power Class	D

Tractive Effort	25,500lbs
Driving Wheel Size	5ft 8in
Cylinder Dimensions	18½in x 30in
Wheelbase	8ft 9in + 7ft 0in + 7ft 9in
Boiler Class	Standard 4
Dates Withdrawn	1938 (for rebuilds) – 1964

The birth of the class, drawn by Holcroft to Churchward's instructions, is described in the introduction. It was, in effect, virtually a tender engine version of the 3150 class 2-6-2 tank. For the first batch Holcroft used the Saint cab, as being the smallest, to reduce the length for short turntables. With few new drawings required the type went into production with no prototype.

4301-4320 were turned out in 1911, the first engines built new with top feed. They were standard in most ways. An unusual feature was the elongated splasher over the middle driving wheel on the right hand side, which provided a cover for the brake vacuum pump.

The running department found the area under the cab to be somewhat cramped, so when 4321-4330 followed in 1913, they had the nine inches longer County cab and matching longer frames, as did all subsequent locos.

The versatility of the design – equally capable of running passenger services at close to express speed and quite heavy goods traffic – is shown by the fact that no other secondary line designs were produced under Churchward's reign. At one stage, they comprised 7 per cent of the locomotive stock and were running 14 per cent of the annual locomotive mileage. A drawback was that they could run short on steam on higher speed runs with heavy loads. A number were sent to France to serve the War department behind the lines in 1917.

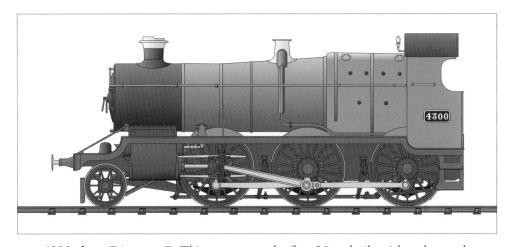

4300 class. *Diagram G. This represents the first 20 as built with a short cab.*

The class continued in production almost unchanged until 1917, with another six lots, by which time they consisted of 4300-4399 and 5300-5319. In 1917, a change was made to the pony truck and the weight distribution altered; 5320-5383 followed with this configuration.

From 5384, in 1920, the motion bracket design was changed to the smaller flanged type, possibly the first class to have this feature. From 5390, the reversing rod was moved outboard and the design of the splasher was changed. Production continued and numbers reached 6341 in 1921. At this point, the production history gets rather complicated and the locomotives were not built in numerical sequence. An order for fifty was placed with Robert Stephenson and Co, although in the event they only completed thirty-five of these, numbered 6370-6399 and 7300-4, in 1921/2. Then 7305-7319 were erected at Swindon, using components manufactured by Stephenson's, from Nov 1921 to Jan 1922. 6342-6361, entirely Swindon products, followed in 1923.

In 1925 6362-6369 and 7320/1, filling up the gap in the number series, were built at Swindon. These were built with outside steam pipes from new.

The first significant change in the 4300s was the weight distribution change made by moving the pony truck fulcrum in 1917. All the earlier locomotives received this modification, and the change was considered sufficiently important that, until all the class had been modified, the updated locomotives carried a red letter K (the change was documented as diagram K) under the number plate.

No locomotives were built as 8300s. Experience had shown that in areas with severe curves the leading driving wheels on the 4300s were experiencing severe flange wear. This resulted in uneconomically frequent wheel returning and tyre replacements. Originally, in late 1927, three locos between 4351 and 4395 were fitted with a heavy – approx. two tons – casting behind the front buffer beam, which moved the buffer beam forward a foot and changed the weight distribution. This brought them into red route restriction, but reduced the tyre wear. They were renumbered in the 8300 series by having 3950 added to their numbers: 4351 became 8300 and so on. However, these were soon reverted, and in early 1928 sixty-five locos in the 5300 series gained the ballast weight and had 3000 added to their numbers to put them in the 8300 series.

Outside steam pipes started to appear from 1928.

One hundred 43s (including twelve in 8300 configuration) were withdrawn between 1936 and 1939 for renewal into Manors and Granges. About half of the components from the 43s were used in the new locomotives. These were all from the 43 and 53 series: the 6300 series was left intact.

In 1944 there was a shortage of blue route locomotives, due to the conversion of 4300s to Granges and the withdrawal of older 4-4-0s, and the surviving 83s had the buffer beam casting removed. They returned to their 53xx numbers, mostly in 1944, with the last two in 1946 and 1948.

6320 was included in the oil burning programme in 1948, but was not renumbered, unlike other oil burning conversions.

3,500 gallon tenders were almost universal and most twentieth century variations were found on class members at one time or another.

There were nine diagrams. They were a late enough design not to have had the variations in superheater design seen on other Churchward classes. Most of the diagrams covered the weight distribution changes detailed above. The original batch with short cabs always had their own diagrams. Very late on, there were a small number of increased superheat boilers which also resulted in different diagrams.

Of the original 322, 221 survived to British railways, 100 having been renewed as 4-6-0s and one having been scrapped after an accident. Withdrawals began in 1948, with the last two of the first lot with the small cab going in 1952.

The majority, including all the 6300 series, survived until at least 1956 and scrapping in earnest started in 1958. 128 lasted into the 1960s, and the last twenty nine went in 1964.

Only one has survived: 5322, a Great War veteran, is owned by the Great Western Society.

9300 and 7322 classes

Builders	GWR/Swindon
Dates Built	1932 (converted to 7322 1956-9)
Number Built	20
Route Colour	Red (9300), Blue (7322)
Power Class	D
Tractive Effort	25,500lbs
Driving Wheel Size	5ft 8in
Cylinder Dimensions	18½in x 30in
Wheelbase	8ft 9in + 7ft 0in + 7ft 9in
Boiler Class	Standard 4
Dates Withdrawn	1961-1964

This was a Collett version of the 8300. Built in 1932, 9300-9319 had screw reverse and a 6ft frame extension to fit a side window cab. They were given the extended buffer beam and extra front end weight of the 8300 series and so were red route limited from new. As would be expected, they also had outside steam pipes. The boiler was raised fractionally: by 5/16 of an inch.

9300s, in common with other side window classes, had the side windows plated over during the Second World War.

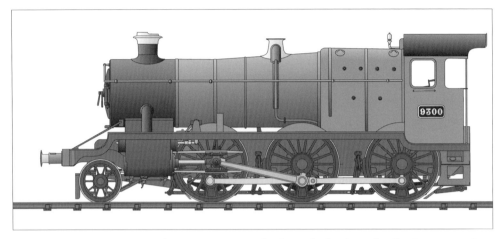

9300 class. *Diagram R. The 9300 series as built with the front buffer beam weight.*

From 1956 to 1959, the 9300s had the buffer beam ballast weight removed to bring them down to blue weight restriction. They were renumbered 7322-7341, bringing them into the 4300 number series.

There were three diagrams, one for the 9300 configuration, and two for the 7322s, one being for the increased superheat boilers.

They all lasted into the 1960s, six until 1964. One survived, is owned by the Severn Valley Railway, and has run in preservation.

Absorbed Class at the Grouping
Midland and South Western Junction Railway
Beyer Peacock 2-6-0.

Builders	Beyer Peacock & Co
Dates Built	1896
Number Built	2 (see notes)
Route Colour	Uncoloured
Power Class	B
Tractive Effort	21,000lbs
Driving Wheel Size	4ft
Cylinder Dimensions	18in x 26in
Boiler Class	Own/Standard 9
Dates Withdrawn	1930

The MSWJR had had two of these, but only one, built in 1896, was taken over by the GWR, the other having been sold in 1918. The survivor became GWR 24 and received the nickname 'Galloping Gertie'. In 1925, it received a Standard 9 boiler and a Swindon cab. It was withdrawn in 1930.

CHAPTER 4

Ten Wheeled Tender Engines

The GWR moved very quickly from a fleet of predominantly six wheeled engines to ten wheeled. This was surely Churchward's doing, and may not have been completely supported by his directors: one of them has been quoted as saying privately of Churchward's locomotives, '… unnecessarily big and heavy, causing us to spend too much money on track and bridges … and too expensive to build.'

4-6-0s, 4-4-2s and the 4-6-2

7828 (**Manor class**) *running on the West Somerset Railway bearing the name 'Norton Manor'. (Photo: Jim Champ)*

Boilers

Boiler Class	Name	Barrel			Firebox length
		length	diameter		
Z	Standard 14	12ft 6in	4ft 7⅝in	5ft 3in	8ft 8in
O	Standard 15	12ft ¼in	5ft 0in	5ft 8¼in	9ft 9in
A	Standard 1	14ft 10in	4ft 10¾in	5ft 6in	9ft 0in
H	Standard 8	14ft 10in	5ft 2in	5ft 9in	10ft 0in
W	Standard 12	16ft 0in	5ft 6in	6ft 0in	11ft 6in
	'Standard 6'	23ft 0in	5ft 6in	6ft 0in	8ft 0in

GWR Classes
Dean
No. 36 – the Crocodile

Builders	GWR/Swindon
Dates Built	1896
Number Built	1
Driving Wheel Size	4ft 6in
Cylinder Dimensions	20in x 24in
Boiler Class	special
Dates Withdrawn	1905

It was something like a small-wheeled (4ft 6in) Duke 4-4-0 with two extra driving wheels. The boiler was unusual, with 'Serve' tubes, which had internal fins to increase the heating surface. The double frames turned into single external frames after the rear driving wheels in order to make room for a wide firebox. Built in 1896, it was withdrawn in 1905, having had changes only to wheel diameter (the normal thicker tyres at that period) and boiler water feed. There doesn't appear to be any evidence to suggest that the locomotive was a failure, although it did not run an especially high mileage in its eight years of life, but clearly by 1905 there was little point to keeping it alongside a fleet of 2800s.

2601 – Kruger

Builders	GWR/Swindon
Dates Built	1899
Number Built	1
Tractive Effort	28,000lbs

Driving Wheel Size	4ft 7½in
Cylinder Dimensions	19in x 28in
Wheelbase	5ft 6in + 4ft 6in + 7ft 6in + 7ft 6in
Boiler Class	Special
Dates Withdrawn	1904

It does no-one's reputation with posterity any harm to get their mistakes out of the way under their predecessor's name and Churchward certainly did this in 1899 with 2601, nicknamed Kruger by his railwaymen. This was roughly the equivalent of nicknaming the loco Adolf Hitler in 1940 or Osama Bin Laden in 2011. Naturally it never actually carried that (or any) name.

Although it had a similar chassis, in many ways 2601 was the complete antithesis of No. 36, being, amongst other things, irredeemably ugly, whereas 36 was quite attractive in a Victorian sort of way. The 4-6-0 was followed by nine 2-6-0s that were little better, and are dealt with above. The boiler started off running at 200psi, but this was later reduced to 180psi and possibly later to 165psi. Suspension was by nests of volute springs, not the conventional leaf springs.

2601 is recorded as having been withdrawn in 1904 after running only 67,000 miles. There was one diagram for the 4-6-0 Kruger.

Churchward
2900 (Saint) class

Builders	GWR/Swindon
Dates Built	1902-1913
Number Built	77
Route Colour	Red
Power Class	C
Tractive Effort	20,500- 25,000lbs
Driving Wheel Size	6ft 8½in
Cylinder Dimensions	18in x 30in, later 18½in x 30in
Wheelbase	7ft 0in + 5ft 4in + 7ft 0in + 7ft 9in (No 100 - 7ft 2in + 5ft 3in + 7ft 0in + 7ft 9in)
Boiler Class	Standard 1
Dates Withdrawn	1931-1953

The Saints were arguably the most influential class of British locomotives of the twentieth century. The basic principles they introduced lasted until the end of steam; even Wardale's 5AT proposal (www.5at.co.uk) for a third generation steam locomotive oozes Saint ancestry.

2900 (Saint) class. *Diagram L. Straight frames Saint with top feed and superheater. The Great Western Society are rebuilding a Hall into this configuration to become Saint 2999, 'Lady of Legend'.*

171 (Scott) class. *Diagram B. This shows the early 4-4-2s with non-superheated short cone boilers. Note that the smokebox is considerably shorter on the unsuperheated engines.*

2900 (Saint) class. *Diagram V. 1930s condition with outside steampipes and without compensated suspension.*

The Saint has by far the most complex history of the 4-6-0s, because it was right in the thick of Churchward's development.

As described in the Introduction, the first prototype was No 100, which differed significantly from the production locomotives. The second prototype, no. 98, introduced all of the standard features except for top feed and superheat, which came later. No, 98 was followed by no. 171, which is probably best described as a pre-production locomotive rather than a prototype. It had an improved version of the Standard 1 boiler with 225psi boiler pressure and was soon converted into a 4-4-2 to enable closer comparison with 102 *La France*, the imported French compound 4-4-2. The name *Albion*, for a locomotive built to be tested against *La France*, was inspired! A batch of nineteen followed, 172-190, thirteen as 4-4-2 and six as 4-6-0. This sort of long term trial of different features on closely related locomotives was a key aspect of Churchward's work, and must have been a far better way of evaluating design features than building one off prototypes.

The next batch was 2901-2910, later named as Ladies, which had a mix of short cone and long cone boilers. 2901 was built with a Schmidt superheater – the first modern superheater on any locomotive in the UK. One of the Ladies was involved in a somewhat shadowy incident. It seems there was a desire to see if a new engine could be run, light engine, up to 100mph fresh out of the works (one wonders why). In the course of the exercise, it is claimed that they managed to run the poor locomotive up to the region of 120mph, although not timed in any accurate manner. Goodness only knows how it stayed on the track and avoided major mechanical damage.

Next, in 1907, were 2911-2930, the actual Saints. Still unsuperheated, but with curved end framing, these were the first locomotives to have the full classic twentieth century GWR look. The Saints had screw reverse rather than the big reversing lever of the earlier locomotives.

Finally, in 1911-1913, were the Courts, 2931-55. These were built new with superheating and top feed. From 2941 they were delivered with 18½in diameter cylinders, the bore having been previously increased to 18⅛in from 2902 against the 18in of the prototypes. The Courts had the cylinder centreline aligned with the wheel centres, unlike the earlier locomotives.

The Saints, indeed all the Churchward standard 4-6-0s, were built with compensating beams between the driving wheel suspension units, and, in the case of the 4-4-2s, between driving and trailing wheels.

The first batch of Saints were built without names, but soon acquired them. The 4-4-2s were mostly given names from the Broad Gauge 'Waverley' class, in turn mostly from Sir Walter Scott's *Waverley* novels and the 4-6-0s were named after GWR directors. For some reason, many of this group were renamed again, sometimes more than once.

The early Saints, 171-190, were renumbered 2971-2997 in 1912. The first prototype 100 was renumbered 2900 and the second, 98, 2998.

No. 100 lost its parallel boiler in favour of a short cone taper boiler within eighteen months of being built. Some fifty-five short cone boilers were built up to January 1907; after that only long cone Standard 1 boilers were constructed. The short cone boilers were used interchangeably with long cone boilers on earlier Saints, Stars and 2800 2-8-0s until the early 1920s. Presumably they were scrapped when major repairs were required.

The 4-4-2s were rebuilt as 4-6-0s from 1912 to 1913 and acquired the curved end treatment at both front end and cab at the same time. Older engines tended to get the upgrades built into the later batches. After 1930 locomotives received outside steam pipes when new front ends were fitted. The cabs were not altered with the new front ends so those few locomotives that retained the old straight framing received the curved front end, but not the altered cab. Compensation was removed in the 1930s when improved suspension was fitted. There were a considerable number of minor changes and variations over the years – safety valve covers, chimneys and the like.

2931 *Caynham Court* was rebuilt with rotary cam poppet valve gear in 1931. Although not considered a great success, it was retained until the locomotive was scrapped in 1948, but not used on any other GWR locomotives.

The prototypes were initially fitted with 4,000 gallon tenders, of which a small batch was built in the early twentieth century. Thereafter, the class normally ran with various 3,500 gallon units, although 4,000 gallon tenders similar to the Castle class were occasionally seen.

Although there were fifteen locomotive diagrams issued for the 29xx, the vast majority were from the development years under Churchward. After Diagram V was issued for the batch from 2941 on, the only other new diagrams issued were for *Caynham Court*'s poppet valves and *Saint David*'s conversion to the prototype Hall.

Withdrawals started from 1931, albeit slowly. Forty-seven lasted into BR days, but all were gone by 1953. Really one should have been preserved. At the time of writing, the Great Western Society are rebuilding an early Hall, 4942, into a Saint, to be 2999 *Lady of Legend*.

Nos 102-104 (The Frenchmen)

Builders	SACM France
Dates Built	1903, 1905
Number Built	3
Route Colour	Blue (102), Red
Power Class	B
Tractive Effort	24,000, 27,000lbs

Driving Wheel Size	6ft 8½in
Cylinder Dimensions	13⅛in (HP, outside) & 22¹⁄₁₆in (LP, inside) x 25³⁄₁₆in, 14³⁄₁₆in (HP, outside) & 23⅝in (LP, inside) x 25³⁄₁₆
Boiler Class	Special, Standard 1
Dates Withdrawn	1926-1928

Much has been written about 102, 103 and 104: *La France, Alliance* and *President*. It is difficult to think of many other examples of a major British line bringing in radically different locomotives from another country in order to evaluate their performance. The object of the exercise was to see whether a good compound locomotive was superior to the good simple locomotive the GWR already had in the Saint prototypes. It made a lot more sense to buy in known good locomotives rather than attempt to build their own and risk comparing a poor compound with a good simple expansion loco. Most British compounds had been unsuccessful, not least the GWR's own ones built under Dean. It is clear that no great advantage was established from compounding, but many detail features from the Frenchmen were adopted, most notably aspects of bogie and inside big end design. The advantages of the 4 cylinder layout led to the introduction of the Stars.

The locomotives were obviously considered useful, because they were adapted so that they could carry Standard 1 boilers and thus go through the works faster than if they had to wait until their own boilers had been repaired. They were also superheated with other express classes in the 1913-1915 period and were as powerful as the native classes.

They were bought without tenders and built so they could use standard GWR units. 102 initially ran with a 4,000 gallon tender, but used a 3,500 gallon one from 1916, whilst 103 and 104 were only recorded with 3,500 gallon units.

They were withdrawn between 1926 and 1928 when Castle production was in full swing after running between 700,000 and 800,000 miles – around half the life of a Saint or a Star.

4000 (Star) class

Builders	GWR/Swindon
Dates Built	1906-1923
Number Built	73
Route Colour	Red
Power Class	D
Tractive Effort	25,000-28,000lbs
Driving Wheel Size	6ft 8½in

Cylinder Dimensions	14½in x 26in-15in x 26in (4)
Wheelbase	7ft 0in + 5ft 6in + 7ft 0in + 7ft 9in
Boiler Class	Standard 1
Dates Withdrawn	1925-1940 (rebuilt as Castles), 1933-1957

Churchward is considered to have been very impressed with certain aspects of the design of the deGlehn Compounds he had bought from France to run up against the Saints - in particular the smooth running provided by the divided drive – the term used for having the two pairs of cylinders driving different wheel sets.

The Stars were very similar indeed to the Saints. They were a foot longer at the front to allow for the inside cylinders, but otherwise most of the critical dimensions were identical and they must have had many parts in common. One distinctive difference – and identification point – between the 2 cylinder and 4 cylinder locomotives is the shape of the slide bars. The relationship between cylinders and wheel position on the 4-cylinder locos meant the motion bracket that supports the end of the slide bar had to be some way behind the actual end of the bearing surfaces. The 'forked' end of the slide bars provided clearance for the connecting rod.

No. 40 (later 4000) was built in 1906 as a direct comparison with the Frenchmen, with 4-4-2 wheel arrangement. The cylinders were 14½in x 26in, and the boiler was a No. 1. The valve gear was very unusual. It was a variation of Walschaerts gear, but had no eccentrics: instead the equivalent movement was taken from the other side of the engine. It looks elegant and efficient, but it was not repeated, and several different reasons for this are proposed by various writers. There is a discussion in appendix F.

The first batch of production Stars, 4001-10, came out about a year after the prototype. They had curved ends to the framing and a more conventional arrangement of inside Walschaerts valve gear. The second batch, Knights, in 1908, had improved front bogies based on concepts from the Frenchmen.

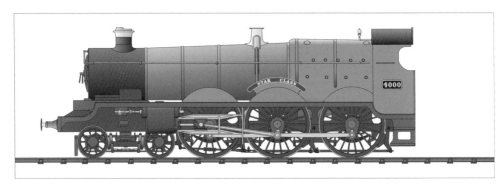

4000 (Star) class. *Diagram M around 1911.*

They were followed by ten Kings in 1909 – essentially the same – and were not superheated, with the exception of 4011, which carried the first style of Swindon designed superheater. Ten Queens, all with standard superheaters, followed in 1910/11. Five Princes were built in 1913, the first being turned out with 15in diameter cylinders. Fifteen Princesses were built in 1914, all with the larger cylinders. These were the first to be built with the large 4 cone ejector running down the right hand side of the boiler which had become standard equipment for the larger passenger classes. A last batch of Stars, the twelve Abbeys, were built in 1922, so, Churchward having retired at the end of 1921, these were nominally under Collett's watch. There were some minor changes to the crank axle and its balancing and initially some had fluted coupling rods.

Knight of the Black Eagle was hastily renamed after war was declared on Germany in 1914 and the King series of Stars were renamed *The British Monarch*, *The Belgian Monarch* etc. when the King class was introduced. A number of these had their names removed in 1940 and 1941, when the monarchs in question came under Nazi subjection or declared war on Great Britain!

Stars 4063-4072 were renumbered 5083-5092 when rebuilt into the Castle class, as these were officially renewals into new locomotives. Earlier Star rebuilds normally kept the existing numbers, although 4009 was renumbered/renamed 100A1 *Lloyds*, with 100, 100A1 and just A1 used as the number at different times and on different parts of the locomotive.

All Stars were built with long cone Standard 1 boilers, but short cone boilers were interchanged with long cone boilers up until the early 1920s. Twenty-four of the class are recorded as having had short cone boilers at some stage in their life, but none of the Princess or Abbey batches and only one of the Princes. From 1929, outside steam pipes started to be fitted. These were of two types – the elbow type and the Castle type. The elbow type allowed boilers with outside steam pipes and matching internal arrangements to be used on locomotives that still had cylinders set up for inside pipes, as only a few Stars (other than conversions to the Castle class) received outside steam pipe cylinders.

Between 1925 and 1929, five Stars were upgraded to Castle class specification by extending the Star frames and adding new cylinders, boilers and cabs whilst reusing other components. These were classed as rebuilds and kept their original numbers. 4000 lost its non-standard valve gear during the rebuild. By contrast, between 1937 and 1940, Stars 4063-4072 from the Abbey series were scrapped and new Castles (5083-5092) were built by extending the Star frames and adding new cylinders, boilers and cabs whilst reusing other components. The difference between the rebuild and the scrapping and replacement exercises might seem purely notional, but it was a vital distinction – in the books…

Stars were initially fitted with various designs of 3,500 gallon tender. Two of the class ran with *The Great Bear*'s 8 wheel bogie tender during 1936; from 1938

4,000 gallon tenders, both low sided and high sided, became the usual fitment. Two were observed with slab sided Hawksworth 4,000 gallon tenders after WW2.

There were eleven diagrams, mostly concerned with superheater variations and cylinder size, and one covering the 4,000 gallon tender.

Withdrawals started in the 1930s, from the Star, Knight and King batches, but only ten had been withdrawn by the time the war came, which, with the fifteen Castle conversions, brought the class down to forty-eight at the end of the war. Forty-seven (plus all the conversions) survived to British Railways, but the majority were gone by 1953, the last surviving until 1957. One is preserved, 4003 *Lode Star*, in non-running but ex Swindon Works condition.

No 111 (The Great Bear)

Builders	GWR/Swindon
Date built	1908
Number Built	1
Route Colour	Special Red
Power Class	D
Tractive Effort	28,000lbs
Driving Wheel Size	6ft 8½in
Cylinder Dimensions	15in x 26in (4)
Wheelbase	7ft 0in + 5ft 6in + 7ft 0in + 7ft 0in + 8ft 0in
Boiler Class	Standard 6
Dates Withdrawn	1924 (rebuilt as Castle)

The Great Bear, the Great Western's only 4-6-2, was Churchward's most prominent disappointment. The front end is almost pure Star. The firebox had a wide grate of about 30 per cent greater area than a Standard 1 boiler (and therefore about a foot shorter). This was located immediately behind rear driving wheels which had been moved as far forward as possible. The tubes filled the gap in between the firebox and the smokebox. That meant a 23ft barrel! Then there was a tiny cab tacked on the back – to try and keep the length and weight down. The long barrel also meant that the superheater surface area was very large by contemporary standards. The firebox tube plate was vertical and, unlike later Stanier and Gresley Pacifics, there was no combustion chamber to increase the volume of the firebox, so the heating surface was small in proportion.

The tender had 3,500 gallon water capacity as on most 4-6-0s at the time, but it was a special unit carried on two 4 wheel bogies which were based on locomotive front bogies. Apparently, this was purely for aesthetic reasons!

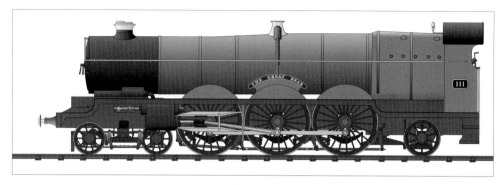

111, The Great Bear

There were two rebuilds of the boiler. The original boiler design featured an early superheater design with three rows of relatively small flue tubes containing elements of the Field type in which the steam flow is through two concentric tubes. This was changed to two rows of standard size flue tubes, firstly with 8 standard U shaped elements per tube and latterly with 6 of larger diameter, which was a change made across all the larger standard boilers. On both rebuilds, the superheater heating surface was reduced and by the end of its life, the superheater area was down to 75 per cent of the original figure.

In 1924, with a new inner firebox required, the locomotive went into the works to be converted into a Castle. The frames were cut between the second and third driving wheels and an extension to Castle dimensions welded on. It also came out of the shops with a new name, *Viscount Churchill*, but, like the early Star conversions, the same number.

Collett
4073 (Castle) class

Builders	GWR/Swindon
Dates Built	1923-1950
Number Built	171 (see notes)
Route Colour	Red
Power Class	D
Tractive Effort	31,500lbs
Driving Wheel Size	6ft 8½in
Cylinder Dimensions	16in x 26in (4)
Wheelbase	7ft 0in + 5ft 6in + 7ft 0in + 7ft 9in
Boiler Class	Standard 8
Dates Withdrawn	1950-1962 (rebuilt Stars), 1959-1965

The Castle was something of a compromise. Early studies for the design show the big Standard 7 boiler from the 47xx class, but this could not be made to work within the weight limits on the line. A smaller barrel was used to keep the weight down whilst the firebox was very similar to the Standard 7. As compromises go it was brilliant. There is some evidence that the Castle could not cope with poor coal as well as some other line's locomotives but the remedy for that is obvious.

It is surprising that the number series for the Castle follows straight on from that of the Stars rather than, say, starting at 5000. In that respect, perhaps they were originally seen as a further batch of Stars – as indeed in most ways they were.

The design had a great influence on other railways. There was a swap between the LNER and the GWR in 1925, when the Castle, matched against early Gresley Pacifics, demonstrated lower fuel consumption, with at least equal power, and superior adhesion and acceleration up the gradient out of King's Cross. The Gresley locomotives were soon modified with Churchward style long travel valve gear and higher boiler pressure. Another exchange, with the LMS, was not competitive, but simply for evaluation and the result was that the LMS first asked the GWR for fifty Castles, or the drawings to build their own. When refused, they went to the Southern Railway, whose new Lord Nelson class had considerable GWR influence, for drawings and a 3 cylinder version was designed and built by the North British Locomotive company, somewhat over the head of Fowler, the LMS CME. This was the genesis of the Royal Scot class. Not so many years later the LMS came to the GWR for a new CME, W.A. (later Sir William) Stanier. He was a loss to the GWR but a far greater gain to the LMS.

The first batch was 4073-4082, built 1923/4. 4083-92 followed in 1925 and 4093-5012 in 1926/7. 5013-22 in 1932 comprised the first significant improvement to the Castles. They had a fire iron tunnel, a revised casing over the inside cylinders and were also the first to be built without compensating

4073 (Castle) class, *Diagram W. Note Bogie brakes and compensating beams in the suspension.*

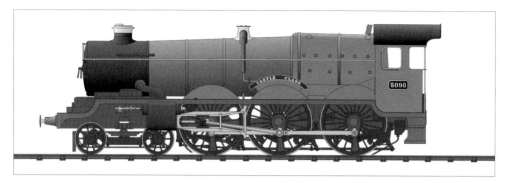

5098 (Castle) class. *Diagram A22.*

5098 (Castle) class *Diagram A30. 4 row superheater and double chimney.*

beams on the springing. There was also a boiler design change, with a slightly smaller grate and wider water space to improve water circulation. This was the class HB boiler.

A really important but completely invisible change came in the next batch, 5023-5032 in 1934 – this was the first to be assembled using Zeiss optical alignment equipment, which brought a big advance in precision of assembly.

5033-5042 were built in 1935, 5043-67 in 1936/7 and 5068-5082 in 1938/9. 5083-5092, between 1937 and 1940, were the Star rebuilds mentioned above and 5093-7 in 1939 were the last all new Castles until after the war.

5098 class

In 1946 came the next significant change. 5098/9 and 7000-07 and on were built with new design (HC) boilers with three row superheaters and improved steam passages to the cylinders. They were known as the 5098 class. These came with slab sided Hawksworth style tenders. As a footnote, 7007, the last Great Western-built Castle in August 1946, was renamed *Great Western* in January 1948.

7008/27 followed in 1948/9 and so were purely BR locomotives. 7017 was named *G.J. Churchward* after the great man. The last of all were 7028 to 7037 in 1950, with 7037 named *Swindon* by Princess Elizabeth, the future Queen. This was the last batch of Castles, but not the end of the changes...

A handful of Castles, seemingly chosen at random, were renamed after Army regiments over the years, a couple before the Second World War, one after Korea. Castles 5043-5063 were renamed as Earls in 1937 after the noble Lords objected to their names being put on Dukedogs. 5071-5082 were renamed in 1940/41 after aircraft that were prominent in the Battle of Britain. There were some later renamings under BR, mainly to names associated with the Great Western.

The renamings saw some Castle names carried by more than one locomotive. The most extreme case was *Ogmore Castle*, the original name for 5056 *Earl of Powis*, 5080 *Defiant*, and 7007 *Great Western* until it found a permanent home at the fourth try on 7035. Thus, that name was involved in all three significant Castle renaming exercises.

Castles were built from 1923 to 1950, which is probably the longest lifespan of any British express steam locomotive class. The last ones were built after the first (albeit a Star conversion) was withdrawn.

There were various design improvements over the life of the class, with differing frame arrangements and cylinder design and, as mentioned, some of these were significant enough to be regarded as sub classes. The Castles were rather less homogenous than most Collett era classes. The first significant change was removal of compensated springing from those earlier locomotives that were built with it. Five Castles were temporarily converted to oil burning in 1946/7, but unlike other classes were not renumbered. All returned to coal firing in 1948. The three row superheater boilers designed for the 5098 series were used on older engines, but there is some evidence that they tended to be restricted to the later ones. There was further work on draughting arrangements in the 1950s.

A four row superheater boiler was designed in 1947, and from 1953 all new boilers were to this design. Towards the end of the 1950s this was coupled with a radical draughting change and a double chimney. This arrangement was fitted to over sixty members of the class, including some of the very earliest locomotives and even a couple of the Star conversions. The result was a significant increase in performance. Some of these upgrades had a very short life – less than a year in one case, which is most likely to have been a result of policy changes at Paddington.

The first Castles were built with 3,500 gallon tenders, but in 1926 a new design of 4,000 gallon tender was introduced and this became standard by 1930. After the Second World War, a slab sided Hawksworth design tender was fitted to new builds, and of course spread round the class. Unusual tender fitments included an 8 wheel 4,000 gallon tender with rigid frames, *The Great Bear*'s bogie tender and an experimental tender with an aluminium alloy water tank.

There were no less than eleven diagrams for the Castle class, but three were tender variations and one was a rather half-hearted exercise in streamlining. The rest were concerned with boiler/superheating variants.

Withdrawals started with the rebuilt Stars (and *The Great Bear*), which went between 1950 and 1957. From 1959 steam traction started to be run down and locomotives requiring heavy repairs started to be withdrawn instead, the majority going from 1963 to 1965. It is appropriate that a Castle hauled the last pre-preservation steam train out of Paddington Station.

Eight Castles have survived into preservation and most have run or are running with just one still in scrapyard condition at the time of writing. Castles are regular main line performers.

6000 (King) class

Builders	GWR/Swindon
Dates Built	1927-1930
Number Built	30
Route Colour	Double Red
Power Class	Unclassified
Tractive Effort	40,300lbs
Driving Wheel Size	6ft 6in
Cylinder Dimensions	16¼in x 28in (4)
Wheelbase	7ft 8in + 5ft 6in + 8ft 0in + 8ft 3in
Boiler Class	Standard 12
Dates Withdrawn	1962

The tale of the genesis of the Kings has been told in many places and, perhaps unsurprisingly, details vary between sources. Sir Felix Pole, the then General Manager, related a 1926 conversation between himself, one of the Directors and Collett, in which the Castles were criticised as being slightly unsatisfactory in some respects. Collett replied to the effect that he was hamstrung by the weight limits and if he were only allowed to build to a 22½ ton axle load limit he could build a much better locomotive.

The next development was when Pole asked the Civil Engineering department what weight limit they designed new and replacement structures to. He was astonished to be told that it was 22 tons, and had been since 1904, when the new guideline had been agreed between Churchward and the civil engineers. Pole instructed Collett to build a 22½ton axle weight locomotive for the summer of 1927 and the Chief Engineer to have the main line to Plymouth ready for it.

Pole also says that the early designs had tractive effort coming out at just under 40,000 pounds, and he asked if it could be increased. He states it was done by reducing the driving wheel diameter by ¼in, but Pole's memory failed him in this minor detail, even though his statement has been reproduced; the extra TE was obtained by boring out the cylinders by an extra ¼in. It is probable that later locomotives were delivered with 16in cylinders.

The Kings had a non-standard driving wheel size of 6ft 6in, which was fixed at an early stage of design. A Castle was run for a limited time with tyres turned down to 6ft 6in – slightly under scrapping thickness for a Castle – to evaluate this feature. There were also detail improvements to the valve gear over the Castles and Stars.

An interesting side line on GWR accounting practice concerns 6007. It was damaged in the Shrivenham disaster in 1936 and was condemned. Officially it was replaced by a new locomotive. In fact, the original engine was repaired. This was another example of use of the renewal account.

In their middle age the frames tended to become tired at the front end, where the cylinder loads came, and all had new front ends with cylinders welded on at a point ahead of the leading wheels. They also required some reinforcement to the leading bogie during the 1950s. There were also new design outside steam pipes which had easier curves and so were more flexible.

Like the Castles, the biggest change to the Kings was the installation of four row superheaters and later double chimneys, together with considerable changes to the smokebox arrangements which made a very significant difference to the power output.

The Kings had new 4,000 gallon tenders. They were basically of the same design as other contemporary 4,000 gallon tenders but there were changes in various fittings, notably the water delivery pipes.

There were four diagrams for the Kings, one as built, one for a streamlining exercise similar to that on the Castle, one for the four row superheater and the last for the double chimney.

6000 (King) class. *Diagram Z, but some features are from 6020 upwards.*

The entire class was withdrawn between June and December 1962. Three have survived and all have now run in preservation.

4900 Hall class

Builders	GWR/Swindon
Dates Built	1924 (rebuild), 1928-1943
Number Built	259
Route Colour	Red
Power Class	D
Tractive Effort	27,000lbs
Driving Wheel Size	6ft 0in
Cylinder Dimensions	18½in x 30in
Wheelbase	7ft 0in + 5ft 4in + 7ft 0in + 7ft 9in
Boiler Class	Standard 1
Dates Withdrawn	1959-1965 (1 destroyed in air raid, 1941)

Churchward/Holcroft's versatile little 43xx 2-6-0 was, apparently, much loved by the locomotive department, but it had one significant limitation. With the standard Churchward front end, it could, if run faster or with a bigger load than normal, use rather more steam than the relatively small No. 4 boiler could deliver. The running department were making noises that what they needed was a 43xx with a No. 1 boiler. So in 1924, Collett took a Saint and rebuilt it with 6ft diameter wheels. Why 6ft rather than the standard 5ft 8½in is unclear. Anyway, this conversion spent four years being trialled round the system. The success of the trials can be gauged by the fact that the first order was for eighty!

The first batch, 4901-4980 came between December 1928 and February 1930. These were very much built up to the current standards, with outside steam pipes and a side window cab like the Castles. They had compensating beams between the driving wheels. The cylinder and wheel centres were in line, unlike the early Saints.

4981–5920 followed between December 1930 and August 1931. These, and all subsequent batches, did not have the compensated suspension. From 5911 in 1931 they had smaller piston valves – 9in diameter, the same as the Kings. The next batch, 5921-5940, came in 1933 and these had a fire iron tunnel on the fireman's side. Further batches, essentially the same, were built every year until 1943, 6958 being the last.

Side window cabs had the side windows plated over as an air raid precaution during the war. The windows were reinstated after the war; those built without

4900 (Hall) class. *Diagram A2. This is one of the early batches of Halls while they still had compensated suspension.*

them had them added. Eleven Halls were converted to oil firing in 1946/7 and renumbered. Five with numbers under 4972 (i.e. from the first batch) were numbered in the 3900 series; the other six, all from post 1937 lots, were numbered from 3950. When the experiment was abandoned, and all were returned to coal firing, they resumed their old numbers. Three row increased superheat boilers, as found on the Modified Halls, started to appear on Halls in the course of normal boiler swaps during overhauls in the 1950s. In the 1950s, the locomotives fitted with 9in valves tended to have them replaced with 10in valves.

The first forty or so started life with Churchward pattern 3,500 gallon tenders, the next few a Collett design 3,500 gallon unit, but from 4958 on most were given Collett 4,000 gallon tenders when new. Later on, Hawksworth slab sided tenders appeared on the class, as did the experimental 8 wheel tender noted in the Castle section.

There were six diagrams altogether for the Halls. One was for the prototype, *Saint Martin*, and three for the standard locomotives with different tenders. There was another diagram for the oil burners and finally one for three row superheater boilers

4911 was scrapped in 1941 due to air raid damage, otherwise all reached BR. The first two or three were withdrawn in 1959 and they started to be withdrawn in numbers in 1962, with the majority going between 1963 and 1965.

Eleven Halls have survived into the preservation era, but one is being converted into a Saint, and some of the others are still essentially in scrapyard condition.

6800 (Grange) and 7800 (Manor) classes

Builders	GWR/Swindon
Dates Built	1936-1939 (partial rebuilds), 1950

Number Built	80 (6800)
	30 (7800)
Route Colour	Red(6800)
	Blue (7800)
Power Class	D
Tractive Effort	29,000lbs (6800)
	27,000lbs (7800)
Driving Wheel Size	5ft 8in
Cylinder Dimensions	18½in x 30in (6800)
	18in x 30in (7800)
Wheelbase	7ft 0in + 5ft 4in + 7ft 0in + 7ft 9in
Boiler Class	Standard 1 (6800)
	Standard 14 (7800)
Dates Withdrawn	1960-1965

It seems odd to have built the Granges, which in so many ways were similar to the Halls; and like the Halls they were 4300 replacements. Finance was probably the principle factor. 4300s were withdrawn and about half the parts from them – wheels, valve gear, minor fittings and the like – were used on the new Granges. Quite a few more parts could be used on the Granges than would have been possible if the 4300s had been scrapped in favour of Halls, so the exercise must have been a good deal cheaper. The Granges had a different cylinder design to the Halls with some improvements based on Chapelon's design work in France. The steam chest volume was increased which provided better steam flow. These cylinders had 9in piston valves. The footplate had a small raised section over the cylinders and the splashers were of course smaller, but otherwise they were very similar to the Halls. Unlike their 4300 precursors, but like the Halls, the cylinder and wheel centrelines were aligned, not offset.

The Manor was a 4-6-0 to run on the lighter routes. The Granges were still red route engines and so were heavily restricted in the lines on which they could be used. They could be used instead of 8300s, but not replace 4300s on the blue restricted routes which still made up 17 per cent of the GWR in 1938. Thus they could not replace the 4300s and surviving 4-4-0s on many duties. There was a lot of design work before the Manor boiler was settled on. One of the reasons for the 4-6-0 conversions was to get more steam capacity than the 43s, so clearly a Standard 4 boiler would not be enough. Equally, though, a Standard 1 would be too heavy. Designs were worked out with modified Standard 1, Standard 2 and Standard 4 boilers, but in the end the Manors were fitted with a brand new boiler design, the Standard 14. This boiler was smaller in diameter than a Standard 1, and in particular the firebox was a foot shorter,

6800 (Grange) class. *Diagram A8. The Granges can be distinguished from the Hall by the raised footplate over the cylinders, and from the Manor by rear splashers which do not reach the cab.*

7800 (Manor) class. *Diagram A9. The Manor is shorter than the other 4-6-0s, the splashers merge into the cab unlike the Halls and Granges, and the safety valve cover is placed much closer to the firebox than on the other 4-6-0 classes.*

and so the engine too was shorter with a 5ft 3in rear overhang – the same as the 4300s. Cylinders were essentially the same design as the Granges, but started off at 18in bore rather than 18½in. Like the Granges the Manors – or at least the pre-war ones – were built with components from withdrawn 4300s.

101 4300s were withdrawn and dismantled, in a reasonably steady stream between February 1936 and March 1939. Granges and Manors were built to replace them incorporating the resulting parts. The first forty were used to build two lots of Granges, 6800-6819 in 1936 and 6820-6859 in 1937. Then came two lots of Manors, 7800-7811 in 1938 and 7812-7819 in 1939, and finally a last batch of Granges, 6860-6879, were erected later in 1939.

Another lot of Manors, 7820-7029, were built, officially from all new components, in November and December 1950. There was an attempt by the Western Region to commission another batch of Manors in 1954, but predictably this was overruled by British Railways Head Office – Swindon referred to them as 'The Kremlin'.

The Granges started life with their own design of chimney which was smaller than that used on Halls. As a result of boiler swaps during overhauls, a variety of chimneys could be seen on classes with No. 1 boilers by the 1950s. Thus, the Grange chimneys migrated to other classes and vice versa.

The small boiler on the Manor did not steam well as originally designed, but in the early 1950s the Swindon development team under S.O. (Sam) Ell developed great expertise in front end design and locomotive testing and in the case of the Manors they succeeded in doubling the steam output of the boiler with changes to blast pipe, chimney and fire bars.

The Granges started life with Churchward 3,500 gallon tenders as fitted to the donor 4300s. Later on, Collett style 3,500 and 4,000 gallon units were also fitted to class members. Manors always had 3,500 gallon tenders, again initially Churchward designs, but with Collett ones appearing later on some locomotives.

There were two diagrams for the Granges, A8 and A28, the difference being 3,500 or 4,000 gallon tenders, and just a single diagram issued for the Manors.

One Grange was withdrawn in 1960, but the majority lasted until 1964 and the end of WR steam in 1965. All were scrapped, but there is a project to build a new Grange based at the Llangollen Railway. This will have new frames and cylinders, a boiler from a modified Hall, chassis components from another Hall and, most appropriately, a set of driving wheels that were last used on a 4300.

The Manors were withdrawn between 1963 and 1965. From a class of thirty, no less than nine have survived, mainly because, unlike any of the Granges, they were bought by Woodham's scrapyard at Barry. All have been restored from scrapyard condition and have run in preservation.

Hawksworth
6959 Modified Hall class

Builders	GWR/Swindon
Dates Built	1944-1950
Number Built	71
Route Colour	Red
Power Class	D
Tractive Effort	27,000lbs
Driving Wheel Size	6ft 0in
Cylinder Dimensions	18½in x 30in
Wheelbase	7ft 2in + 5ft 4in + 7ft 0in + 7ft 9in
Boiler Class	Standard 1
Dates Withdrawn	1963-1965

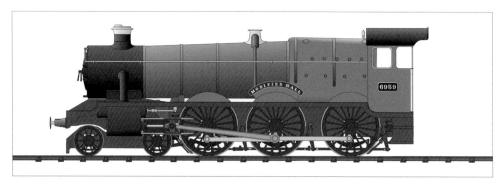

6959 (Modified Hall) class. *Diagram A25.*

Hawksworth's Modified Halls started with 6959 in March 1944. Although superficially they looked much the same as their predecessors there were, for the first time, some significant departures from Churchward's standard 2 cylinder layout.

The combined cylinders and smoke box saddle and the extension frames were gone: instead there were full length plate frames and separate cylinder and saddle assemblies. This was not really new territory since the 4 cylinder locomotives did not have extension frames either. There was also a new bogie design with quite different springing arrangements and a slightly longer wheelbase. The full length plate frames are visible above the running plate in front of the boiler, so the Modified Halls are readily distinguishable from their predecessors. They also had a new style of Standard 1 boiler, with a large three row superheater, although a few of the early ones carried a normal two row superheat Standard 1.

Two row lower superheat boilers appeared on Modified Halls in the course of routine overhauls; they did not use the high superheat ones exclusively.

The first few were given Collett 4,000 gallon tenders and 6979 and on were built with slab sided 4,000 gallon Hawksworth tenders. It seems unlikely that any ran with 3,500 gallon tenders. There were three diagrams for the modified Halls, two row and three row superheaters, plus Collett and Hawksworth 4,000 gallon tenders.

Seven modified Halls have survived, but one has been used as a chassis for a recreation of the 4-6-0 County class, and not all of the others have yet been restored from scrapyard condition.

1000 (County) class

Builders	GWR/Swindon
Dates Built	1945-1947
Number Built	30

Route Colour	Red
Power Class	D
Tractive Effort	32,500lbs (29,000lbs later)
Driving Wheel Size	6ft 3in
Cylinder Dimensions	18½in x 30in
Wheelbase	7ft 2in + 5ft 4in + 7ft 0in + 7ft 9in
Boiler Class	Standard 15
Dates Withdrawn	1962-1964

There is a good deal of criticism and speculation about the decision to build the County class as opposed to more Castles or Halls. Notably there are claims that Hawksworth had intended some of the design features to be experiments to inform the design of a 4-6-2 express locomotive. Hawksworth appears not to have had the slightest intention of building a pacific, and some unauthorised work in the design office has been magnified into a myth.

They were the ultimate development of the two cylinder line which started with no. 100. The chassis was straightforward enough – basically a Modified Hall chassis but with the new and non-standard wheel size of 6ft 3in. Like all the later 4-6-0s there was no offset between cylinder and wheel centrelines.

Above the footplate, however, there was a lot of new design. There are a good number of design proposals in existence for the Counties, and it is clear that a larger boiler than the Standard 1 was an early requirement. The Standard 7 boiler would be too heavy – this had been established in the Churchward era. The Standard 8 (Castle) boiler might have been an alternative, but as noted above this had its drawbacks with poor fuel. Swindon had available the tooling to make Stanier 8F boilers, which had been built at Swindon during the war. These boilers were just a little smaller in diameter than the Castle one, but

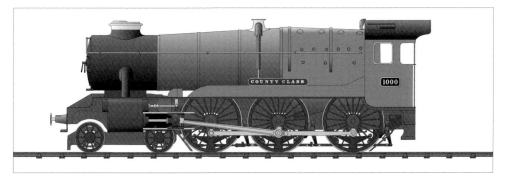

1000 (County) class. *Diagram A17, which is of the original double chimney fitted to 1000, not the later design used on the whole class.*

appreciably greater than a Standard 1. The eventual boiler used this tooling and was only 12ft 7in long in the barrel, much shorter than the 14ft 10in Standard 1 and 7, with a firebox slightly shorter than that of the Standard 7 and 8 and consequently slightly less grate area. It was also designed for a working pressure of 280psi. The short barrel resulted in a long smokebox and a generally tubbier appearance than most GWR boilers.

Hammer blow was an issue with the Counties. It restricted where they could be used and how fast they were allowed to run. The first County had a double chimney, but thereafter they were built with single chimneys.

The boiler pressure was reduced to 250psi from 1956 in order to reduce the hammer blow, a new design of double chimney was installed and other draughting improvements were made. There were three diagrams – 1000 as built with its experimental double chimney, the main batch with single chimney and then the revised double chimney arrangement.

They were withdrawn between 1962 and 1964, and none survived. However, the Great Western Society is building a replica County using a modified Modified Hall chassis and large portions of a Stanier 8F boiler as a foundation.

8 Coupled Classes
Boilers

Boiler Class	Name	Barrel			Firebox Length
		length	diameter		
A	Standard 1	14ft 10in	4ft 10¾in	5ft 6in	9ft 0in
H	Standard 7	14ft 10in	5ft 6in	6ft 0in	10ft 0in

GWR classes
2800 class

Builders	GWR/Swindon
Dates Built	1903-1919
Number Built	84
Route Colour	Blue
Power Class	E
Tractive Effort	30,000-35,000lbs
Driving Wheel Size	4ft 7½in
Cylinder Dimensions	18½in x 30in
Wheelbase	8ft 9in + 5ft 5in + 5ft 5in + 6ft 0in
Boiler Class	Standard 1
Dates Withdrawn	1958-1965

3822 (2884 class) *at Didcot Railway Centre, in the GWR wartime black it most likely bore when new. (Photo: Jim Champ)*

The prototype 2-8-0, No 97, was built concurrently with the first pre-production Saint, 98 and was arguably as important a locomotive. The various novel features of the pair are discussed in the introduction. 2801-2820 followed in 1905. They had larger piston valves, and the improved short cone 225psi Standard 1 boilers were set noticeably higher than on 97. 2821-2830 came in 1907. Like their contemporaries, the Lady series of Saints, they had a mix of short and long cone boilers.

   2831-2835 in 1911 introduced 18½in cylinders. All were built with long cone boilers, full length smoke boxes, superheating and curved framing.2836-2849, 1912 were the first with top feed, followed by 2050-5 a year later. The last Churchward batch, 2856-2883 in 1918/19 were significantly different. They were heavier, using some large and heavy castings in the frame, and this improved the weight distribution and increased adhesion. 2846 had been used as a prototype for these changes. Otherwise these were similar to the previous batch.

2800 class. *Diagram B. Representative of early class members as built from 1905. Unsuperheated, with short smoke box and short cone boiler, straight frames and no top feed.*

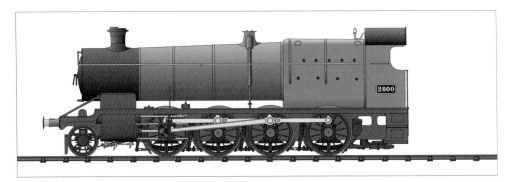

2800 class. *Diagram I. This was the final configuration of the class, curved frames, superheated, top feed and long cone boiler. The only significant visual change after this was outside steampipes on many of the class.*

2884 class

Builders	GWR/Swindon
Dates Built	1938-1942
Number Built	83
Route Colour	Blue
Power Class	E
Tractive Effort	35,000lbs
Driving Wheel Size	4ft 7½in
Cylinder Dimensions	18½in x 30in
Wheelbase	8ft 9in + 5ft 5in + 5ft 5in + 6ft 0in
Boiler Class	Standard 1
Dates Withdrawn	1962-1965

Building of 28s resumed from 1938 to 1942, when Collett built several lots, 2884-2899 and 3800-3866, lightly updated with the outside steampipes that were now standard replacement on the older locomotives, side window cabs and a fire iron tunnel. They were not fitted with compensated springing on the driving wheels. These were known as the 2884 class. They had similar weight distribution to the 2856 batch, but were slightly heavier. 3814-3866, built at the height of the war, were originally built without the side windows as an air raid precaution.

97, the prototype, was renumbered 2800 in the 1912 renumbering.

From 1945/48, twelve 28s were renumbered from 4800 (the range having been cleared by renumbering the 0-4-2 Tanks in the 1946 renumbering) when they were converted in the oil burning trial, and 8 2884s were renumbered from 4850. When the experiment was abandoned the locos reverted to their old numbers as they were converted back.

The early short cone boilers shuffled between Saints and 28s until all were gone, and superheating, introduced in 1909-11, soon stabilised with the Swindon No. 3 design superheater. Top feed was introduced in 1911. Beyond that, outside steam pipes came to the 28s from 1930. Initially, locomotives with straight frames kept the straight frames with the new cylinders, but latterly some of the straight frames locomotives acquired curved framing.

Locomotives with side window cabs had the side windows plated over as an air raid precaution during the war. The windows were reinstated after the war, and those built without them had them added.

No. 97 was first coupled with one of the few Churchward 4,000 gallon tenders. The earlier locomotives were mostly used with 3,000 gallon tenders, but from around 1911, 3,500 gallon tenders became general for the class.

There were seven diagrams for the 28s, most concerning variations, especially of boilers, in the early years, but there were two diagrams which covered 2846 and the 2856 batch. The last was for the oil burning conversion. There were just two diagrams for the 2884, respectively for coal and oil power.

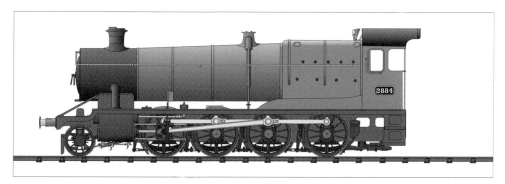

2884 class. *Diagram M. This diagram covered all the coal burning 2884s.*

97/2800 was the first to be withdrawn, in 1958 after 55 years and 1.3 million miles of service. It was the last of the Churchward prototypes in service in original form. About fifty 28s went fairly steadily from then to 1960, supplanted by the short-lived BR Standard 9F 2-10-0s. A few were withdrawn in 1961/2. The rest went in 1963/4: just one survived until Jan 1965.

A few 2884s were withdrawn in 1962 and 1963, but the majority went in 1964 and 1965.

Sixteen have survived; seven 2800 and nine 2884.

Of the 28s, two have run in preservation, both with curved frames and outside steampipes and one, the last with both inside steam pipes and straight frames, is in fully conserved preservation as part of the National Collection. Two of the others are or will be stripped as spares donors. The last two, including the only other with inside steam pipes, are essentially unrestored.

Four of the 2884s have run in preservation, and two of the others are under active restoration at the time of writing.

4700 – The Night Owls

Builders	GWR/Swindon
Dates Built	1919-1923
Number Built	9
Route Colour	Red
Power Class	D
Tractive Effort	30,000lbs
Driving Wheel Size	5ft 8in
Cylinder Dimensions	19in x 30in
Wheelbase	9ft 3in + 6ft 6in + 6ft 6in + 7ft 0in
Boiler Class	Standard 7
Dates Withdrawn	1962-1964

Sometimes regarded as Churchward's masterpiece, these were the last Churchward design. 4700 was initially fitted with a Standard 1 boiler because the design for the Standard 7 had not been completed on time. It was replaced two years later with the larger Standard 7, which all the others had from new. The Standard 7 boiler was based on the tooling created for *The Great Bear*, but was much better proportioned with a shorter barrel and a longer narrow firebox. Their intended role was fast freight trains, and part of the rationale for the design was that *The Great Bear* had been successful with such workings.

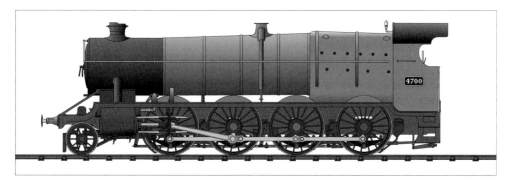

4700 class. *Diagram J*

In some ways they were like an enlarged 4300, but they used various components from a number of classes. They could not have the same wheel spacing as the 2800s because of the wheel size. Unlike the 2800s, which drove the third pair of main wheels, the 4700s drove the second, as did the 2-8-0 tanks.

They were sometimes known as the Night Owls because their chief usage was running fast vacuum fitted freight trains on the main line to facilitate 'next day' freight delivery. However, they were true mixed traffic locomotives, used as such. Although only nine were built, the running department wanted more in the 1930s, although in the end, Collett decided that it would be better to build a batch of Castles. The 4700s' one recorded fault was that they tended to 'nose about' at speeds over 60mph and accordingly were given a speed restriction. However, within this limitation, they were still used for passenger traffic as well as fast freight, even, and perhaps especially in their later days.

Everyone who came into contact with them seems to have admired them. There is a well-known quote from a locomotive inspector who declared that the entire work of the running department could be completed with a fleet of Churchward 47s and Collett Granges.

They were little altered over their lives. They were given extended cab roofs in the 1930s and received 4,000 gallon tenders a few years later. Durrant, who designed screw reversing gear for the class in BR days which in the event was never fitted (though the drawings do still exist in the NRM archive), comments on how few changes had been made to the working drawings compared to other classes.

They are interesting to look at from the point of view of understanding maintenance. Cook gives some numbers – around 100,000 miles between repairs, and 300,000 miles between heavy boiler repairs. He comments that with one spare boiler between the nine, they had to schedule maintenance carefully not to be caught with two in the shops at once. The ten original boilers lasted until 1955/7, when British Railways built ten more, so presumably they were intended for many more years of service when the axeman came.

The 47s were originally equipped with 3,500 gallon tenders, but from around 1932 4,000 gallon tenders became the standard fitment.

There were four diagrams. One for 4700 as built with the No 1 boiler, two variations on the Standard 7 boiler, and finally one for the class fitted with a 4,000 gallon tender.

The entire class survived until June 1962, very late for such a small class to remain complete, and the last went in May 1964. None survived, but the Great Western Society is building a new one using various pieces from the GWR 'kit of parts' including components from a 5101 2-6-2T, a 5205 2-8-0T and a 2800 2-8-0.

Absorbed Classes at the Grouping
ROD 2-8-0

Dates Built	1917-1919
Number Built	100 (see notes)
Route Colour	Blue
Power Class	D
Tractive Effort	32,000lbs
Driving Wheel Size	4ft 8in
Cylinder Dimensions	21in x 26in
Boiler Class	own
Dates Withdrawn	1927-1931, 1946-1958

A particularly complicated history, and not the best loved locomotives on the GWR. A straightforward outside cylinder 2-8-0 designed by Robinson for the Great Central Railway. Something over 500 were built to MOD specification between 1917 and 1919 by various builders, using steel fireboxes. Those acquired by the GWR were built by the North British Locomotive Co, Nasmyth, Wilson & Co, and Robert Stephenson and Co.

The GWR first bought twenty, which were practically new, in 1919. These became 3000-3019. Next they hired eighty-four, all used to a greater or lesser extent, which were numbered 3020-3099 and 6000-6003. These arrived between 1919 and 1920 and were returned in 1921/1922. Finally, in 1925, they purchased, at a considerably reduced price, eighty. These too were numbered from 3020-3099. Nineteen of these had been in the hired batch, most retaining the numbers they had had before when on hire.

After only four months of service, the eighty locomotives purchased in 1925 were brought together at Swindon works and inspected. To simplify a complicated affair, the thirty best of the second eighty were considered 'good'. Between 1926 and May 1927 these were given new copper fireboxes, GWR safety valves, top feed and superheaters, painted GWR green and treated as part of the normal locomotive

3000 (ROD) class. *Based on diagram K, amended with various GWR fittings as on post WW2 photos.*

stock. The original twenty were given the same treatment a little later on. As each upgrade was complete the locos were sent out on service; all were modified and in full service by October 1929. 3000-3019 kept their numbers whilst the 'best thirty' were renumbered 3020-3049. The remaining fifty were given GWR safety valves, a minimal overhaul, left in ROD black livery and renumbered from 3050. They too were sent out on service as each one was ready and, it seems, run until they dropped, which in some cases was not a very great mileage.

There were no very major changes to the westernised locomotives once they had gone into service, although the fitting of Standard 1 boilers was considered at one time. Piston tail rods disappeared, probably from the 1930s, resulting in new cylinder covers and there were some changes of chimneys and smokebox doors.

The RODs came with tenders, so the GWR rapidly came to have rather more of these than were required for the ROD fleet. They were used on the Aberdare and later the 2251 classes and even in the end as sludge tanks.

The unmodified locomotives all went between 1927 and 1931.

Withdrawals of the fully westernised locos started in 1946, the last going in 1958. Oddly, most went in either 1946-1948 or 1956-1958. Presumably, once the war was over, there were surplus locomotives and some were run until they dropped – again.

None of the GWR owned and modified RODs have survived, but one Great Central locomotive survives and has run in preservation, and there are three ex ROD locomotives in Australia.

Barry 0-8-0

Builders	Sharp, Stewart and Co.
Dates Built	1986-1888
Number Built	4
Route Colour	Uncoloured

Power Class	C/D
Tractive Effort	32,000lbs
Driving Wheel Size	4ft 8in
Cylinder Dimensions	19in/20in x 26in
Dates Withdrawn	1927-1930

Four outside cylinder 0-8-0 locomotives from Sharp Stewart. They were unusual in having small 4 wheel tenders with just 1800 gallons of water. The boilers were rebuilt by the GWR, and there were changes to safety valves, chimneys and cab sides. All were gone by 1930.

Second World War Classes
LMS Stanier 8F 2-8-0s
The GWR was loaned twenty-five Stanier 8Fs in November 1940, all numbered between 8226 and 8300. These were returned in 1941. In 1943, Swindon built eighty more for the MOD, numbered 8400-8479 and used on the GWR system. These were delivered to the LMS from January 1946. The 8Fs were always in LMS livery. One Swindon built 8F has survived in the UK and has run in preservation. There are a reasonable number of other survivors.

Austerity 2-8-0s
The Austerities were loosely based on the LMS 8F, but much simplified in construction with iron castings rather than steel, fewer of them and given a simple parallel boiler. A number were loaned to the GWR until they were required on the continent. In a reprise of events after the Great War, British Railways bought a large number of these after Nationalisation, some of which were used on the Western region, presumably supplanting the ROD 2-8-0s that were scrapped about this time. Those on the Western region were fitted with GWR style top feed and fire iron tunnels. One Austerity 2-8-0 has survived, but from Sweden, and is not one of the WR modified locos.

USA S160 class 2-8-0s
Over two thousand of these were built in America to a design by the US Army Transportation Corps. 173 were loaned to the GWR during the war and returned when they were required on the continent after D-Day. There were problems in the early days with the water gauges and fusible plugs which resulted in the fatal scalding of a fireman at Honeybourne. Fusible plugs are tapped into the firebox crown (top) and contain a lead core which melts if the boiler water is dangerously low, reducing the boiler pressure and warning the crew.

There are around twenty-five surviving S160s in various locations round the world, including some in the UK.

CHAPTER 5

Locomotive Tenders

Tenders have never received as much attention as the locomotives they served. Cook, in *Swindon Steam*, barely mentions them. The development of tenders was a process of steady improvement and enlargement and the few major changes of design didn't always match with changes of CMEs. It's hard to imagine a CME getting very excited about tender design, although Churchward is believed to have specified the long bogie tender for *The Great Bear* primarily for cosmetic reasons.

By the twentieth century, GWR policy was to own fewer tenders than locomotives as they spent less time being repaired. This both saved capital and having loose tenders taking up space. The result is that tenders were highly standardised and to a considerable extent interchangeable. Kings, for example, averaged over twenty changes of tender during their thirty to thirty-five year working lives, and one preserved tender was attached to twenty-six different locomotives in a thirty-one year working life, after which it was used as an oil storage tank for another twenty-three years until it reached preservation.

Early Absorbed and Contractor built Tenders before 1870.

The early tenders, like the locomotives they were attached to, were essentially a rather random collection from a variety of manufacturers. There were about 260 that meet this description. About thirty-four of these were small 4 wheeled units, but the majority were 6 wheeled with wheels between 3ft and 4ft diameter. Water capacity, where recorded, was usually something under 2,000 gallons. Tenders built for the Gooch designed classes normally had sandwich frames to match the locomotives.

Like the earlier locomotives, many of these tenders were rebuilt/renewed at Wolverhampton in the 1870s and 1880s. The least satisfactory were scrapped around the 1870/80 era, but the rebuilds often survived until the turn of the century, with the last going in the 1920s.

GWR built Sandwich frame Tenders and Broad Gauge conversions.

The earlier Swindon tenders had sandwich frames with springs above the footplate and were generally 6ft + 6ft wheelbase with 4ft 0in wheels and a water capacity of around 1,800 gallons. All these early tenders had well tanks that came down between the frames to a greater or lesser extent.

Like so many of the early locomotives, the tenders were rebuilt/renewed at Wolverhampton in the 1870s and 1880s and these rebuilds tended towards a standard 6ft 2in + 6ft 10in wheelbase with 4ft 0in wheels, and water capacity between 2,000 and 2,500 gallons. Like the locomotives, they might have few or no original parts.

When broad gauge tenders, especially the later ones, were rebuilt to the narrow gauge, they were altered to a similar specification, also with the 6ft 2in + 6ft 10in wheelbase and 4ft 0in wheels. As with the locomotives, the nominal 4ft 0in wheels increased in diameter at the end of the nineteenth century as thicker tyres came into use, finishing with a standard 4ft 1½in.

Lastly, twenty-two new 2,500 gallon tenders were built at Wolverhampton in 1890-1905, which were classified as renewals. These are also believed to have had sandwich frames and the 6ft 2in-6ft 10in wheelbase.

These sandwich frames tenders mostly lasted until around the Great War, and were withdrawn in large quantities in the 1920s along with older locomotives. One of the Wolverhampton built tenders survived until 1934, and was probably the last one.

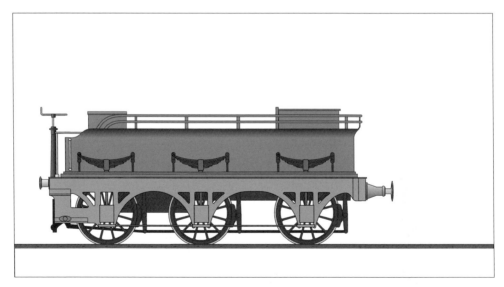

2,350 gallon (typically) sandwich frame tender. *This is one of the 6ft 2in + 6ft 10in wheelbase rebuilds in turn of the century condition with coal rails.*

Swindon Built Tenders 1866-1877

From 1866, Swindon-built tenders had iron plate frames, not sandwich frames. The first three lots had 6ft 4in + 6ft 8in wheelbase, but the rest were all the now standard 6ft 2in + 6ft 10in. 306 were built, similar enough to be included on a single diagram produced in 1898, probably to document water scoop installation. The tanks were typically 1,800 gallon capacity. A few of these went abroad in the First World War, not only with locomotives of the Standard Goods class, but also as water tanks. The last of these plate frame tenders was withdrawn from use as a tender in 1929.

Absorbed Tenders, 1870 – 1905

Few of the tenders from locomotives absorbed by the GWR over this period lasted very long in service. A few tenders from the Llanelli Railway and Dock Co lasted into early years of the twentieth century. Some of the tenders taken over from the Bristol and Exeter lasted long enough to be used as water tanks in France during the Great War.

Swindon Tenders, 1884-1906
3,000 gallon Tenders

In 1884, a single tender to a new design 3,000 gallon tender was built. This had the new feature of springs below the footplate. 396 more were built between 1890 and 1906 to basically similar designs, with various detail improvements in suspension, changes in fittings and so on. Even after 1906 the early Churchward era 3,500 gallon tenders, although extensively updated, still had significant parts in common with these units. Such was Swindon economy of design that the principal dimensions of these tenders were still present in the Hawksworth 4,000 gallon tenders, eighty years later.

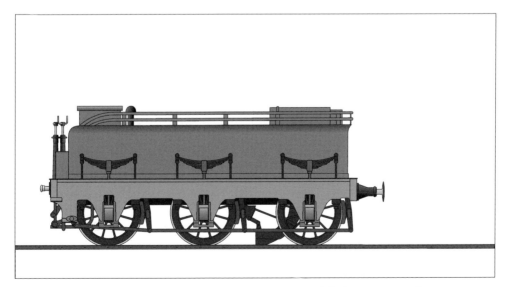

1,800 gallon Swindon built plate frame tender *as modified in 1898 with water scoop equipment.*

3,000 gallon Dean era Tender. *Lots A10 onwards. This is from an 1898 drawing showing coal rails and water scoop.*

Coal rails were introduced in the 1890s and solid fenders from 1903. The nominal coal capacity was five tons. Coal rails were abandoned on new builds about 1904, replaced with short fenders about fifteen feet long. The coal rails were rapidly replaced with fenders on existing tenders of all capacities.

Water scoops would have been fitted from the mid-1890s, as the first set of water troughs went into use in 1895. The water scoop gear incorporated not only the actual scoop at the bottom, but also apparatus above the tank. The uprushing water hit a dome where it spread out and fell back into the tank. At this time, the dome and the filler cap were combined in a single roughly D shaped casing. These were sometimes replaced with a separate water filler and round dome later on.

There were small variations in footplate height, hand rail arrangements and even the width of the tender to match different locomotives requirements.

The first was withdrawn in 1927 and 104 of this type were sold to the war department in 1940, associated with Dean Goods. However, there were still some in use in 1964, when the WR stopped keeping records of tenders. *City of Truro* is preserved with one of these tenders, fitted with coal fenders rather than coal rails, and with separate water filler and dome casings.

2,500 gallon tenders from 1884

At this time, 2,500 gallon tenders had 6ft 6in + 6ft 6in wheelbase. 301 were built of these between 1884 and 1903. Often used with 0-6-0s, many went overseas in the Great War, and three were sold to the war department in 1940. In time they received coal rails and fenders like the 3,000 gallon units. The coal capacity is recorded as 4.5 tons.

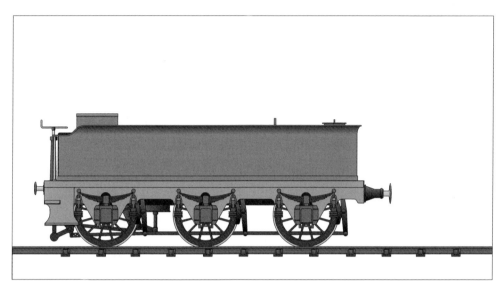

2,500 gallon Dean era tender. *This is an 1887 built tender in original condition without coal rails or fenders.*

Withdrawals started from 1927. One is preserved with Dean Goods 2516 at Steam Museum, Swindon, again fitted with fenders, not coal rails, but with a single casing for filler and scoop dome. This tender, built in 1898, is recorded as having had replacement frames in 1919.

2,000 gallon short wheelbase tenders

These very short (5ft 6in +5ft 6in) wheelbase tenders were built from 1895 to 1899. Sixty were built altogether; at least the first twenty-five were originally

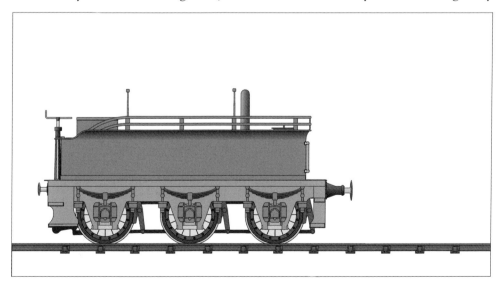

2,000 gallon short wheelbase tender. *As built in 1895/6 with Mansell wood centre wheels and the supports for an early communication cord apparatus.*

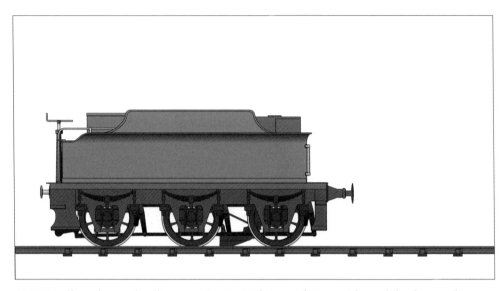

2,000 gallon short wheelbase tender *in 20thC condition with coal fenders and water pickup scoop.*

fitted with Mansell type wheels with solid wooden centres rather than spokes. The coal capacity was listed as 2.5 tons, but by the time they had received coal fenders, water scoops and other extras later in their lives the loaded weight had gone up some 2.5 tons, and it seems reasonable to assume some of this was extra coal between the fenders.

The first was withdrawn in 1927, although some had gone overseas in 1917.

2,400 gallon short wheelbase
There were twenty of these, built in 1900/1901. They also had 5ft 6in + 5ft 6in wheelbase but the coal capacity was 4.5 tons. None of these short wheelbase tenders have survived.

Non-standard tenders, 1884-1900
A 2,800 gallon tender was built in 1886, originally for use with a prototype 2-2-2. It was similar to the early 3,000 gallon units, but is recorded as having 4ft 6in wheels. It was condemned in 1928. A 2,600 gallon tender with the same wheelbase as the 2,500 gallon ones was built in 1896, originally to partner the 4-6-0 no 36. This one was condemned in 1949.

Churchward and Collett Standard Tenders, 1900-1946
A distinction is often made between Churchward and Collett tenders. However the main design boundary was in 1925/6, some years after Churchward retired so the label is somewhat confusing. Tenders from this era get a little complicated. The source of problems is not so much that the designs changed radically, in

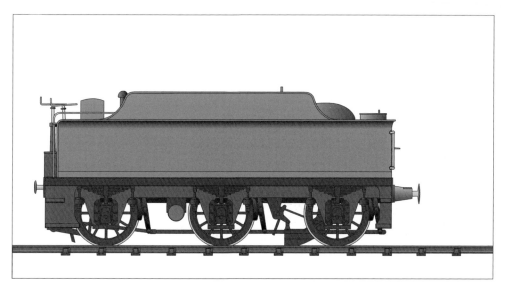

3,500 gallon Tender *as built around 1906 with short coal fenders and separated water dome and filler.*

3,500 gallon tender *from around 1910 to 1924.*

fact rather the opposite. There was continuous background development going on through the lifespan of these tenders and a policy of fixing what needed fixing, whilst not fixing what was still serviceable. And, rather like the 4-4-0s at the turn of the century, the frames were not really strong enough, so between 1925 and 1948 there were a number of significantly different treatments of the area round the horn plates and spring hangers.

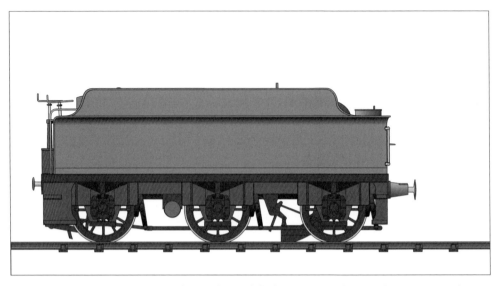

3,500 gallon *pre 1925 tender with modified springs and riveted on rectangular hornplate reinforcements.*

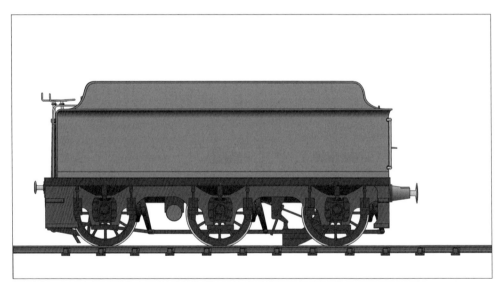

3,500 gallon tender *from 1925/6 with scalloped frames. This sketch shows the high sided variant, so has all features described as 'intermediate'.*

Construction Features
Chassis.
Almost all tenders of this era had the 7ft 6in +7ft 6in wheelbase used on the 3,000 gallon Dean tenders; indeed, some components were from the Dean era. Until 1925, the tenders had relatively shallow mainframes and deep horn plates, essentially similar to their predecessors, although a revised frame design was introduced in 1900 and another in 1910. In 1925/6 a batch of ten, lot A112, had

deeper frames in the region of the spring hangers, but the frame was then scalloped upwards to roughly the same depth as its predecessors. This two stage design was somewhat reminiscent of outside frame locomotives of the previous century.

From 1926 until 1931, the frames omitted the scalloping and were straight between the spring hangers, so somewhat deeper. From 1931, the horn guides on the frames were very much wider at the base, but the same depth as their 1926 design.

A significant number of tenders built with earlier design frames had them replaced with later designs or reinforced. All surviving pre-1910 tenders, with the exception of that preserved with *City of Truro*, have later design frames. Identification of surviving tenders is problematic, since most lost their identification plates before reaching preservation, but around half of the surviving pre-1931 tenders now have later style frames.

There was a distinctive style of strengthening fitted to quite a number of pre-1926 tenders, in which rectangular plates with generous flanges were used to reinforce the horn guides and support later style flat springs. There are photos of both 3,000 and 3,500 gallon tenders with this arrangement. One such tender has survived.

Springs and Spring Hangers
There were several designs of spring hanger, both to cope with varying designs of spring and chassis and to match frame reinforcements on older tenders. The spring gear used on the first 3,500 and 4,000 gallon tenders was the same as that used on the Dean 3,000 gallon tenders. Revised springing came with the revised frames in 1910 and again with the 1925, 1926 and 1931 frame designs.

Collett's team did some significant work on spring design for tenders as well as locomotives. The later springs had more and flatter leaves, without the curvature of earlier types. To complicate things further, it was by no means uncommon for older tenders to be uprated with later design springs.

Water tanks.
From around 1905, the water filler and dome, instead of being combined in a single casing, were separated and the dome became a flattened hemisphere. Up to and including the scalloped frame batch in 1925/6, the water tanks included a well section between the frames; consequently the water tank above the frames was relatively shallow. From 1926 on, the well tank was abandoned and the tenders had a simple flat bottomed (called flush) tank above the frames, which consequently was somewhat higher. The flush tank tenders had rather lower coal capacity than their predecessors.

Tender sides, Coal Rails and Coal Fenders
Longer coal fenders, around 18ft, were used on new construction from around 1910. There was a variant type 3,500 gallon well tank tender with sides some

four inches higher than standard and very long fenders almost to the back of the tender. This was produced in the 1920s and is usually described as high sided and often, but not exclusively, associated with the scalloped type frames. Tenders with these features are often described as intermediate. Oddly no known official general arrangement drawing shows the high sided variant, and it is not clear which tenders were built with high sides - see Appendix F.

From 1926, on flush tank tenders, the coal fender was continued round the back of the tender at a lower level, not simply truncated after the coal space. Post 1926 tenders without well tanks naturally had slightly taller tanks and thus tender sides than their predecessors.

4,000 gallon well tank tenders, 1900-1904
The first of these tenders was turned out with Churchward prototype 4-6-0 No. 100 and had coal rails. All the rest had fenders from new. They were rated for seven tons of coal. Only twenty were built, between 1900 and 1904 and they were usually, but not invariably, used with Stars. At least some survived until the 1960s, but none have been preserved.

3,500 gallon well tank tenders, 1905-1926
639 of these tenders were built between 1905 and 1925, also with nominal seven ton coal capacity. Although most were built at Swindon, thirty-five were constructed by Robert Stephenson & Co with the 4300 2-6-0s they built. The last ten 3,500 gallon well tank tenders had the scalloped frame type. A single 8 wheel tender using two shortened locomotive bogies was built for *The Great Bear.*

A good number of the pre-1925 tenders have survived into preservation, several of which have had replacement Collett era frames. Water tanks are naturally very vulnerable to corrosion and many of these tenders have had new or partially new tanks and bodies in service or in preservation, not all of which are the original design or capacity. A single tender to the scalloped frame design of Lot A112 has survived.

3,500 gallon flush tank tenders
Only a single lot of twenty-seven of these were built, in 1929/30. They were similar to the 4,000 gallon tenders of this period, with deep frames and narrow horn plates. They were intermediate in height between those and the earlier 3,500 gallon tenders with well tanks and had 5.5 ton coal capacity. It seems likely one has survived, but had been fitted with a 4,000 gallon tank during its working life.

4,000 gallon flush tank tenders, 1926-1946
Thirty-three lots were built, amounting to 481 tenders. The coal capacity was 6 tons: less than the earlier 3,500 and 4,000 gallon tenders. The policy in the 1930s and '40s was that new 4,000 gallon tenders were built with new

4,000 gallon flush tank tender *from around 1930. This sketch shows the 1926-1931 era frames*

4,000 gallon flush tank tender *with the post 1931 frame design.*

locomotives, even classes like the Manors and 2884s that did not run with them. The new tenders were coupled to Castles, Stars and Halls, and the new locomotives left the works with second hand 3,500 gallon units.

One 8 wheel 4,000 gallon tender was built as an experiment – apparently axle box wear was quite high on the 4,000 gallon units – and another experiment was an aluminium alloy tank. Seventeen of these tenders were temporarily converted to carry oil fuel rather than coal in the 1946 oil fuelling experiment.

A good number of these tenders have survived into preservation and they are the most numerous type. A number of the earlier ones have had their original frames replaced with the later design during their service life. Many tanks have been replaced in preservation and again, not all are the original design or size.

3,000 gallon flush tank tenders

There were fifty of these, built from 1940 to 1948. Thus they all had the later design deep frames with wide horns. The coal capacity was just 4.25 tons. They were mostly found on the 2251 class, but were also used on some of the Bulldogs towards the end of their lives. No 3,000 gallon tenders had been constructed since 1906, so presumably 1890s vintage units were coming to the end of their lives. At least two of these tenders have survived into preservation.

Hawksworth Straight Sided Tenders, 1948 on
4,000 Gallon for 8ft 6in Cabs

The first of what are generally called Hawksworth tenders were built for the Counties. They were 8ft 6in wide – wider than standard – to match the wider cabs on the Counties; thirty were built for the thirty Counties. They were never used on other classes. With flush sides and deep slotted frames, they were distinctly reminiscent of the 8F units. They had 7 ton coal capacity. The spring gear and axle boxes were unchanged from those used on the later Collett tenders.

All of the 8ft 6in tenders were scrapped with the Counties. The Great Western Society is building a new one, using parts from a Collett tender.

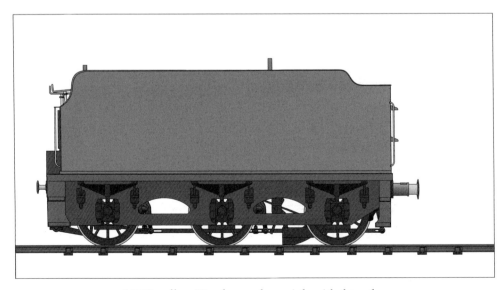

4,000 gallon Hawksworth straight sided tender.

4,000 Gallon Standard

107 of these were built from 1947 and were mainly used with Castles and Halls, although a few were seen on Stars. The water capacity was the same as the wider model, but the coal capacity was only 6 tons. The last two built had slightly reduced water capacity and were fitted up with coal-weighing apparatus in order to provide detailed data on coal consumption in tests. Unlike the others these two were occasionally used on Kings.

Several of these tenders have survived and are in active use both on preserved lines and on the mainline behind both Halls and Castles.

Twentieth century Absorbed Tenders
ROD Tenders, 1919

These were 4,000 gallon tenders with 7 ton coal capacity. The GWR bought many ROD locomotives that were soon scrapped so they had some fifty spare tenders. They were not built with vacuum brake gear, but some were fitted with train vacuum brake gear and used with Aberdare and later 2251 class locomotives. The first withdrawals were as early as 1927, the last surviving until 1961. Several were converted for service tasks and continued in use after the end of steam. One, which lost its centre wheel set when it was converted to a 4 wheeled sludge tank, survives unrestored.

Absorbed Tenders, Grouping

Tenders came to the GW from the Barry, Cambrian, Taff Vale and MSWJR lines, mostly on 4-4-0s and 0-6-0s. They were normally withdrawn at the same time as the accompanying locomotives, although Taff Vale and MSWJR units in particular were reused as water tanks or sludge tanks.

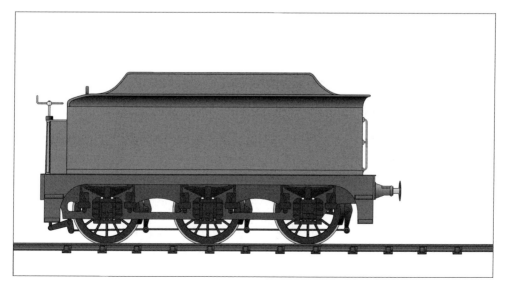

4,000 gallon ROD tender. *Based on the Robinson design for the Great Central, but with increased coal capacity and without any water pickup apparatus.*

CHAPTER 6

Four and Six Wheeled Tank Engines

2-4-0s, 0-4-2s and 0-4-0s

Perhaps more than any other classes, the 4 coupled tanks show the alternate Swindon and Wolverhampton lines of development and maintenance during the nineteenth century. There were two classes built in large numbers; the 0-4-2 517 class and the slightly larger 2-4-0 Metro class. The 517s were designed and built at Wolverhampton and the Metros at Swindon, but both factories would repair and rebuild both classes. The two works maintained separate design teams and did not even maintain common drawings for the same class, so Swindon rebuilds of 517s could be readily distinguished from Wolverhampton ones.

3567, a condensing equipped Large Metro, *this is most probably late 1920s, early 1930s. (Photo: Brian Stephenson Collection)*

Over the Armstrong/Dean/Churchward era, all classes had steady design improvement going on. It seems clear that the policy was to update older stock as and when they came into the shops for repairs, rather than institute a programme to rebuild a whole class. The degree of rebuild that a locomotive might receive in the works varied greatly. One may speculate that it depended on how busy the works in question was when a locomotive came in for repair and how desperately it was needed back in traffic.

Boilers

Boiler Class	Name	Barrel			Firebox Length
		length	diameter		
B	Standard 2	11ft 0in	4ft 5in	5ft 0in	7ft 0in
C	Standard 3	10ft 3in	4ft 5in	5ft 0in	7ft 0in
P	2301	10ft 3in	4ft 5in		5ft 4in
R	850	10ft 0in	3ft 10in		4ft 0in
S	517	10ft 0in	3ft 10in		4ft 6in
SS	4800	10ft 0in	3ft 10in		4ft 6in
T	Metro	10ft 6in	4ft 3in		5ft 1in
U	2021	10ft 0in	3ft 10in		5ft 0in

GWR Classes
Early Locomotives
Some of these early 4 coupled tanks, predating any kind of standardisation, had very long lives, even lasting into the Collett era.

Beyer Peacock 0-4-2T
Two basic 0-4-2 saddle tanks, 91 & 92, were built by Beyer Peacock in 1857 and in 1877/8, one good one, 92, was made from the two. It was rebuilt as an 0-4-0ST in 1878 and in 1893 received a very major rebuild at Wolverhampton. Amazingly, it then survived until 1942, albeit only as a stationary engine in its latter years. A similar loco, 342, was built by Beyer Peacock in 1856, and bought by the GWR in 1864. This had a similar life to 92, converted to 0-4-0ST in 1881, rebuilt in 1897, surviving until 1931.

Wolverhampton 2-4-0T
Wolverhampton built twelve 2-4-0Ts from 1864-1866. 1002, 1A (soon 17) and 2A (soon 18) in 1864, then 1003, 11, 227 and 344-349 in 1865/6. Much detail

has been lost over the years, but they varied in both boiler size and wheelbase. As built, they were cabless and had well tanks and a notably tall chimney on a low slung boiler, later on acquiring open cabs and saddle tanks. All went in the 1880s and 1890s.

320 class

Builders	GWR/Swindon
Dates Built	1864
Number Built	2
Tractive Effort	10,500-15,000lbs
Driving Wheel Size	5ft 6in
Cylinder Dimensions	15in x 24in
Dates Withdrawn	Converted to tender engines 1867, 1873 withdrawn 1881.

Swindon built two outside cylinder 2-4-0 Well tanks in 1864, 320 & 321. A Gooch design, they were the first standard gauge locomotives to be fitted with condensing gear on any British line. They had steeply inclined outside cylinders, located above the footplate and were very similar to the broad gauge 'Metropolitan' class.

They were not a great success as condensing engines and were converted into tender engines in 1867 and 1873, and withdrawn in 1881.

320 Class. *Gooch designed well tank with condensing apparatus under the smokebox.*

No 45

Wolverhampton built an 0-4-0ST, No. 45 in 1880. Noteworthy only for being the only conventional 0-4-0T built at any GWR works, it was scrapped in 1938 after running only 430,000 miles in those fifty-eight years.

Armstrong Designs
Wolverhampton 517 class

Builders	GWR/Wolverhampton
Dates Built	1868-1885
Number Built	144
Route Colour	Uncoloured/Yellow
Power Class	Unclassed
Tractive Effort	10,500-15,000lbs
Driving Wheel Size	5ft 0in†
Cylinder Dimensions	15in x 24in-16½in x 24in
Wheelbase	7ft 4in + 6ft 3in (517-522) 7ft 4in + 6ft 4in (523-552) 7ft 4in + 7ft 4in (553-576 7ft 4in + 7ft 8in (826-849, 1154-1165, 202-5, 215-222, 1421-1444 plus conversions of 517-576) 7ft 4in + 8ft 2in (1483-8 plus conversions)
Boiler Class	R, S, U
Dates Withdrawn	1904-1947

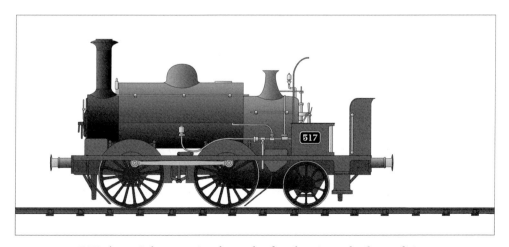

517 class. *A locomotive from the first lots in as built condition.*

517 class. *Diagram E. This is a Wolverhampton rebuild, of the style turned out between 1911 and 1930.*

517 class. *Diagram L. This is a Swindon rebuild from the 1930s.*

144 of the 0-4-2 517 class were built between 1868 and 1885. As might be expected with the GWR at that time, the last batches were significantly different from the first, indeed perhaps more so than most classes. As built the first ones (517-522) were quite stylish but very Victorian looking saddle tanks, with small saddle tanks that only covered the boiler barrel, so both firebox and smokebox were uncovered. They had no enclosed cab or even a cab roof, only a 'spectacle sheet' to give the crew a little shelter when running chimney first. They had a short (7ft 4in + 6ft 3in) wheelbase, 15in diameter cylinders and R class 140psi boilers.

Another twelve lots followed, which can be divided into three groups.

Firstly, 523-576, built from 1868-1870. 523 onwards had 7ft 4in + 6ft 4in wheelbase (still regarded as short for the purposes of this treatment), 553 on

7ft 4in + 7ft 4in wheelbase (also regarded as short) and 571-576 had side tanks rather than the saddle tank.

Then, from 1873-1878 came 826-849, 1154-1165, 202-5, 215-222, 1421-1444. These were built with medium length wheel base (7ft 4in + 7ft 8in). From 202, they gained spectacle plates on the back of the bunker and from 1433, open cabs with a short roof and reinforcing plates on the side tanks which overlapped the footplate valance.

The third main group were 1465-1488, built from 1883-1885. They had larger bunkers and 16in cylinders. Finally, 1483-8 had a long wheel base (7ft 4in + 8ft 2in) with outside axle boxes on the trailing wheels. There was little superficial resemblance between 1868 and 1885 batches.

The 517 class history is of almost unrivalled complexity – perhaps only the Metros approach them. Few 517s can have looked quite alike and just about all of them changed radically in appearance over their lives – sometimes several times. However some general trends in development are visible.

1876-1886. All the earlier short wheel base locomotives were converted to medium wheel base (MWB), still with inside bearings for the trailing axle. At the same time they were normally given side tanks.

1880-1883. Locomotives with 15in cylinders were given 16in diameter cylinders.

1870s/1880s. Open cabs were fitted to those without cabs, sometimes with and sometimes without spectacle plates on the bunker.

1883-1886. Some MWB locomotives were converted to long wheelbase with outside trailing wheel bearings, with variations in detail design.

1890 on. S class boilers, which had a longer firebox than the R class, were introduced, becoming the normal boiler for the class. Few R class boilers were fitted after 1900.

1894-1902. U class boilers, with a longer yet firebox, were fitted on eleven locomotives, which kept them until withdrawal, making these almost equivalent to the 3571 class.

1891-5. A few MWB locomotives were given longer frames, a bigger bunker and the S class boiler.

1894-1915. Many MWB (including conversions from SWB) locomotives were converted to LWB. The conversion included new frames. Only fifty were never converted.

1896 on. Most received 16½in diameter cylinders.

1902-1923. A good number were given narrow closed cabs.

1911 on. S and U class boilers with Belpaire fireboxes started to be fitted.

1924 on. Further conversions to enclosed cabs were given a Collett style cab and bunker. By now, these locomotives were starting to look very similar to their eventual successors, the 4800/5800 classes.

1904 on. Autofitting. Many of the class were autofitted. It seems likely that none of the locomotives with U class boilers were ever autofitted.

Bunkers were in a state of constant flux. They tended to get larger and Swindon, Wolverhampton and even Newton Abbott had their own designs! Water tanks varied too – Wolverhampton tended to fit larger tanks – 900 gallons was the most common eventual size, whilst Swindon preferred smaller ones, 620 being the most common size earlier on, and 800 gallon later. Those with 900 gallon tanks were given Yellow Route availability.

At the beginning of their lives, the 517s were much used on suburban traffic, especially, as might be expected, in the northern areas of the GWR. Once autofitting came in, the usage changed considerably and they scattered all over the system. The autofitted locos were kept smart, used mainly for passenger work. Indeed at the beginning of the twentieth century, when GWR carriages were painted 'lake' (a rather reddish brown), not the more familiar chocolate and cream, quite a number of 517s were painted the same colour. Two 517s were even encased in dummy bodywork to make them better match the rest of the train.

The non-autofitted locomotives were used for whatever light work was required, which could, to the confusion of chroniclers, include hauling autocoaches in passenger trains. A little side line on the Victorian psyche is that in 1896, when a lightweight engine was required to take a Royal Train over the Woodstock branch, 517 1473 was given the name *Fair Rosamund*. 'Fair' Rosamund Clifford was a mistress of Henry II who was reputed to have lived at Woodstock. The locomotive kept the name and worked on the Woodstock branch for many years.

One was scrapped as early as 1904. A few went in the 1910s, but the majority went from the late 1920s to the late 1930s, with just a handful surviving the Second World War and none lasting to British Railways.

Wolverhampton '196' class

Builders	GWR/Wolverhampton
Dates Built	1879-1881
Number Built	3
Driving Wheel Size	6ft 0in
Cylinder Dimensions	17in x 24in
Boiler Class	Q, O
Dates Withdrawn	1884/5 (rebuilt with tenders)

These 2-4-0T with 6ft driving wheels, actually numbered 197, 199 and 201 were Wolverhampton renewals – to all intents and purposes new locomotives –

of 2-4-0 tender engines absorbed from the West Midland Railway. The rest of the 196 class were renewed as tender engines. They were built from 1879-1881. They had something of the look of earlier large Metros, but without the volute springs. One was fitted with condensing gear. They were converted back to tender engines in 1884/5.

Wolverhampton 3571 class

Builders	GWR/Wolverhampton
Dates Built	1895-7
Number Built	10
Route Colour	Uncoloured/Yellow
Power Class	Unclassified
Tractive Effort	12,500lbs
Driving Wheel Size	5ft 2in
Cylinder Dimensions	16½in x 24in
Wheelbase	7ft 4in + 8ft 2in
Boiler Class	U
Dates Withdrawn	1928-1949

Just ten of these 0-4-2Ts were built in 1895-7. They can be considered to be an enlargement of the 517 class, having a larger (U class) boiler and different external framing for the trailing wheels.

These had a quiet life compared to the 517s. Belpaire fireboxes appeared from 1912. Various enlarged bunkers were fitted and often rear spectacle plates on the bunkers. None were autofitted and only one received an enclosed cab.

Two went in 1928/9, but the rest survived into the 1940s. Three lasted until 1949 and British Railways, but by then they do not appear to have been in use for revenue trains.

Swindon Metro class

Builders	GWR/Swindon
Dates Built	1869-1899
Number Built	140 (see notes)
Route Colour	Yellow
Power Class	Ungrouped
Tractive Effort	12,000-14,000lbs

Driving Wheel Size	5ft 0in[†]
Cylinder Dimensions	16in x 24in
Wheelbase	7ft 3in + 8ft 0 in (455-470) 7ft 3in + 8ft 3in (613-632) 7ft 9in + 8ft 0 in (455-470 rebuilt) 7ft 9in +8ft 3in ((967-986, 1401-1420, 613-632 rebuilt)
Boiler Class	T
Dates Withdrawn	1905-1949

The 2-4-0T 'Metros' – short for Metropolitan as many worked over the Metropolitan Railway lines – did not exist in quite such variety as

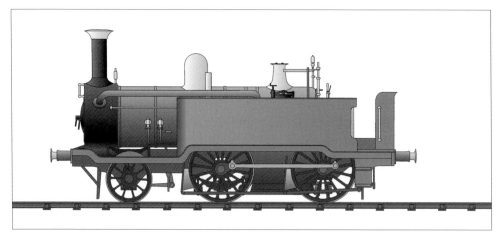

455 (**Small Metro**) class. *Arrangement of condensing equipped engine as built 1865.*

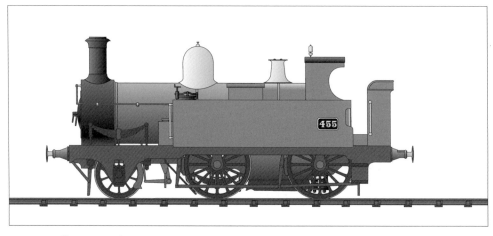

455 (**Small Metro**) class. *Diagram K with open cab and Belpaire firebox from 1910 on.*

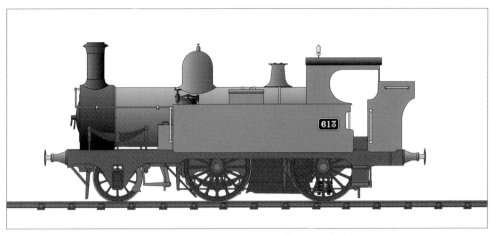

613 (Medium Metro) class. *Diagram I with extended frames. 1920s on.*

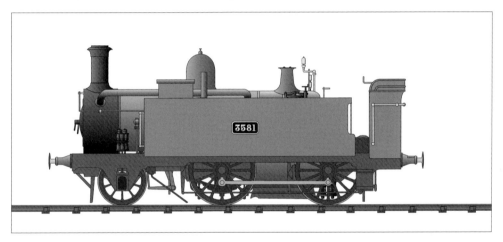

3581 (Large Metro) class. *Diagram C, condensing equipped with round top firebox.*

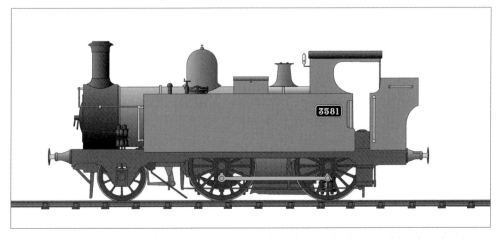

3581 (Large Metro) class. *Diagram H with Belpaire firebox and enclosed cab.*

the 517 class, but it was perhaps a close run thing. They were built between 1869 and 1899 and some of the first built ones were withdrawn as early as 1903/4.

As well as the different wheel arrangement, they had bigger boilers than the 517 class, tending to be longer and heavier, although the ranges of weights overlapped slightly. The first lot of Metros, the 455-470 series, had 740 gallon tanks and T class 140lbpsi boilers. They had a rather odd footplate arrangement, swept down over the leading wheels from buffer height, up over the driving wheels, then back down to buffer height for the crew, who had no cab. Add to this a decidedly primitive looking flared chimney and as built they appeared to be very much an 'early' locomotive.

Like the 517 class, new design features came in with successive lots to emerge from the works. 613-632 came out in 1871 and were a little larger with longer wheelbase and 800 gallon tanks.

From 1874 to 1878, 967-986 and 1401-1420 featured even longer wheelbase, external axle boxes for the leading wheels, a straight running plate and 820 gallon tanks.

In 1881/2 1445-1464 were built with domeless boilers that were of different dimensions to those used by the rest. Those of this lot that were not fitted with condensing apparatus were given open cabs.

1491-1500 and 3561-3570 followed in 1892-4 and returned to the standard T class boiler dimensions. Finally, in 1899, 3581-3600 were built with much larger 1100 gallon tanks and revised front suspension in the form of a nest of volute springs.

The first major changes affected the 455 and 613 series, which were rebuilt with straight running plates, and a six inch increase in the wheelbase between the leading wheels and the driving wheels. The 455 series always retained this shorter wheelbase.

Boilers started to be replaced in the normal course of things from late in the nineteenth century, but these were always variations on the T class rather than different styles of boilers as happened in so many other classes. At the same time, they normally gained larger tanks and various increases in bunker capacity. In 1898/9, thirty of the post-1878 built engines with 820 gallon tanks received larger 1080 gallon tanks and revised front springing to make room for them; they were then, with the 3581 series which was built shortly afterwards, known as Large Metros. So the twenty Small Metros were those of the initial lot with the three inch shorter wheelbase, the fifty Large Metros (thirty of which had started life as Medium Metros) were those built from 1878 which carried 1080 gallon tanks and volute springs for the leading wheel suspension, and the seventy Medium Metros were those of the 100 built between 1871 and 1894 which retained tanks of 800-820 gallons.

A complication with the Metros is condensing gear. Until electrification of the Metropolitan lines in 1903, the GWR maintained a fleet of about fifty locomotives with condensing gear for use on the underground – or at least surface – lines, the majority of which were Metro tanks. The gear seems to have been readily removable and locomotives gained and lost the gear from time to time and with it cabs, as locos with the condensing gear were normally cabless – sometimes known as the 'get wets'. The gear tended to be used on 'large metros', once they were available, but there were exceptions in plenty. After electrification, only about a dozen condensing locomotives were required, six of them Metros, mainly to run freight trains to Smithfield Market. The other condensing fitted locomotives were 633 class 0-6-0Ts.

One locomotive, 3593, was converted to a 2-4-2 in 1905. It gained an enclosed cab and a very much enlarged bunker, but the experiment was not repeated. Belpaire fireboxes appeared from 1910. Yet larger bunkers appeared from this time and earlier engines received an 11in rearward extension of the frames to support a larger bunker, which later ones had from new. From 1924, Collett-style bunkers with the overhanging extension at the top of the bunker appeared, as did (other than on condensing fitted locomotives) fully enclosed cabs. A great variety of shapes and sizes of bunker were fitted: there appears to have been no pattern at all. Around forty were autofitted in the late 1920s and early 1930s, presumably to compensate for withdrawn life-expired 517s until the 48xx class were available.

Non-condensing locomotives were extensively used on London area suburban services, but were also used on other branch and local work, mostly in the Southern division. They were also used on some quite fast main line trains – a Gloucester to Cardiff service for instance. Once autofitted, they scattered even more widely.

A few of the class were scrapped around 1905/8, presumably surplus to requirements after the Metropolitan electrification. Of the rest, a few started to go from 1928, but the majority ran into the 1930s when withdrawals started in earnest. Around twenty-five survived until after the war, all of them from the lots built after 1891. Ten large Metros from the last two lots survived to British Railways. All were gone by 1950.

Dean/Churchward
No 1 2-4-0T (built as 4-4-0T)

Builders	GWR/Swindon
Date built	1880, rebuilt as 2-4-0T 1882
Number Built	1

Tractive Effort	15,000lbs
Dates Built	5ft 6in[†]
Cylinder Dimensions	17in x 26in
Wheelbase	8ft 6in + 9ft 0in 5ft 6in + 6ft 6in + 9ft 0in (as built)
Boiler Class	N
Route Colour	Blue
Power Class	Unclassed
Date Withdrawn	1924

This was an experimental locomotive, having an unusual, and unsuccessful, design of front bogie in its 4-4-0T form. It was soon rebuilt as a 2-4-0T, retaining the non-standard boiler it was built with. It received an N class boiler in 1899 and a Belpaire firebox boiler in 1914, and lasted until 1924.

Swindon 3501 & 3511 (Stella Tank) classes.

Builders	GWR/Swindon
Dates Built	1885
Number Built	10 (see note)
Tractive Effort	14,500lbs
Driving Wheel Size	5ft 1in[†]
Cylinder Dimensions	17in x 26in
Boiler Class	P
Dates Withdrawn	1894/5 (rebuilt as tender engines)

Built in 1885, the ten double framed 3511 2-4-0Ts were a tank engine version of the Stella class 2-4-0s, presumably a part of Dean's standardisation exercises. They were a much larger engine than the Metros with 17in by 26in cylinders and class P (Dean Goods) boilers. Originally they carried condensing apparatus for use in the Severn Tunnel. 3501-10 were similar, but built as convertibles for the broad gauge.

The 3501s were all converted to tender engines, some whilst they were still running on the broad gauge. All were running as members of the 2-4-0 Stella class by 1892. The 3511 series followed them into the Stella class and lost tanks and gained tenders in 1894/5.

Swindon 3521 class

Builders	GWR/Swindon
Dates Built	1887-9
Number Built	40 (see notes)
Tractive Effort	18,000lbs
Driving Wheel Size	5ft
Cylinder Dimensions	17in x 24in
Wheelbase	7ft 6in + 10ft 6in (3521-3540 as built) 7ft 0in + 10ft 4in + 4ft 6in (3521-3540 as 0-4-4T) 7ft 0in + 9ft 10in + 4ft 6in (3541-3560 as 0-4-4T)
Boiler Class	P
Dates Withdrawn	1899-1903 (rebuilt as 4-4-0)

3521-3540 were built in 1887/8 as double framed 0-4-2 tank engines with a short coupled wheelbase and a long gap to the trailing wheel. This made them reluctant to stay on the track and yet twenty of them were built. They had P class (Dean Goods) boilers – larger than any other 0-4-2s. A further twenty, 3541-3560, were built in 1888/9 as convertible broad Gauge saddle tanks.

The last of the broad gauge locos was turned out as an 0-4-4T with a very short wheelbase trailing bogie which made some improvement to its ability to stay on the track and all were converted to 0-4-4T by the end of 1892. Holcroft went on a trial trip on one as an apprentice. He recorded:

'The outward journey was made bunker first and at a moderate speed ... the driver went "hell-for-leather" on the return trip to give the engine a good shake-up – and he succeeded! Although I have travelled extensively since on all kinds of engines and at speeds over 100mph there was never a trip like this one. It had to be experienced to be believed, for the lateral oscillation was terrific: the motion imparted to the footplate could be likened to that of a terrier shaking a rat!'

Even in this form they were very prone to derailment and so from 1899 to 1903 all were converted to 4-4-0 tender engines! See the 4-4-0 section for more details.

No 101 0-4-0T

Builders	GWR/Swindon
Dates Built	1902
Number Built	1

Tractive Effort	11,500lbs
Driving Wheel Size	3ft 8in
Cylinder Dimensions	13in x 22in
Dates Withdrawn	1911

This was the only 0-4-0T built at Swindon works. It was a side tank used for experimental boilers. The first two iterations used oil firing on a system devised by James Holden, a former assistant to Dean, who was the locomotive superintendent of the Great Eastern Railway. This boiler had no water space round the firebox; instead the firebox was lined with firebrick. The initial firebox was very large in proportion to the rest of the boiler, and was soon replaced by a smaller one. The third variation, fitted in 1903, was a design by the Austrian Hugo Lenz, known as a Lentz boiler. This featured a corrugated inner firebox, was tapered and still oil fired. In the final iteration the Lentz boiler was converted to coal burning and a small bunker added. It was condemned in 1911, having only been used at Swindon Works. The locomotive is perhaps most notorious for being the inspiration for the entry level Hornby model which has featured in many a child's first train set.

Collett
1101 class

Builders	Avonside Engine Co
Dates Built	1926
Number Built	6
Route Colour	Red
Power Class	B
Tractive Effort	19,500lbs
Driving Wheel Size	3ft 9½in
Cylinder Dimensions	16in x 24in
Boiler Class	own
Dates Withdrawn	1959/60

Six powerful and business-like looking 0-4-0 side tanks ordered from Avonside of Bristol and delivered in 1926. They were fundamentally of a standard Avonside design with some small modifications for the GWR. The most obvious change was that the side tanks were cut away at the front to resemble pannier tanks. The boilers were always the Avonside design and never replaced with a GWR type.

The 1101s had their cab roofs rounded off to improve clearances within a very few years of purchase, and gained GWR safety valves and covers by the 1930s.

1101 class. *Diagram T. Note: the valve gear drawn on this sketch is conjectural.*

Other than that they were little altered until withdrawn in 1959/60. None were preserved, but Cadbury's No. 1, also built by Avonside and with the Birmingham Railway museum, is clearly a close relative.

4800/1400 class

Builders	GWR/Swindon
Dates Built	1932-1936
Number Built	75
Route Colour	Uncoloured
Power Class	Unclassed
Tractive Effort	14,000lbs
Driving Wheel Size	5ft 2in
Cylinder Dimensions	16in x 24in
Boiler Class	SS
Dates Withdrawn	1956-1965

By the mid twentieth century, the 517s and Metros were wearing out and needed to be replaced. The 4800s essentially followed the Wolverhampton lines of development. It was very much a case of taking a proven configuration and redesigning it, using the best features of their predecessors in their fully developed state, and adding all the latest engineering improvements for increased running time between overhauls and easier maintenance. The drawing office had a shopping list of mutually exclusive features, including a desire to have leading and trailing wheels, even bogies, through light weight, good adhesion, low build cost and low running costs. In the end, they picked on almost exactly the same compromises as their predecessors of fifty years before. The final design had

4800 (later 1400) class. *Diagram M. The sketch shows the class as built without top feed.*

similar major dimensions to the ultimate LWB configuration of the 517 class. The boiler pressure was increased to 165psi, the cylinders reduced to 16in, and the locomotives were fitted with generous sized cabs. The boiler, called the SS class, was very similar to the S class, but with a drum head smokebox.

Collett is often criticised about the supposedly antiquated nature of the 4800s, but from a business point of view using a 41 ton six wheel locomotive to haul one and two coach trains would appear to make far more sense than using a 63 ton ten wheel locomotive as was done by other lines. The use of inside cylinders is also criticised, but a short wheelbase outside cylinder 0-4-2 would have given passengers in the leading carriage a rather uncomfortable journey.

In 1948, they were renumbered in the 1400 series, as the 4800 series was required for oil burning 2800s. This saw many of them assuming numbers that had previously been used for the 517 class or for Metros.

As with most Collett designs, changes were few over their lifetime. The last batch were fitted with whistle shields to divert steam from the whistle, and a larger pattern was eventually fitted to all of the class. Steps on the fireman's side of the bunker were gradually added, starting in 1936, and top feed was introduced from 1944.

They started to be withdrawn from 1956 as branch lines were closed or DMUs took over light passenger traffic; the last went out of service in 1964. Four survived, three of which have run in preservation and the fourth is a museum exhibit. 1466 (4866) is particularly notable as being the first locomotive bought by the nascent Great Western Society.

5800 class

Builders	GWR/Swindon
Dates Built	1932-1936
Number Built	19

Route Colour	Uncoloured
Power Class	Unclassed
Tractive Effort	14,000lbs
Driving Wheel Size	5ft 2in
Cylinder Dimensions	16in x 24in
Boiler Class	SS
Dates Withdrawn	1957-1961

The nineteen members of the 5800 class were essentially the same as the 4800s, but not autofitted.

They received the same updates as the 4800s. This sub class ran out of work rather earlier than the autofitted engines; by 1954 six of them were in store, out of use. The majority were withdrawn from 1957-1959, with one surviving until 1961. None have been preserved.

Absorbed Classes (Nineteenth Century and Early Twentieth Century)

A good number of 4 coupled tank engines came into GWR ownership with absorbed lines. The GWR seemed very reluctant to build 0-4-0T and a few of these nineteenth century acquisitions had long lives in quiet corners of the system, although most had gone by 1914.

One odd survival was *Prince*, a South Devon railway 2-4-0, which was converted for stationary use in 1896 and then meandered to all sorts of locations until finally being scrapped in 1935!

Fox, built for the West Cornwall Railway in 1872 by Avonside, was a small industrial type 0-4-0, and became GWR 1391 until being resold to the Gloucester Carriage and Wagon works, who used it as a works loco until scrapped in 1948.

Lady Margaret, 1902 Sharp Stewart 2-4-0T

Built in 1902 for the Liskeard and Looe railway. As GWR 1308 it received a major rebuild in 1929 to look something like a small version of the Cambrian Sharp Stewart 2-4-0s and finally went in 1948.

South Devon Railway Avonside 0-4-0ST

Builders	Avonside Engine Co
Dates Built	1874/5
Number Built	5
Driving Wheel Size	3ft 0in
Cylinder Dimensions	14in x 18in
Dates Withdrawn	1906-1910 (sold), 1929.

This small class was built for the broad gauge, on which 7ft gauge their 7ft 6in wheelbase must have looked distinctly odd. They had outside cylinders and the GWR numbered them 2175-2179. They were rebuilt as standard gauge locomotives in 1892, receiving new boilers and renumbered 1329-1333. They were all sold between 1906 and 1910, one going to the Wantage Tramway where it was cut up in 1920, and the other four to Powlesland & Mason at Swansea Docks. Three of these were sold to the Ministry of Munitions during the Great War, and the last remained with Powlesland & Mason to return to the GWR in 1924, and be finally withdrawn in 1929.

Monmouthshire Railway 1345 class 0-4-4ST

Builders	Avonside/Dubs, rebuilt GWR Swindon
Dates rebuilt	1892-2
Number Built	8
Driving Wheel Size	4ft 1½in
Cylinder Dimensions	17in x 24in
Dates Withdrawn	1906-1913

This was one of Swindon's odder conversions. A class of 8 0-6-0ST, absorbed with the Monmouthshire railway in 1880, were converted into 0-4-4ST. They retained saddle tanks, but were given large bunkers which included additional water tankage. The result was decidedly odd with a short wheelbase bogie spaced well back from the driving wheels – rather reminiscent of the 3521 class in their 0-4-4T guise. They were withdrawn from 1906 to 1913.

Absorbed Classes at the Grouping
Alexandra (Newport and South Wales) Docks and Railway
1341. 0-4-0ST 'Alexandra'
This was a small outside cylinder loco of unrecorded manufacture. It was given a light rebuild in the 1920s and survived until 1946.

Avonside 0-4-0ST

Builders	Avonside Engine Co
Dates Built	1897
Number Built	1

Route Colour	Uncoloured
Power Class	Ungrouped
Tractive Effort	11,000lbs
Driving Wheel Size	3ft 0in
Cylinder Dimensions	12½in x 19¾in
Dates Withdrawn	1932 (sold)

This was another small outside cylinder 0-4-0ST, built in 1897. It kept its name, *Trojan* and was numbered 1340 when it reached the GWR. It received a Swindon rebuild in the 1920s which involved larger cylinders and boiler work. It worked on the GWR until 1932, when it was sold into industrial service. In 1968, it came into the hands of the Great Western Society and, after acquiring a new boiler, has steamed in preservation.

Brecon & Merthyr Railway
Stephenson 2-4-0 class

Builders	R. Stephenson & Co
Dates Built	1888/9, 1898, 1904
Number Built	6
Route Colour	Yellow
Power Class	Ungrouped/A
Tractive Effort	13,000lbs
Driving Wheel Size	5ft 0in
Cylinder Dimensions	16in x 24in
Boiler Class	Own
Dates Withdrawn	1921-1924

This class of six, four built in 1888/9, with two more following in 1898 and 1904, were effectively copies of GWR 'medium' Metro 2-4-0s, one having been borrowed by the B&M in 1888. One was withdrawn just before the grouping and its boiler repaired for reuse. The GWR allocated numbers 1402, 1412, 1452, 1458 and 1460, which were all numbers previously used by withdrawn GWR built Metros. In the event though, only 1460, which was given the repaired boiler from its scrapped cousin, survived long enough to actually carry its GWR number, the others being scrapped more or less on sight in 1922/3. However it only lasted until 1924.

Cambrian Railway
Small Side Tank class 2-4-0T

Builders	Sharp, Stewart & Co
Dates Built	1866
Number Built	3
Route Colour	Uncoloured
Power Class	Ungrouped
Tractive Effort	9,000lbs
Driving Wheel Size	4ft 6in
Cylinder Dimensions	14in x 20in
Wheelbase	6ft 0in + 6ft 3in
Boiler Class	Own
Dates Withdrawn	1929, 1948

Three small side tank locomotives from Sharp Stewart, delivered in 1866. All survived to the GWR, who proposed to scrap two of them immediately, but they were reprieved and numbered 1192, 1196 and 1197. They soon received the full GWR treatment above the footplate. The boilers were thoroughly overhauled with top feed added and they were given new GWR smokeboxes, tanks, cab and bunkers. Thus utterly transformed they resumed work, normally on the very weight-restricted Tanat Valley line. One was scrapped in 1929 but the other two soldiered on until 1948, becoming British Railways locomotives and running over a million miles each.

Cardiff Railway
Kitson 0-4-0ST

Builders	Kitson & Co
Dates Built	1898/9
Number Built	2
Route Colour	Uncoloured
Power Class	Ungrouped
Tractive Effort	14,500lbs
Driving Wheel Size	3ft 2½in
Cylinder Dimensions	14in x 21in
Boiler Class	own
Dates Withdrawn	1932, 1963

There were two of these 0-4-0 saddle tanks, delivered in 1898 and 1899. They had a rather unusual valve gear, J Hawthorn Kitson's, which was a modified Walschaerts type with the link above the footplate. They were given GWR safety valves and cover. One, 1339, was withdrawn in 1932, but the other, after a period in store and then a loan to an industrial user, returned to revenue service at Bridgwater Docks and joined British Railways. In 1960, it went to Swansea Docks, and when withdrawn it was the last GWR/absorbed locomotive left in service with BR. 1338 was preserved and has run in preservation.

Neath and Brecon
Sharp Stewart 2-4-0T

Builders	Sharp, Stewart & Co
Dates Built	1889/90
Number Built	1
Route Colour	Blue
Power Class	A
Tractive Effort	15,000lbs
Driving Wheel Size	5ft 3in
Cylinder Dimensions	17in x 24in
Boiler Class	Own
Dates Withdrawn	1926

This was effectively a copy of a Barry class C. Already somewhat in Swindon condition it was allocated 1400 at the grouping and withdrawn in 1926.

Powlesland & Mason
Ex South Devon Railway Avonside 0-4-0ST
See South Devon Railway Avonside 0-4-0ST above.

Brush Electrical 0-4-0ST

Builders	Brush Electrical
Dates Built	1903, 1906
Number Built	2
Route Colour	Uncoloured/Yellow
Power Class	Ungrouped
Driving Wheel Size	3ft 6in

Cylinder Dimensions	14in x 20in
Boiler Class	Own, 1376 (Class YD)
Dates Withdrawn	1928/9 (sold)

The Falcon Engine & Car Works Ltd had built earlier steam locomotives for P&M amongst others, and were taken over by Brush in 1889. This is the same Brush company, give or take a few mergers and acquisitions, that was and is a significant builder of diesel electric locomotives. These two were among their last steam locomotives.

Powlesland & Mason locomotives came to the GWR in January 1924, late in the grouping, and were given a rather random collection of numbers – and number plates – reused from locomotives absorbed earlier that had already been withdrawn. The Brush locomotives were numbered 726 and 921 by the GWR. 726 was given a considerable rebuild in 1926. This included a new boiler to a different design, and, uniquely for an 0-4-0T, pannier tanks. These were short tanks and didn't cover the firebox. 921 didn't receive such dramatic changes but did receive a GWR combined dome/safety valve cover. Both were sold on to industry in 1928/9. 726 was scrapped in the early 1960s, but 921 survives and is preserved, although has not run in preservation.

Peckett Class E 0-4-0ST

Builders	Peckett & Sons
Dates Built	1906-1918
Number Built	7 (see notes)
Route Colour	Blue
Power Class	Ungrouped
Tractive Effort	14,000lbs
Driving Wheel Size	3ft7in
Cylinder Dimensions	15in x 21in
Boiler Class	Own
Dates Withdrawn	1928, 1952,1960,

Both the SHT and Powlesland & Mason owned examples of this Peckett standard class, and the GWR treated them all as a single class. All but one received a combined dome/safety valve cover in GWR service, and all but one had long lives, surviving into the 1950s and even 1960s.

The SHT locomotives were 929 (later 1141), withdrawn in 1952, 968 (1143), withdrawn 1960, and 1098 (1145) withdrawn 1959. The P&M locomotives were 927, which went early in 1928, 935 (1152) which lasted until 1961, 696 (1150) withdrawn 1952 and 779 (1151) which was sold to a scrap merchant in 1963 and worked on in their yard until it was cut up in 1965.

Andrew Barclay & Co 0-4-0ST
A similar locomotive to 701/1140, owned by the SHT, it was built in 1912, numbered 928 by the GWR, and withdrawn in 1927.

Hawthorn, Leslie 0-4-0ST
This was a smaller locomotive than most of the P&M stock. Purchased around 1919, it was numbered 942 by the GWR. In 1926 it received a significant rebuild with a boiler similar to that of 726 above, but unlike 726 942 retained a saddle tank. It was renumbered 1153 in 1947, and withdrawn in 1955.

Swansea Harbour Trust
Peckett Class W4 0-4-0ST

Builders	Peckett & Sons
Dates Built	1899-1904
Number Built	8 (see notes)
Route Colour	Uncoloured
Power Class	Ungrouped
Tractive Effort	12,000-13,000lbs
Driving Wheel Size	3ft3in[†]
Cylinder Dimensions	14in x 20in
Boiler Class	Own
Dates Withdrawn	1927-1929

SHT Locomotives came into GWR hands in October 1923, late in the grouping. Like the P&M locomotives the allocation of numbers was a little random. At one stage a contractor for the SHT had had 8 of these standard Peckett designs working on the line, but only four, with slight variations in specification, reached the GWR. They were numbered 886, 926, 930 and 933. They were scrapped or sold in the late 1920s, replaced by the new 1101 class.

Hudswell Clarke & Co 0-4-0STs
The SHT bought three small 0-4-0STs from Hudswell Clarke in 1905, but only one survived to the GWR. They were very similar in size to the Peckett W4s, and the one survivor, as GWR 701, was scrapped in 1929.

They bought a further, slightly larger locomotive from Hudswell Clark in 1911, which was numbered 943 when it came into GWR hands. Renumbered 1142, it was withdrawn in 1959.

Andrew Barclay & Co 0-4-0ST

Builders	Andrew Barclay & Co
Dates Built	1905
Number Built	3 (see notes)
Route Colour	Uncoloured
Power Class	Ungrouped
Tractive Effort	14,000lbs
Driving Wheel Size	3ft 5in
Cylinder Dimensions	14in x 22in
Boiler Class	Own
Dates Withdrawn	1958

Only one of these three locomotives was handed over to the GWR. It was little altered in GWR and BR service, receiving a safety valve cover and GWR safety valves in the 1930s, but as GWR 701 and then 1140 it was in service until 1958.

Peckett Class E 0-4-0ST
See Peckett E class under Powlesland & Mason.

Hawthorn, Leslie 0-4-0ST
This locomotive was of broadly similar power to the Andrew Barclay 0-4-0STs. Built in 1909, it was numbered 974 by the GWR, and given 1144 in the 1974 renumbering. It was withdrawn in 1960 and scrapped. A similar but much later Robert Stephensons & Hawthorn locomotive, works no 7058, is preserved and has in the past been painted and numbered as 1144.

Taff Vale
S & T 0-4-0STs
The Taff Vale ordered two very small shunters from Hudswell, Clarke & Co in 1876. The second was slightly larger than the first, and was classified as 'Class' T in the 1890s, and the smaller classified S. They were numbered 1342 (S) and 1343 (T) respectively, and withdrawn in 1925 and 1926.

0-6-0 Tank Locomotives

633 class. *The crew's rain tarpaulin is partially rigged. (Photo: Brian Stephenson Collection)*

Preserved 8750 Class *3728 at Didcot, wearing GWR wartime black in the Oxfordshire sunshine. (Photo: Jim Champ)*

Boilers

Boiler Class	Name	Barrel			Firebox Length
		length	diameter		
K	Standard 10	10ft 3in	4ft 5in	5ft 0in	6ft 0in
T	Metro	10ft 6in	4ft 3in		5ft 1in
O	Standard Goods	11ft 0in	4ft 5in		5ft 4in
P	2301	10ft 3in	4ft 5in		5ft 4in
Q	Sir Daniel	11ft 0in	4ft 3in		5ft 4in
R	850	10ft 0in	3ft 10in		4ft 0in
U	2021	10ft 0in	3ft 10in		5ft 0in
Q (later)	Standard 16	10ft 1in	3ft 10in		5ft 0in
F (later)	Standard 21	10ft 6in	4ft 3in		5ft 6in

The class letters for boiler classes which became extinct were later used for other types.

Early Absorbed Class
231 class 1853

Builders	E.B. Wilson & Co
Dates Built	1856
Number Built	4
Line	Oxford, Worcester and Wolverhampton Railway
Driving Wheel Size	4ft 8in
Cylinder Dimensions	15in x 20in
Dates Withdrawn	1877-180

These were four inside frame locos with back tanks, of a standard Wilson design used at many collieries.

GWR Classes

There were very many classes and types of 0-6-0 tank, including various absorbed engines and small classes for special purposes. However, the majority can be roughly divided into two main groups, 'large' and 'small' and in both a line of development over some eighty years can be seen.

Design Trends

It is easy to think that, because few 0-6-0 tanks were nominally built under his charge, Churchward had no interest in the type. However, the RCTS volumes detail a great deal of work while he was CME: subtle and less subtle boiler changes, top feed, superheating and much else.

Side tanks were used on some of the earliest locomotives, but were soon replaced with saddle tanks, which give better access to the motion. When the GWR started to put Belpaire fireboxes on their 0-6-0 tank locomotives, they decided that the saddle tanks were excessively complicated to fabricate. The pannier tanks consisted of pair of tanks, one each side of the boiler and roughly rectangular in section so were much simpler to construct. The concept was first seen on the 4-4-0 tank, number 1490. Conversions to pannier tanks started before 1914, but were very much as and when, with a very few locomotives retaining saddle tanks even after 1948. Many, but not all, were given enclosed cabs. Pannier tanks were designed to fit the boilers used, which varied over time as well, so quite a selection of different sized tanks, boilers and cabs could be seen at various times on locomotives that had started life in the same batch. It must have made life interesting for train spotters and makes life equally interesting and research essential for the discerning modeller.

Through Churchward's time and going on into Collett's, the earlier 'large' 0-6-0 tanks tended to receive larger boilers than had been originally fitted, mainly Q and then P class units. An engine would have looked rather different with the longer and thinner Q class boiler than it would with the shorter and wider P class, even though it was still the same locomotive class. Some of the earlier locomotives had very considerable increases in weight over the years – the early 302 class for instance, 35 tons 13½cwt when built, weighed 43tons 2cwt in their final condition with P class boilers and other changes. There was also a steady increase in the boiler pressure used: taking the 302 class as an example again, they started life with 140psi boilers and by the end had at least 165psi boilers, whilst the later classes sometimes went up to 180psi. With the increased boiler pressure came an increase in tractive effort, so the weight increases were probably desirable to provide increased adhesive weight and thus traction. Another development was quite widespread use of superheating in the 1920s, which tended to be removed in the 1930s. Superheating tended to give a lag in the regulator response, which was quite acceptable in a traffic locomotive, but undesirable whilst engaged in shunting.

The number of diagrams issued for the nineteenth century classes does not cover many of their variations, because the diagram system was only commenced in the twentieth century under Churchward.

Autofitting
As noted in the introduction, autofitting was fitted and removed from individual locomotives in various pre-grouping classes. The 'small' 2021 was the most frequently autofitted class, and a few examples of the 1901 also received the gear from time to time. Amongst 'large' classes, there were quite a few examples amongst 655s and 1076/1134s, while odd ones and twos of the 1501 and 1016 classes also received the gear from time to time. Thus there was a mixture of 'small' and 'large' classes fitted, although the 'large' ones selected were among the less powerful types.

As discussed below, the 'small' 5400 and 6400 Collett classes would have been equally capable as the 'large' 655 and 1134, and no 5700 or 9400s ever received the gear. When some more powerful autofitted engines were required in BR days, the equipment was fitted to 4500 class small prairie locomotives.

Gooch Design
Nos. 93 & 94

Builder	GWR/Swindon
Dates Built	1860
Number Built	2
Driving Wheel Size	4ft 2in
Cylinder Dimensions	15in x 22in
Dates Withdrawn	Renewed 1875/7

The first GWR built 0-6-0T were quite small engines with 4ft 2in (or possibly 4ft) wheels. They were fairly typical Gooch designs with domeless boilers, raised fireboxes and Gooch valve gear. They had inside frames, small side tanks and a well tank under the bunker. When renewed, they were turned out as members of the 850/1901 class, so it is probable that no significant parts were reused.

Large Engines - Outside Frames
Wolverhampton 302 class

Builder	GWR/Wolverhampton
Dates Built	1864/5
Number Built	8
Route Colour	Uncoloured/Yellow

Power Class	Ungrouped/A
Tractive Effort	13,500-17,500lbs
Driving Wheel Size	4ft 6in†
Cylinder Dimensions	16in x 24in-17in x 24in
Wheelbase	7ft 4in + 8ft 2in
Front Overhang	4ft 6in
Rear Overhang	5ft 2in
Boiler Class	Special, Q, P
Dates Withdrawn	1918-1932

The large tanks started with outside framed saddle tank engines, all with the barest minimum of weather protection for the crew – just a spectacle plate and waist level cab sides. The progenitors started at Wolverhampton with the 302 class (1864/5) of eight engines. They were built with short saddle tanks that only covered the boiler barrel and left firebox and smokebox uncovered.

This class had a particularly complex history with many variations of boiler, dome position, tank size and other components. They received 17in cylinders from the late 1870s, open cabs from the 1880s and full length saddle tanks towards the end of that decade.

The original boilers were similar to but smaller in diameter than the Q class. They first received Belpaire Q class boilers from 1911 and then P class from 1922. Pannier tanks appeared with the Belpaire fireboxes and had higher capacity than the saddle tanks, putting them into the Yellow weight group. A few P class boilers were superheated. Some of the later survivors received larger bunkers and enclosed cabs. They were mostly scrapped in the 1920s and

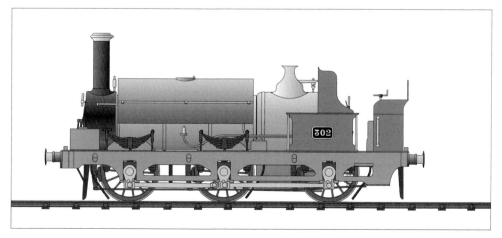

302 class *as running about 1880 with short saddle tank and no cab.*

early 1930s. The P class boilers and some of the later Q class boilers had high enough pressure to being the locos into power class A.

There were five diagrams for the 302s, covering saddle tank and boiler variations.

Wolverhampton 1016 class

Builder	GWR/Wolverhampton
Dates Built	1867-1871
Number Built	60
Route Colour	Yellow
Power Class	Ungrouped/A
Tractive Effort	13,500-17,500lbs
Driving Wheel Size	4ft 6in[†]
Cylinder Dimensions	16in x 24in-17in x 24in
Wheelbase	7ft 4in + 8ft 2in
Front Overhang	5ft 3½in
Rear Overhang	5ft 11in
Boiler Class	Special, Q, P
Dates Withdrawn	1910-1935

The 1016 class was very similar to the 302, but formed a class of sixty. Like their precursors, they were built as outside framed saddle tank engines with the barest minimum of weather protection for the crew. The 1016s had the same wheel spacing as the 302s but were somewhat longer.

1016 class *as running about 1880 with short saddle tank and open cab.*

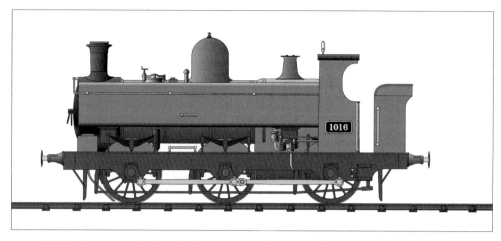

1016 class *with P class boiler and pannier tanks, late 1920s. Diagram B17*

1016 started life as 238, and the first five were probably 1132-6 until renumbered in 1870.

The history of the locomotives was generally similar to the 302 class with many changes of tanks and boilers in the Victorian era. They received 17in cylinders from 1879-1895. The subsequent history of the class continued to be similar to the 302s, with higher pressure P class boilers and increased water capacity bringing them into the higher weight and power classifications. Quite a number of them received superheated boilers in the 1920s, a few lasting long enough to have the superheater elements removed again in the 1930s.

There were four diagrams for the 1016s, covering saddle tank and boiler variations. Four were withdrawn before the Great War, but the vast majority went between 1925 and 1936, having run over a million miles each.

Wolverhampton Nos. 60, 67
Two of the 57 class tender engines, 60 and 67 were renewed as saddle tanks in 1876/7. They were converted back to tender engines in 1884.

Wolverhampton 119 class

Builder	GWR/Wolverhampton,
Dates Built	1878-1883 (renewals)
Number Built	11
Route Colour	Yellow
Power Class	Ungrouped/A
Tractive Effort	14,500-17,500lbs

Driving Wheel Size	4ft 6in†
Cylinder Dimensions	17in x 24in
Boiler Class	Special, Q
Wheelbase	7ft 4in + 8ft 4in
Dates Withdrawn	1910-1933

There were eleven members of the 119 class, which were Wolverhampton renewals of 79 class tender engines. They were double framed with sandwich frames outside and plate frames inside, full length saddle tanks and open cabs. Three of the class were built with a style of condensing apparatus, not for use on underground lines but for feed water heating.

They underwent the normal late nineteenth century changes of thicker tyres and a variety of boilers. Pannier tanks came from 1913 and a few gained enclosed cabs and enlarged bunkers. No larger boiler than the Sir Daniel (Q class) was ever fitted. There were two diagrams, covering Saddle and Pannier tanks. They were withdrawn gradually between 1910 and 1933.

119 class *as running around 1890. This sketch is based on diagram A, but some features have been changed to reflect available photographs.*

Wolverhampton 322 class

Builder	Beyer, rebuilt GWR/Wolverhampton
Dates Built	1878-1885 (rebuilds)
Number Built	6
Route Colour	Yellow
Power Class	Ungrouped/A

Tractive Effort	14,500-18,000lbs
Driving Wheel Size	5ft 0in[†]
Cylinder Dimensions	17/17½in x 24/26in
Boiler Class	Special, Q, P
Wheelbase	8ft 0 + 8ft 3in
Front Overhang	4ft 9in
Rear Overhang	6ft 9in
Dates Withdrawn	1921-1932

The 322 class consisted of six Wolverhampton conversions from tender engines of the 'Beyer' class. They had open cabs and full length pannier tanks as was conventional at this period.

They received a variety of boilers in the late nineteenth century, receiving the Sir Daniel type in various configurations. After 1918, they mostly received pannier tanks, and those that survived into the 1930s had all received superheated P class boilers. Only one received an enclosed cab. One was scrapped in 1921, and the rest between 1928 and 1932.

There were two diagrams, saddle tank and Q class boiler and pannier tanks and P boiler.

Swindon 1076/727/1134 class

Builder	GWR/Swindon
Dates Built	1870-1881
Number Built	266
Route Colour	Yellow
Power Class	Ungrouped/A
Tractive Effort	15,000-17,500lbs
Driving Wheel Size	4ft 6in[†]
Cylinder Dimensions	17in x 24in
Boiler Class	Special, Q, O, P
Wheelbase	7ft 4in + 8ft 4in
Front Overhang	4ft 9in
Rear Overhang	5ft 2in (1076-1081) 6ft 0in (727-756, 947-966) 6ft 9in (1134-1153, 1166-1185, 1228-1297, 1561-1660)
Dates Withdrawn	1903-1946

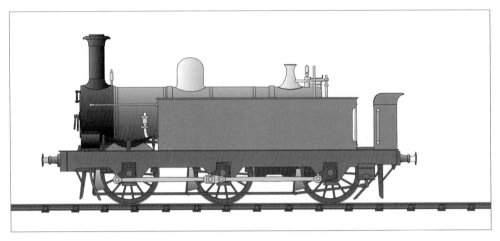

1076 class *in original condition with side tanks.*

1076/727/1134 class *in final configuration: P class boiler, full cab and large bunker. This sketch is based on diagrams B23 and B24 which represent superheated and saturated boilers.*

727 (1076) class *in the 1890s. Still with a short saddle tank, but with an open cab.*

1134 (1076) class. *Earlier members of the 1134 series as built without a cab. Note wooden brake blocks.*

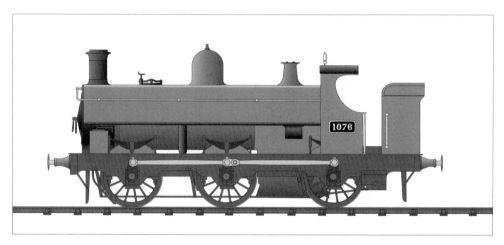

1076/727/1134 class. *Diagram A22. Q class boiler.*

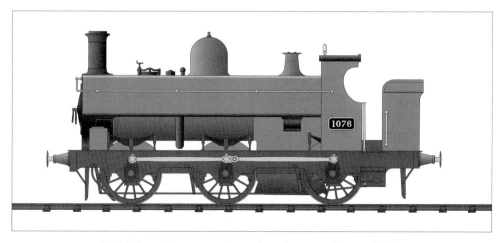

1076 class. *Diagram A61. This shows a class O boiler.*

These were really three classes, which were later merged into one, a trend which, to an extent, happened with all the large pannier classes. This class/set of classes is being used to demonstrate the variety in mid nineteenth century locomotive classes and how they tended to merge in the twentieth century, which is why there are so many sketches.

They started with the six members of the 1076 class in 1870. They had side tanks, and boilers similar to but smaller in diameter than the Q class.

They were followed by the fifty of the 727 class of 1872/3, substantially similar but with short saddle tanks and a greater rear overhang. The last twenty of these were numbered 947-966.The rest of the class, 210 in all, were the 1134 or Buffalo class with greater yet rear overhangs and full length saddle tanks. They were built in ten lots between 1874 and 1881, and the configuration changed between lots. By 1878 they were being turned out with open cabs. The cab roofs were initially very short, but the design was soon changed to a slightly longer style. Middle batches had boilers close to O and Q class in dimensions and some of the last batches a shorter boiler, nearer to the P class. 1228 to 1234 and 1561-1565 were built as broad gauge convertibles with wheels outside both sets of frames.

As well as those noted as having been built as broad gauge convertibles, 1238-1257 were converted to broad gauge in 1887-8, and 1566-80 converted in 1884. Some of them ran as 0-4-2T on the broad gauge by the simple expedient of removing the rear set of coupling rods. All the convertibles were converted to standard gauge in 1891/2.

They tended to receive Q class boilers from the end of the nineteenth century, and Belpaire fireboxes and pannier tanks from 1911. Around twenty of the class were given auto gear from 1917 and these were typically fitted with screw reverse rather than the normal lever reverse. Some of these later received enclosed cabs with large rectangular windows.

About half the class received enclosed cabs with larger bunkers in the 1920s and many of the rest just the enlarged bunkers. A few received the slightly larger O class boiler in 1920 and some of the later survivors received P class from 1925. Superheating was used for a time on some of the P class boilers. They were mostly withdrawn between 1928 and 1939, but a handful survived the war. 1287, in use as a stationary boiler, made it to 1953.

There were nine diagrams for the class, but two of these cover the fitting of spark arresting chimneys.

Swindon 1661 class

Builder	GWR/Swindon
Dates Built	1886-1887

Number Built	40
Route Colour	Blue
Power Class	Ungrouped/A
Tractive Effort	14,500-18,500lbs
Driving Wheel Size	5ft 0in†
Cylinder Dimensions	17in x 26in
Boiler Class	P
Wheelbase	7ft 9in + 8ft 0in
Front Overhang	4ft 7in
Rear Overhang	5ft 9in (later 6ft 4¼in)
Dates Withdrawn	1911-1934

A variation was the 1661 class, which used frames which had originally been intended for 2361 class 0-6-0 tender engines. As discussed above, although the 2361 superficially looked like an outside framed Dean Goods, these locomotives actually had many parts, notably motion, in common with the Stella class 2-4-0 and 2-4-0T. Consequently this design was rather different to the rest of the 'large' tank engine classes. They had open cabs, boilers similar to the P class, and 5ft 2in wheels.

They had started life with rather short rear overhangs, but most if not all had the frames extended. The class does not seem to have been greatly valued, and several were sold off to Welsh lines, only to return at the grouping. Belpaire boilers started appearing around 1901, pannier tanks about 1914. About half got enclosed cabs and/or further enlarged bunkers. They were scrapped early, mostly in the late 1920s, the last going in 1934.

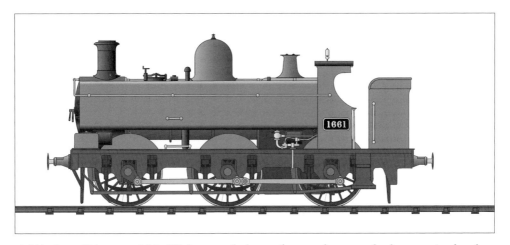

1661 class. *Diagram A29. With extended rear frames, but not the largest size bunker.*

Large Engines - Inside Frames
Wolverhampton 633 class

Builder	GWR/Wolverhampton
Dates Built	1871/2
Number Built	12
Route Colour	Uncoloured
Power Class	A
Tractive Effort	13,500-17,500lbs
Driving Wheel Size	4ft 6in†
Cylinder Dimensions	16in x 24in-17in x 24in
Wheelbase	7ft 3in + 8ft 3in
Front Overhang	4ft 8in
Rear Overhang	5ft 3in (some extended later to approx. 6ft)
Boiler Class	Special/T
Dates Withdrawn	1930-34

Inside frames started with the Wolverhampton 633 side tank class of 1871/2, which never acquired saddle or pannier tanks. Their 7ft 3in, 8ft 3in wheel base was to become standard for almost all subsequent large 0-6-0T designs. The last two were built with condensing gear to work over the Metropolitan 'underground' lines in London. As with the other early classes they later acquired the thicker tyres which brought the wheel size up to 4ft 7½in.

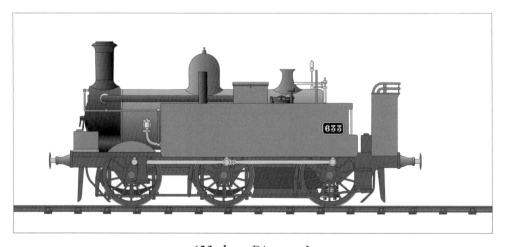

633 class. *Diagram J.*

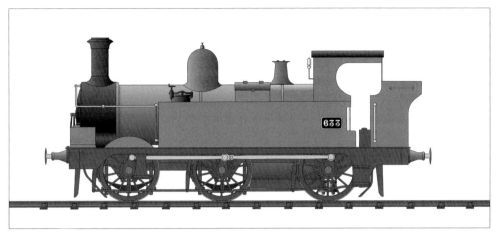

633 class. *Based on a 1926 photograph.*

More of the class were fitted with condensing gear at the end of the nineteenth century and the half dozen so fitted worked freight traffic on the Metropolitan lines until they were withdrawn in the late 1930s. Curiously, these six were never fitted with cabs. The others acquired open cabs and three later received enclosed cabs. A majority received enlarged bunkers of various sizes, some at least with a rearward frame extension. Three of the class went to the Rhondda & Swansea Bay Railway in 1907, returning in 1919 and 1922.

There were three diagrams for the class, one for a round top firebox and two for Belpaire box boilers, with and without condensing gear.

Wolverhampton 645 and 1501 classes

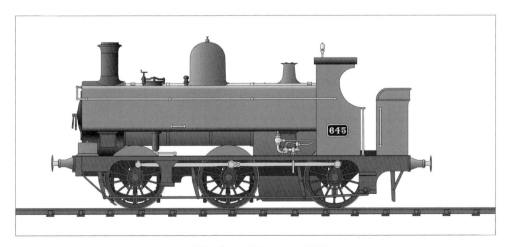

645 class. *Diagram A35*

Builder	GWR/Wolverhampton
Dates Built	1872/3, 1878-1881
Number Built	35 (see notes), 72
Route Colour	Yellow
Power Class	Ungrouped/A
Tractive Effort	13,500-17,500lbs
Driving Wheel Size	4ft 6in[†]
Cylinder Dimensions	16in x 24in, 17in x 24in
Wheelbase	7ft 3in + 8ft 3in
Front Overhang	4ft 8in
Rear Overhang	5ft 3in (645-656, 757-775) 5ft 9in (1501-1560, 1801-1812) 6ft 4in (later frame extensions)
Boiler Class	T, P
Dates Withdrawn	1928-1949

The 645 class was built at Wolverhampton in 1872/3. Five of these did not go into GWR service but were sold new to the South Wales Mineral Railway (3) and the Carmarthen & Cardigan Railway (2). They were built without cabs, and had short saddle tanks and a small bunker.

The 1501 class, or perhaps subclass, followed from 1878. They had T class boilers and more conventional full length saddle tanks and open cabs from new. They had a longer rear overhang and thus a larger bunker.

The SWMR and C&C purchased, second-hand, an additional locomotive each in 1875 & 1876 respectively. The Carmarthen & Cardigan locomotives returned to the GWR in 1881 and were numbered 902-4. The SWM locomotives came under GWR control again in 1908, but were scrapped before the fleet was officially absorbed in 1922 and not numbered as GWR stock. Three of the 1501s went to the SWMR in 1910/11 and these did return to GWR stock in 1922, resuming their original numbers

The detail of modifications and changes is complex, but the 645s tended to receive longer saddle tanks with replacement boilers, larger cylinders and short cabs towards the end of the nineteenth century.

Some 645/1501 received lengthened frames and bunkers, tending to merge them with the 655 class. P class boilers appeared from 1902. Pannier tanks were introduced from about 1913, always with P class boilers. Superheating was fitted to about half of the class at one stage, but later removed. A few carried top feed.

Around fifteen received enclosed cabs. Most were scrapped in the 1930s, but a few survived the war and four even into the first year or two of British Railways. There were seven diagrams, covering saddle and pannier tanks, T and P boilers, and superheating variations.

Wolverhampton 655 (1741) class

Builder	GWR/Wolverhampton
Dates Built	1892-1897
Number Built	52
Route Colour	Yellow
Power Class	Ungrouped/A
Tractive Effort	15,500-17,500lbs
Driving Wheel Size	4ft 6in[†]
Cylinder Dimensions	17in x 24in
Wheelbase	7ft 3in + 8ft 3in
Front Overhang	5ft 0in
Rear Overhang	6ft 0in (6ft 6in later)
Boiler Class	T,P
Dates Withdrawn	1929-1950

The fifty-two members of the 655 class, last of the large Wolverhampton engines, were built from 1892. They were essentially similar to the 1501s, but were larger again with longer overhangs front and rear. Again they were built with T class boilers. They were numbered rather eccentrically: the first two,

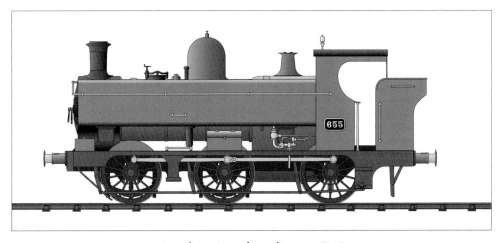

655 class. *Based on diagram B65.*

655 and 767, were given numbers previously used by 645s that had been sold. The rest were numbered 1741-1750, 1771-1790 and 2701-2720.

655s tended to receive P class Belpaire boilers and pannier tanks a little later than the 645s. The majority were given enlarged bunkers. Again, around half were superheated at one stage in their lives and a number gained enclosed cabs.

Some were scrapped in the 1930s, but most survived the war. Some twenty-one made it onto the BR books and the last were scrapped in 1950.

There were five diagrams for the 655s, covering the variations in boilers and tanks. The last diagram, B65, was common to both 645 and 655 classes, demonstrating how the two classes had merged as they were updated.

Swindon 1813 class

Builder	GWR/Swindon
Dates Built	1882-1884
Number Built	40
Route Colour	Yellow
Power Class	Ungrouped/A
Tractive Effort	15,000-19,000lbs
Driving Wheel Size	4ft 7½in
Cylinder Dimensions	17in x 24in
Wheelbase	7ft 3in + 8ft 3in
Front Overhang	4ft 6in
Rear Overhang	6ft 0in
Boiler Class	Special, P
Dates Withdrawn	1928-1949

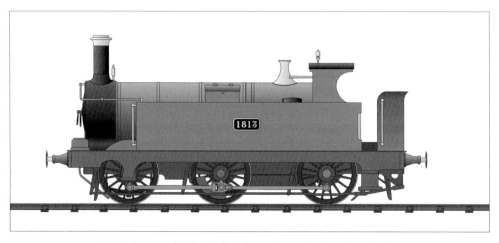

1813 class *as built with side tanks and domeless boiler.*

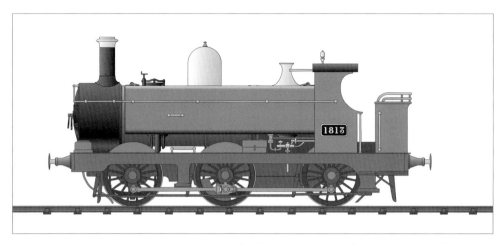

1813 class. *Diagram A9. No 1813 as rebuilt in 1903 with short pannier tanks. Later in life they looked very similar to the 1854 class.*

The first inside framed Swindon class was the 1813 class of 1882. Like the 633s, these were built as side tank engines, but with open cabs. The original boiler was effectively a slightly thinner P class. Forty were built. They were unusual in being built with a vertical pivot in the connecting rods forward of the centre wheels.

1813 herself was sold to the Pembroke and Tenby Railway in 1883, being taken back when that line was absorbed in 1897. It kept the nameplate *Holmwood* through several changes of tank.

Most 1813s received saddle tanks and true P class boilers from 1894, but one retained side tanks as late as 1907. This class was also amongst the earliest to receive pannier tanks, one as early as 1903. Some of the early pannier tank installations were 'short', finishing at the smokebox. Thus four tank styles, side, saddle, short and long pannier, could be seen together on the same class of forty engines, although the short pannier tanks were replaced fairly quickly. The new tanks did not start to be widespread until 1910/11. A majority were superheated in the middle of their lives, but, in common with other 0-6-0PTs, this was later removed. Most got enlarged bunkers in the 1920s, about half with enclosed cabs. Most were withdrawn in the 1930s, with just one surviving to BR ownership.

There were five diagrams, covering tank and superheater variations.

Swindon 1854/1701 classes

Builder	GWR/Swindon
Dates Built	1890-1895
Number Built	120

Route Colour	Blue
Power Class	A
Tractive Effort	16,500-19,000lbs
Driving Wheel Size	4ft 6in[†]
Cylinder Dimensions	17in x 24in
Wheelbase	7ft 3in + 8ft 3in
Front Overhang	4ft 6in
Rear Overhang	6ft 6in
Boiler Class	P
Dates Withdrawn	1928-1951

The 1813s were followed by the 1854 (or 1701) series of 1890-95, numbering 120. These had P class boilers and a longer rear overhang, adopted by all subsequent classes until the 9400.

Belpaire boilers appeared from 1901 and pannier tanks from 1911. In the end, all the class had Belpaire fireboxes and only one was never fitted with pannier tanks. At one stage, the majority of the class had superheaters fitted, but these were later removed again. About a third of the class received enclosed cabs and in that state closely resembled the Collett 5700 class.

Withdrawals started in the 1930s and '40s. 1729 was scrapped in 1943 after having been virtually torn apart in an air raid. Twenty-three made it to BR ownership, but the last were scrapped in 1951.

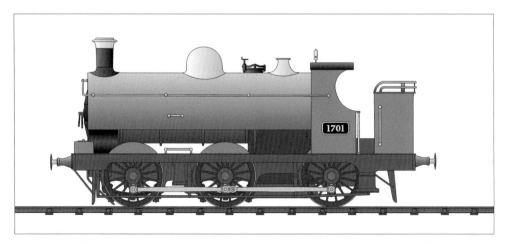

1854 (1701) class. *Diagram E. The last members of the class were built in this configuration, and it was typical around 1900.*

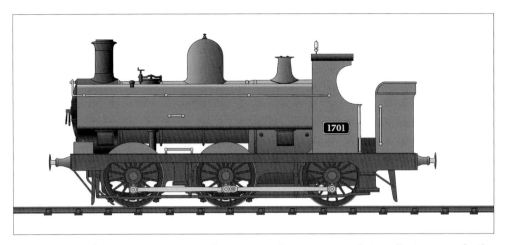

1854 (1701) class. *Diagram A19. This is an early pannier tank installation on a boiler with a round top firebox. Only around 7 class members ran with this configuration.*

Swindon 2721/2779 classes

Builder	GWR/Swindon
Dates Built	1897-1901
Number Built	80
Route Colour	Yellow/Blue
Power Class	A
Tractive Effort	16,500-20,000lbs
Driving Wheel Size	4ft 7½in
Cylinder Dimensions	17in x 24in, 17½in x 24in
Boiler Class	P
Wheelbase	7ft 3in + 8ft 3in
Front Overhang	4ft 6in
Rear Overhang	6ft 6in
Dates Withdrawn	1945-1950

The last nineteenth century 0-6-0T class built at Swindon was the 2721 class, fifty-eight built from 1897-1900 and another twenty-two, the 2779 sub class, built with slightly larger cylinders in 1900/1. The main differences from the 1854s were suspension arrangements – they had nests of coil springs above the leading and driving wheels rather than leaf springs below – and fluted coupling rods. The last five of the 2779s were built with piston valves rather than slide valves.

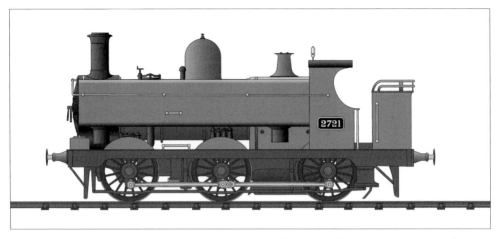

2721 (2796 series) class. *Diagram A11. As first modified with pannier tanks around 1910.*

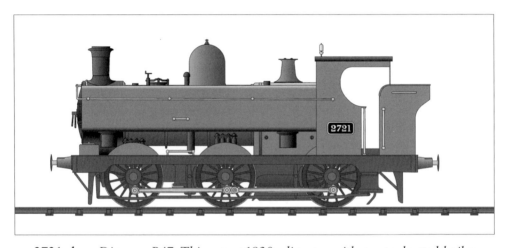

2721 class. *Diagram B47. This was a 1920s diagram with a superheated boiler.*

The last of the class, 2800, was renumbered 2700 when the original number was wanted for the new 2-8-0 class.

The piston valves were problematic, and many designs were tried. The majority of the 2779s were fitted with piston valves of one design or another at some stage, but all reverted to slide valves from the 1920s. Superheating was fitted to the majority, but later removed; several had top feed. Forty-one received enclosed cabs, one whilst still fitted with a saddle tank and most received enlarged bunkers. All had pannier tanks by the 1920s and increased water capacity brought them into the Blue weight group. All survived the war, forty-four (about half) were transferred to BR, but all were withdrawn between 1948 and 1950.

Large Engines - Collett & Hawksworth
5700/8750/9700 classes

Builders	GWR/Swindon, North British, W.G. Bagnall, Kerr Stuart, Yorkshire Engine, Armstrong Whitworth, Beyer Peacock.
Number Built	863 (250 5700, 50 6700, 522 8750, 11 9700, 30 6750)
Dates Built	1929-1950
Route Colour	Blue
Power Class	C
Tractive Effort	22,500lbs
Driving Wheel Size	4ft 7½in
Cylinder Dimensions	17½in x 24in
Wheelbase	7ft 3in + 8ft 3in
Front Overhang	5ft 6in
Rear Overhang	6ft 6in
Boiler Class	P
Dates Withdrawn	1956-1964

By the time Collett took over, the older outside frame engines were getting on for fifty years old and replacements were required. In Collett style, he took the earlier locomotives as a model and the 57xx could be regarded as being essentially a 1930s condition 1854 with the larger cylinders of the 2779 series of the 2721 class and higher boiler pressure (200psi) for increased power. They

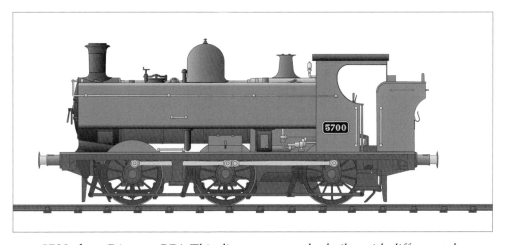

5700 class. *Diagram B74. This diagram covered a boiler with different tube arrangements to the original.*

8750 class. *Diagram B70. This was the first diagram for the class, but it has been amended to include top feed and a whistle shield as fitted to the class from the 1940s.*

9700 class. *Diagram B69. This was the only diagram issued for the sub class.*

had the same rear overhang as the last Swindon saddle tanks, but a slightly increased front overhang. They had many detail improvements in design and construction and could run much greater mileage between overhauls than their predecessors. 250 were built in 1929/31, many by outside companies with loan act government finance. These were 5700-5799, 7700-7799, and 8700-8749. A sub class of 50 from 6700 was also built in 1930/31: these had no vacuum brakes so could only be used for shunting.

There was a need to replace the 'Get Wets'; 633 and Metro class tanks with condensing equipment and still (in 1932!) without any kind of cab. 8700 was given condensing apparatus, which included a water feed pump on the right hand side of the smoke box. This necessitated shortening the pannier tanks, reducing water capacity. Trials showed up a need for the lost water capacity, so when the 9700 sub class of ten was built in 1933, they had distinctive short hybrid pannier/side tanks. They also had a new, more fully enclosed cab. In 1934, 8700 itself was rebuilt again to the same specification as the rest of the class, and renumbered 9700.

In 1933, the 8750 sub-class was introduced which had the improved cab from the 9700s. 522 of these were built up until 1949: 8750-8799, 9711-9799, 3700-3799, 3600-3699, 4600-4699, 9600-9682 and a replacement 8700.

6750-6779 were built from 1947 to 1950 without steam brakes; effectively an 8750 version of the 6700 sub class.

There was little development of the class other than a new form of top feed and one or two temporary conversions to oil fuel. The eight diagrams covered two boiler subclasses with different tubing arrangements and a spark arrestor fitting.

Under British Railways ownership, the 57xx spread around the system; for instance a pair worked as banking engines in Folkestone harbour.

All were withdrawn between 1957 and 1964, with some being sold on to London Transport and the National Coal Board. Sixteen have survived into preservation and all but one have run.

9400 class

Builders	GWR/Swindon, R. Stephenson, W. G. Bagnall, Yorkshire Engine Co
Dates Built	1947-1956
Number Built	210
Route Colour	Red
Power Class	C
Tractive Effort	22,500lbs
Driving Wheel Size	4ft 7½in
Cylinder Dimensions	17½in x 24in
Boiler Class	Standard 10
Wheelbase	7ft 3in + 8ft 3in
Front Overhang	6ft 6in
Rear Overhang	7ft 6in
Dates Withdrawn	1958-1965

The finale to the large pannier tanks was Hawksworth's 9400 class Although substantially similar to the Collett engines below the footplate, these were

9400 class. *Diagram B78, the superheated first batch built at Swindon.*

significantly bigger and heavier engines than their predecessors – two feet longer overall. They had an especially wide cab and tanks that stopped short at the smokebox. However, the wheel base and wheel size remained unchanged from seventy years earlier! The larger Standard 10 boiler made them the heaviest of the pannier tanks and restricted them to red routes, but on the other hand gave them more boiler power and more powerful brakes. The first ten were superheated. They were originally intended to replace absorbed 0-6-2 classes, hence the extra steaming and braking capacity over the smaller 5700s. The first ten were built at Swindon and came out in GWR colours, but the remaining 200 were built between 1950 and 1956 under British Railways, all by outside contractors. In the event, everything changed and many had a very short lifespan. Off the former GWR system, some were used in twos, threes and even fours as bankers on the Lickey Incline. There were two diagrams – one for the GWR built superheated locos and one for the rest. At least some of the early batch did not retain their superheated boilers.

They were withdrawn between 1958 and 1965 but two have survived. One is part of the National Collection and is preserved as a static exhibit, and the other has run in preservation.

Small classes - Armstrong/Dean
850 and 1901 classes

Builder	GWR/Wolverhampton
Dates Built	1874-1891
Number Built	36 (850), 120 (1901), & 2 renewals
Route Colour	Uncoloured

Power Class	Ungrouped
Tractive Effort	13,500-16,000lbs
Driving Wheel Size	4ft 0in[†] 4ft 1½in (1901 class)
Cylinder Dimensions	15in x 24in – 16½in x 24in
Wheelbase	7ft 4in + 6ft 4in
Front Overhang	4ft 7in
Rear Overhang	5ft 6in (6ft 0in and 6ft 3in later)
Boiler Class	R
Dates Withdrawn	1928-1958 (4 sold 1906-1913, 4 more sold 1939)

Twenty-four 850s (850-873, 987-998) were built between 1874 and 1876 as saddle tanks with no cab, just a spectacle plate and side sheets. Twelve more, (1216-1227) were built in 1876/7 with unusual wheels having H section spokes, 16in cylinders and slightly different boilers.

The 120 members of the 1901 class (1901-2020), built 1881 to 1897, were essentially very similar, but had open cabs, and larger tanks on 1941 to 2020. As noted above there were also two locomotives classed as renewals of Gooch 0-6-0T, which as built may have been intermediate in design between the two classes.

The earlier locomotives received cabs and larger tanks towards the end of the nineteenth century. Once they had all received saddle tanks and cabs the two classes were merged, and separate diagrams were never issued.

850 class. *Diagram L. This was the main diagram for saddle tanks. In practice the position of dome and water filler shown here was often reversed, especially towards the end of their lives, and they often had larger bunkers, similar to that on the pannier tank below.*

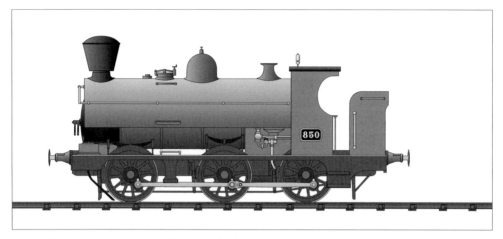

850 class. *Diagram A50. This sketch shows a spark arresting chimney and the later dome position.*

1901 class. *Diagram B51. This was the last diagram for the class, and also covered the 850 class.*

The boilers were always class R, although they differed in detail over the years with the usual variations in dome position. Belpaire fireboxes started to be introduced in 1910, but the round firebox boilers were long lived and a few never received Belpaire boxes. Most were converted to pannier tanks from 1910 through to the 1920s. Quite a number had pannier tanks fitted on boilers with round top fireboxes. A reasonable number retained (or in a couple of cases reacquired) saddle tanks until scrapping. Two even retained saddle tanks into BR days.

Many 850s and 1901s received lengthened frames and rear overhangs and thus larger bunkers from 1924 onwards. Around half gained enclosed cabs. Some were fitted with conventionally spoked wheels to replace the distinctive

H section spoke ones. A few of the class had spark arresting chimneys at one time or other, and several were fitted with bells for working in Birkenhead docks.

There were seven diagrams issued for the class, but most of these covered minor details such as spark arrestors and variant boiler pressure.

Scrapping started in the early 1930s, but forty-three survived to BR and a good few were still active into the 1950s, the last going as late as 1958.

2021/2101/2181 class

Builder	GWR/Wolverhampton
Dates Built	1897-1905
Number Built	140
Route Colour	Uncoloured
Power Class	Ungrouped/A
Tractive Effort	17,000-18,500lbs
Driving Wheel Size	4ft 1½in
Cylinder Dimensions	16½in x 24in
Wheelbase	7ft 4in + 7ft 4in
Front Overhang	5ft 0in
Rear Overhang	6ft 0in (6ft 9in later)
Boiler Class	U
Dates Withdrawn	1938-1958

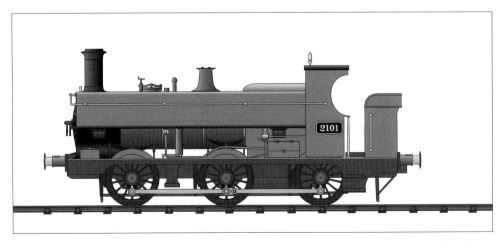

2101 class. *Based on a 1937 photograph, this sketch shows the original size bunker and a domeless boiler. The extent to which the firebox is raised on this boiler variant is quite striking. There was no diagram issued which showed this particular combination of features.*

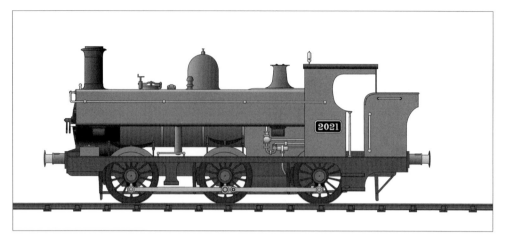

2021 class. *Diagram B52. This was the last diagram issued for the class and shows the extended bunker.*

From 1897 Wolverhampton built the 2021 class, an enlargement of the 850 which had a boiler with a longer firebox, known as the class U. These still had the 4ft 1½in wheels, but a longer wheelbase and were longer overall. The earlier members of the class started life with a rather lower pitched boiler than the rest.

From 1902, the last batches were built with a Belpaire firebox and a domeless boiler with a longer smokebox, but still with saddle tanks. These were the 2101 class.

An odd feature of the development of this class was that, when new boilers were built for the 2021 series around 1906, they were given the extended smokeboxes of the 2101 series, but the tanks were not lengthened to match. This resulted in a smokebox that protruded only a few inches beyond the tanks, with the chimney partially projecting from the front of the tank.

The class was widely used for autofitting; an early oddity was the fitting of two of the class with a dummy coach shell so that they looked more harmonious when running between trailer cars. It's not recorded whether the public attempted to board the locomotive!

Many of the class received extended frames and bunkers from 1924, taking the rear overhang to 6ft 9in. When pannier tanks came along, the 2101 series retained the domeless boilers for a while, but eventually all reverted to domed boilers. Some swapped back to saddle tanks with boiler changes and around sixty had enclosed cabs, some on occasion reverting back to the open ones.

A few of the class were fitted with top feed, a number being fitted with spark arrestors. Quite a number were fitted with bells when working in docks, notably Birkenhead. Two of the class were used by Collett for experimental rebuilds to develop the 5400 and 6400 classes as noted below.

In 1939, ten of the class were given increased brake power and renumbered 2181-2190. Most, but not all of these had enclosed cabs. RCTS list nine diagrams for the class, combinations of different boilers, tanks and spark arrestors. Strangely, no diagram is listed in RCTS for the 2181 sub class, but it seems unlikely none was issued.

A very few were withdrawn before the war, but most survived until the 1940s and '50s, some as late as 1958 to be the last surviving pre-grouping GWR 0-6-0 tanks. None were preserved.

Small classes - Collett/Hawksworth Designs

Although four classes of small 0-6-0T does not seem very much like standardisation (six classes if you include the two varieties of Collett 0-4-2T) in fact these new small classes were closely related with many parts in common; for example, the motion design was common to all and the cylinder casting was basically the same.

5400 class

Builder	GWR/Swindon
Dates Built	1931-1935
Number Built	25
Route Colour	Yellow
Power Class	Ungrouped
Tractive Effort	15,000lbs
Driving Wheel Size	5ft 2in
Cylinder Dimensions	16½in x 24in
Wheelbase	7ft 4in + 7ft 4in
Front Overhang	5ft 2in
Rear Overhang	7ft 7in
Boiler Class	Standard 21
Dates Withdrawn	1957-1963

As with the 5700 class, Collett had to develop replacements for older locomotives reaching the end of their lifespan. His team took an autofitted 2021, fitted a larger (Standard 11) boiler and re-wheeled it with 5ft 2in wheels to create a faster and more powerful locomotive. A batch of new engines, the twenty-five members of the 5400 class, followed from 1931/2 with the last batch in 1935. These had the 5ft 2in wheels, the same wheelbase, and a fully enclosed cab. They had a Standard 21 boiler (basically a Standard 11 but with drum head smokebox). They were fitted with screw reverse – more appropriate

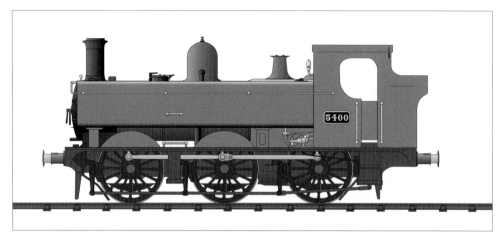

5400 class. *Diagram B61*

for a passenger locomotive anyway, but especially important for an autofitted locomotive: when an autocoach was leading the fireman had to change the reverser settings, even though the driver controlled the regulator.

As with most Collett classes they received few alterations over their life; top feed, whistle shields and bunker steps being the only obvious ones. There was just the single diagram.

The 54s were mostly withdrawn in the late 1950s, with one surviving to 1963. Although three made it to Barry scrapyard, all were cut up by 1965 and so none have been preserved.

6400 class

Builder	GWR/Swindon
Dates Built	1932-1937
Number Built	40
Route Colour	Yellow
Power Class	A
Tractive Effort	16,500lbs
Driving Wheel Size	4ft 7½in
Cylinder Dimensions	16½in x 24
Wheelbase	7ft 4in + 7ft 4in
Front Overhang	5ft 2in
Rear Overhang	7ft 7in
Boiler Class	Standard 21 (165psi)
Dates Withdrawn	1958-1964

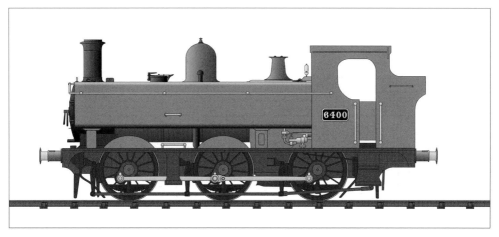

6400 class. *Diagram B62. This shows the earlier cab design and the locos in as built condition.*

For hillier territory, the 5ft 2in wheels of the 5400s were too large, so another 2021 was rebuilt, this time with the 4ft 7½in wheels of the larger tanks. This was the prototype for the autofitted 6400 class, with forty built from 1932 to 1937. They came with two small variations in cab design. The first thirty had the same design as the 5400s, with a small overhang on the roof front and back, plus a curved transition between cab and bunker. The last ten had no lip on the cab and a right angle at the cab/bunker intersection, a variation which had been introduced with the 7400s. Like the 5400s they had screw reverse.

There was just a single diagram issued for the class. Top feed, whistle shields and steps were the only obvious external changes.

The 6400s lasted a little longer than the 5400s. Happily three were preserved, initially by the Dart Valley Railway, although they have since found other homes, and all have run in preservation.

7400 class

Builder	GWR/BR/Swindon
Dates Built	1936-1950
Number Built	50
Route Colour	Yellow
Power Class	A
Tractive Effort	18,000lbs
Driving Wheel Size	4ft 7½in
Cylinder Dimensions	16½in x 24in

Wheelbase	7ft 4in + 7ft 4in
Front Overhang	5ft 2in
Rear Overhang	7ft 7in
Boiler Class	Standard 21 (180psi)
Dates Withdrawn	1959-1965

The 7400 class was almost a non-autofitted version of the 6400 class, but they had a higher pressure boiler and were therefore more powerful. They also had lever reverse. These 'small' engines were as strong as the early double framed 'large' classes such as the 1076, which were now disappearing. There were a number of components on the 7400s that were a little larger and presumably stronger than those on the 6400s and 5400s, notably the connecting rod big end. Thirty were built in 1936/37, before the last batch of 64s, ten more in 1948 and another ten as late as 1950.

They were a good two tons lighter than the 5700s overall, and, perhaps more importantly, the weight distribution was more even, so the heaviest axle was over a ton and a half lighter than the 5700s. This meant that they had significantly wider route availability than the larger 0-6-0 PTs. All the 7400s were built with the later style cab. The pre-war batches were built with a small whistle shield but the post war ones were built new with the larger whistle shield and with top feed.

There was only a single diagram for the class. The earlier locomotives were given top feed, the larger whistle shield and the cab steps in the 1950s. They nearly all lasted until the 1960s, but none have survived.

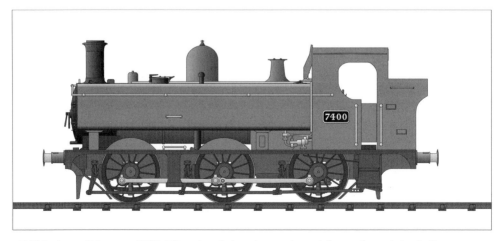

7400 class. *Diagram B72. The sketch has been altered from the original diagram to show the post war condition of the locomotives with top feed, whistle shield and steps on the bunker.*

1600 class

Builder	BR/Swindon
Dates Built	1949-1955
Number Built	80
Route Colour	Uncoloured
Power Class	A
Tractive Effort	18,500lbs
Driving Wheel Size	4ft 1½in
Cylinder Dimensions	16½in x 24in
Wheelbase	7ft 4in + 7ft 4in
Front Overhang	5ft 2in
Rear Overhang	6ft 9in
Boiler Class	Standard 16
Dates Withdrawn	1959-1965

The last pannier tank class of all was Hawksworth's small lightweight 1600 class, built to replace the now very elderly 850s and 2021s. They had the same wheel size and wheelbase as the 2021s, and were shorter than the 54/64/74 series. As well as light in weight, the 1600s were low in height for use on lines with a restricted loading gauge. They were built entirely under British Railways, but were in every sense a Great Western engine. Unlike the 9400s, the 1600 retained a domed boiler. Like the 9400s, they also scattered round the system, two even ending up in Scotland. Eighty were built, the first fifty in 1949/51, and the last thirty in 1954/5. They had a very short life, some being only five years old at withdrawal. One has survived into and has run in preservation.

1600 class, *diagram B81.*

Others
1361 class

Builder	GWR/Swindon
Dates Built	1910
Number Built	5
Route Colour	Uncoloured
Power Class	Ungrouped
Tractive Effort	15,000lbs
Driving Wheel Size	3ft 8in
Cylinder Dimensions	16in x 20in
Wheelbase	5ft 0in + 6ft 0in
Front Overhang	5ft 9in
Rear Overhang	5ft 3in
Boiler Class	VA (special)
Dates Withdrawn	1961-2

1366 class

Builder		GWR/Swindon
Dates Built		1934
Number Built		6
Route Colour		Uncoloured
Power Class		Ungrouped
Tractive Effort		16,000lbs
Driving Wheel Size	3ft 8in	
Cylinder Dimensions		16in x 20in
Wheelbase		5ft 0in + 6ft 0in
Front Overhang		5ft 9½in
Rear Overhang		5ft 9in
Boiler Class		VB (special)
Dates Withdrawn		1960-4

In his book, Holcroft describes how a roll of old drawings was placed on his desk one day and he was instructed to take the basic design of the 1392 class (see below) absorbed from the Cornwall Mineral Railway and

1361 class.

1366 class.

update it with modern details – cab, bunker and the like. The result was the small (in both senses) class of 1361 saddle tanks, the last saddle tanks to be built by the GWR. They retained the round topped fireboxes of their predecessors.

In 1934, the design was slightly updated, given a Belpaire firebox, increased boiler pressure, a larger bunker and pannier tanks. A further six were built, presumably replacing the last of the absorbed locos. The classes were mainly used in docks, on the Weymouth Harbour branch, and in the wagon shops at Swindon Works.

They were little changed over their lives, there was only ever a single diagram for each class and one of each has survived into preservation.

1500 class

Builder	BR/Swindon
Dates Built	1949
Number Built	10
Route Colour	Red
Power Class	C
Tractive Effort	22,500lbs
Driving Wheel Size	4ft 7½in
Cylinder Dimensions	17½in x 24in
Wheelbase	6ft 4in + 6ft 6in
Front Overhang	8ft 0in
Rear Overhang	8ft 6in
Boiler Class	Standard 10
Dates Withdrawn	1959-1963

GWR designed, but introduced under British Railways, these were the most radical change in GWR practice since Churchward's early days. They had outside cylinders and Walschaerts valve gear, virtually no footplate, single bar slide bars and various other new features

The key design aim appears to have been easy maintenance and they were sometimes referred to as '24 hour shunters'. All routine servicing and even some minor repair tasks were intended to be possible from the trackside without the need for a servicing pit. The short wheelbase was intended for use on tight curves, and one of their main roles was empty stock workings at Paddington, which traversed notoriously sharp curves.

1500 class.

Although they appeared after the 9400s, surviving records suggest the design was started first. More conventionally they had other features in common with the 9400s, and looked fairly similar above the footplate.

There were only the ten built, and only one diagram. They were withdrawn between 1959 and 1963. Three were sold to the NCB, and ran at a Coventry colliery until withdrawn by the NCB in 1970. All three were purchased by the Severn Valley Railway. Two were scrapped immediately, with spares being recovered for use on what is now the only survivor of the class, which has run in preservation.

Absorbed Locomotives (nineteenth century and early twentieth century)
919 class

Builder	Sharp Stewart
Line	Llynvi & Ogmore Railway
Dates Built	1865/9
Number Built	5
Driving Wheel Size	4ft 0in
Cylinder Dimensions	16in x 24in
Dates Withdrawn	1876-1892

A class of five side tanks.
924 class

Builder	Black, Hawthorn & Co
Line	Llynvi & Ogmore Railway
Dates Built	1871-3
Number Built	3
Driving Wheel Size	4ft 0in
Cylinder Dimensions	16in x 24in
Dates Withdrawn	1880/1885

A class of three saddle tanks.
1317 class

Builder	Avonside Engine Co
Line	South Devon Railway
Dates Built	1872-4

Number Built	10
Driving Wheel Size	4ft 10in
Cylinder Dimensions	17in x 24in
Dates Withdrawn	1903-1905, 1926,1932

This class of ten saddle tanks were built and absorbed as broad gauge locomotives. They were converted to standard gauge in 1892/3 and renumbered 1317-1325. They were rebuilt with P class boilers between 1897 and 1902 but withdrawn 1903-1905. Two of them were sold to the South Wales Mineral Railway, from whence they were reabsorbed at the grouping. One was scrapped in 1926, and the other, which had acquired pannier tanks, lasted until 1932.

1322 class

Builder	Stothert, Slaughter & Co
Line	Monmouthshire Railway & Canal Co
Dates Built	1853
Number Built	5
Driving Wheel Size	4ft 6in
Cylinder Dimensions	16in x 22in
Dates Withdrawn	1880-1885

Five locomotives with a very odd history! The Monmouthshire Railway had much trouble with its steam locomotive policy. As well as a few classes of locomotive many oddments were passed on to the GWR. Surviving records suggest this class were built as 'bogie tank engines' in which form they were very unsatisfactory. They had been converted to double framed 0-6-0ST by the time they reached the GWR.

1328 class

Builder	Stothert, Slaughter & Co
Line	Monmouthshire Railway & Canal Co
Dates Built	1853
Number Built	6
Driving Wheel Size	4ft 6in
Cylinder Dimensions	16in x 22in
Dates Withdrawn	1877-1888

0-6-0 well tanks with inside frames and outside cylinders.

1334 class

Builder	Vulcan Foundry
Line	Monmouthshire Railway & Canal Co
Dates Built	1865
Number Built	4
Driving Wheel Size	4ft 0in
Cylinder Dimensions	16in x 24in
Dates Withdrawn	1897-1904

Four 0-6-0ST, built to a long boiler design. They were substantially rebuilt at Wolverhampton in 1882, and one was rebuilt again at Swindon in 1894.

1338 class

Builder	Monmouthshire Railway Yorkshire Engine Company
Line	Monmouthshire Railway & Canal Co
Dates Built	1870-1877
Number Built	10
Driving Wheel Size	4ft 1in
Cylinder Dimensions	16in x 24in
Dates Withdrawn	1898-1905

Ten reasonably similar outside cylinder side tanks, perhaps not quite a true class, wheelbase being one dimension that varied. Most were rebuilt at Swindon between 1887 and 1898, whilst one was scrapped without alteration. The rest were withdrawn from 1903 to 1905.

1345 class

Builder	Avonside Engine Co Dubs & Co
Line	Monmouthshire Railway & Canal Co
Dates Built	1870-1877
Number Built	8

Driving Wheel Size	4ft 1in
Cylinder Dimensions	17in x 24in
Dates Withdrawn	Rebuilt as 0-4-4 1891-2

A class of eight double framed saddle tanks somewhat more powerful than the 1338 class. Strangely they were all rebuilt at Swindon as 0-4-4s.

1376/7 Bristol & Exeter 0-6-0T

Builder	Bristol & Exeter
Line	Bristol & Exeter
Dates Built	1874/5
Number Built	2
Driving Wheel Size	3ft 6in
Cylinder Dimensions	12in x 18in
Dates Withdrawn	1927,1934

These two small 0-6-0T were built by the B&E to run the Culme Valley line in 1874/5. Transferred to the GWR in 1876, they had major rebuilds which included a longer wheelbase and new boilers so it seems likely that few original parts were retained. They survived until 1927 and 1934, having received various new cabs and further boilers in the course of their lives.

1378 (Fox Walker 0-6-0ST)

Builder	Fox Walker & Co
Line	North Pembrokeshire & Fishguard Railway
Dates Built	1878
Number Built	1
Driving Wheel Size	4ft 0in
Cylinder Dimensions	16in x 24in
Dates Withdrawn	Sold 1910

This 0-6-0ST was built by Fox Walker & Co for the North Pembrokeshire & Fishguard Railway in 1878 and when that line was taken over by the GWR in 1898 it became GWR 1378. It was then sold by the GWR to the Gwendraeth Valley Railway in 1910. When that line was absorbed by the GWR at the grouping it had been sold to the Kidwelly Tinplate Co, which, very un-coincidentally, was the enterprise the GVR primarily existed to serve. It ran there until the works closed, and became the property of another industrial concern. It remained in service until the 1960s and survives as a museum exhibit, but is not known to have been steamed in preservation.

1392 class (Cornwall Minerals Railway Sharp Stewart 0-6-0ST)

Builder	Sharp Stewart
Line	Cornwall Minerals Railway
Dates Built	1873-4
Number Built	18 (9 to GWR)
Driving Wheel Size	3ft 6in
Cylinder Dimensions	16¼in x 20in
Wheelbase	5ft 0in + 6ft 0in
Dates Withdrawn	1883-1936

The GWR took over the line in 1877, but only acquired nine of the line's eighteen identical locomotives as the other nine were pledged as security against various debts and were sold separately. They had been built as side tanks by Sharp Stewart in 1873/4 to a design by Frances Trevithick and had outside cylinders.

The GWR numbered their locos 1392-1400. In 1883/4 they were all converted to saddle tanks and given a rear frame extension to provide a cab and bunker. They received a variety of cabs, tanks and bunkers over the years, but were otherwise little altered. One was sold in 1883 and another scrapped after a collision in 1906, but otherwise they survived into the 1930s.

At the 1912 renumbering 1400 was renumbered 1398, being the number of the loco sold in 1883.

In GWR history they were significant as being the basis of the design of the 1361 and 1366 classes. By the end of their lives they were carrying 1361 boilers.

Absorbed Classes at the Grouping
Alexandra (Newport and South Wales) Docks and Railway
RW Hawthorn 0-6-0ST

Builder	RR & W Hawthorn & Co
Dates Built	1884
Number Built	2

Route Colour	Blue
Power Class	B
Tractive Effort	18,000lbs
Driving Wheel Size	4ft 0in
Cylinder Dimensions	18in x 24in
Dates Withdrawn	1926, 1930

These were two 0-6-0ST from 1884. The GWR numbered them 664 and 665. 664 received a significant Swindon rebuild, including a GW style bunker, from 1924-1927 – most of which time it presumably spent stored in pieces in dark corners of the works. It was sold in 1930 and worked on until 1945 at a colliery. 665 was scrapped unaltered in 1926.

Stephenson 0-6-0STs

Builder	R. Stephenson & Co
Dates Built	1885, 1894
Number Built	3
Route Colour	Blue
Power Class	A
Tractive Effort	18,500lbs
Driving Wheel Size	4ft 6in
Cylinder Dimensions	18in x 24in
Dates Withdrawn	1925-9

The first was bought new in 1885. The GWR numbered it 668 and like the Hawthorn loco above, it received an extensive rebuild over 1924 to 1927. It was sold to a colliery in 1929 and lasted until 1947. Two more came in 1894, broadly similar and numbered 669/70 by the GWR. They were withdrawn in 1925 and 1926. 670 was sold to a colliery and lasted until 1947.

Builder	R. Stephenson & Co
Dates Built	1898,1900
Number Built	5
Route Colour	Yellow
Power Class	A
Tractive Effort	16,000lbs

Driving Wheel Size	4ft 6in
Cylinder Dimensions	18in x 24in
Dates Withdrawn	1925-9

In 1898/1900 a further five Stephenson 0-6-0ST were bought. These were slightly smaller, numbered 674-678 and given diagram A72. Two received a light Swindon treatment, with new bunkers and chimneys. These two were sold into industry and scrapped in the 1940s. The others were all scrapped when the whole 'class' were withdrawn in the 1920s.

Hawthorn Leslie 0-6-0ST.

Builder	Hawthorn Leslie
Dates Built	1889
Number Built	2
Route Colour	Red (later Blue)
Power Class	A
Tractive Effort	21,000lbs
Driving Wheel Size	4ft 6in
Cylinder Dimensions	18in x 26in
Dates Withdrawn	1924, 1937

Two 1889 built double framed 0-6-0ST. The GWR numbered them 671/2. They were principally notable for odd shaped saddle tanks. One good one (671) was made from the two between 1924 and 1927, including an enlarged GW style bunker. It stayed in service until 1937, then spent nearly a year at Swindon, including a long spell as works pilot, before finally being scrapped.

Peckett 0-6-0ST

Builder	Peckett
Dates Built	1890/1
Number Built	2
Route Colour	Ungrouped
Power Class	Uncoloured
Tractive Effort	11,000lbs

Driving Wheel Size	3ft 6in
Cylinder Dimensions	14in x 20in
Dates Withdrawn	1929, 1948

These standard Peckett designs of 1890/1 with outside cylinders were numbered 679/80 when they reached the GWR. 680 lasted until 1948, and 679 was sold in 1929 and worked on at collieries until the early 1950s.

Ex-ROD Kerr Stuart 0-6-0T

Builder	Kerr, Stuart & Co
Dates Built	1917
Number Built	3 (see notes)
Route Colour	Blue
Power Class	B
Tractive Effort	19,500lbs
Driving Wheel Size	4ft 0in
Cylinder Dimensions	17in x 24in
Dates Withdrawn	1954/5

The ADR had bought two of these from the ROD. They had outside cylinders and were quite powerful locomotives. They were numbered 666/7 on absorption. They received a moderate Swindon rebuild. Another had been purchased by the Brecon & Merthyr. This loco was numbered 2161. It was given a significant overhaul in 1922.

The B&M loco was sold in 1929, and lasted to 1951 in colliery service. Both the ADR locos reached British Railways.

Barry Railway
Class A 0-6-0T

Builder	Sharp, Stewart
Dates Built	1888
Number Built	5
Route Colour	Blue
Power Class	B
Tractive Effort	21,000lbs
Driving Wheel Size	4ft 3in

Cylinder Dimensions	17½in x 26in
Boiler Class	Barry Standard
Dates Withdrawn	1926-31

The majority of Barry classes used a standard design of boiler and cylinders. The first Barry class was an 0-6-0 tank with the standard boiler, class A. There were five, built by Sharp-Stewart in 1888 with a distinctive cab doorway treatment with a shallow arched top, the arch being symmetrical, but the doorway position not.

On arrival with the GWR they were numbered 699-703 and 706. One had a moderate GWR rebuild, enough to justify a new diagram. They did not find favour with the GWR, all being gone by 1931. Three were sold into industry: one of these lasted as late as 1962, the other two being scrapped in the 1950s.

Class E 0-6-0T

Builder	Hudswell Clarke
Dates Built	1889-91
Number Built	5
Route Colour	Uncoloured
Power Class	Ungrouped
Tractive Effort	12,000lbs
Driving Wheel Size	3ft 3½in
Cylinder Dimensions	14in x 20in
Dates Withdrawn	1932-49

A class of five small lightweight 0-6-0T. Numbered 781-5, they received some attention at Swindon. Two survived to join British Railways and were gone by 1950, whilst three went to industrial use in the 1930s and lasted to 1958/60.

Class F 0-6-0ST

Builders	Sharp, Stewart, Vulcan Foundry, North British Loco Co, Hudswell, Clarke
Dates Built	1890-1905
Number Built	28
Route Colour	Blue
Power Class	B
Tractive Effort	20,000lbs

Driving Wheel Size	4ft 3in
Cylinder Dimensions	17in x 26in
Boiler Class	Barry Standard/Standard 9
Dates Withdrawn	1932-1937

These were effectively a saddle tank version of the A class, and no less than twenty-eight came from four builders between 1890 and 1905. There were minor variations, but no subclasses were ever identified. They were given numbers in the ranges 708-729, 742-754 and 776-780, plus 807. With the GWR the majority received major rebuilds with pannier tanks, Standard 9 boilers and other fittings, some superheated and others unsuperheated. The superheating was later removed from most of those that received it. Even the major rebuilds retained the Barry cab profile. They were withdrawn between 1932 and 1937. Like the class E this wasn't the end of the story though, because the majority were sold to collieries rather than scrapped, and several survived into the 1960s, one having become a side tank along the way! None have survived into preservation.

Brecon & Merthyr Railway
4ft 2in Double Framed 0-6-0ST

Builder	R. Stephenson & Co, John Fowler & Co
Dates Built	1884-6
Number Built	12
Route Colour	Yellow/Blue
Power Class	A/B
Tractive Effort	16,500-18,500lbs
Driving Wheel Size	4ft 2in
Cylinder Dimensions	17in x 24in
Dates Withdrawn	1923-1934

This class of twelve was the largest on the B&M. Six were from R. Stephenson & Co, in 1882 and 1883, and six from Fowlers of Leeds in 1884. They had an unusual suspension arrangement with a large balance beam between the frames providing compensation between the leading and centre driving wheels.

All survived to the GWR, and they were numbered 2177-2188. One was given a full Swindon rebuild with a Metro boiler, pannier tanks and all the other details, and two others a less extensive rebuild, with a boiler upgrade, GWR smokebox and chimney etc. These two looked quite different, since one was given pannier tanks and a GW cab and bunker, and the other one retained the original. A couple were condemned in 1923, but the rest, with varying degrees of Swindonisation, were withdrawn between 1925 and 1934, the last survivor being one of the pannier conversions. This loco was sold on and lasted in industry until 1944.

Kitson & Nasmyth & Wilson 4ft 7½in Outside frame 0-6-0ST

Builder	Kitson & Co, Nasmyth, Wilson & Co
Dates Built	1896, 1900
Number Built	5
Route Colour	Blue/Red
Power Class	A
Tractive Effort	17,000lbs
Driving Wheel Size	4ft 7½in
Cylinder Dimensions	17in x 24in
Dates Withdrawn	1927-1932

The first two of these outside framed locomotives were built in 1896. Three more followed from Nasmyth and Wilson in 1900. They were numbered 2169-73 on absorption. Three were rebuilt in 1923/4 with P class boilers, pannier tanks and GWR cabs (oddly for this date two of these had open cabs) and bunkers. A little later one of the other two was given pannier tanks, but retained its original boiler. These two both had strange looking cabs, of different design with the spectacle plate at the back of the bunker; they also received GWR boiler fittings.

Burry Port and Gwendraeth Valley Railway Absorbed Locomotives.
The BPGVR appeared to have a policy of purchasing engines that were similar in broad appearance, but rather different in detail. This makes them hard to summarise. They had long lives, with most surviving into the 1950s. All had inclined outside cylinders.

Chapman & Furneaux 0-6-0ST

Builder	Chapman & Furneaux
Dates Built	1900 /1
Number Built	2

Route Colour	Yellow, Uncoloured,
Power Class	A, Ungrouped
Tractive Effort	16,500-14,000lbs
Driving Wheel Size	3ft 8in, 3ft 6in
Cylinder Dimensions	16in x 24in, 15in x 22in
Dates Withdrawn	1951/2

2192 and 2193. Neither of these were to have been greatly altered by the GWR in spite of lasting until BR days.

Avonside 0-6-0ST

Builder	Avonside Engine Co
Dates Built	1903-1907
Number Built	5
Route Colour	Uncoloured
Power Class	Uncoloured, A
Tractive Effort	13,500, 16,500lbs
Driving Wheel Size	3ft 6in, 3ft 7in
Cylinder Dimensions	15in x 20in, 15in x 22in
Dates Withdrawn	1952-1956

There were five locomotives from Avonside, of which four went to the GWR: two smaller and two larger, given numbers 2194-6 and 2176. They were moderately updated to GWR standards and all lasted to BR ownership. The fifth, BPGVR No. 2, *Pontyberem*, was sold to a colliery in 1914. This locomotive has survived and is now preserved. It has not run in preservation.

Hudswell-Clarke 0-6-0Ts

Builder	Hudswell-Clarke
Dates Built	1909, 1919
Number Built	9
Route Colour	Uncoloured, Yellow
Power Class	Ungrouped, A
Tractive Effort	15,000, 18,500lbs
Driving Wheel Size	3ft 9in

Cylinder Dimensions	15in x 22in, 16in x 24in
Dates Withdrawn	1929, 1951-1959

All of these were side tanks with inclined outside cylinders, and there was a fair bit of variation in design. Basically there were two smaller ones, 2197 and 2198, and seven larger ones, 2162-2168. Four of the larger ones were rebuilt with a modified Standard 11 boiler in the late 1920s. All but one lasted until the mid-1950s.

2198, destined to be the line's last locomotive in BR service, was later reboilered, again with a non-standard boiler.

Cambrian Railway
Ex-Lambourn Railway 0-6-0Ts

Builder	Chapman and Furneaux Hunslet Engine Co
Dates Built	1898, 1903
Number Built	3
Route Colour	uncoloured
Power Class	ungrouped
Tractive Effort	8,500 – 9,000lbs
Driving Wheel Size	3ft 7in
Cylinder Dimensions	12in x 20in, 13in x 18in
Dates Withdrawn	1930-1946

These were three fairly similar outside cylinder 0-6-0 side tank locomotives bought second hand from the Lambourn Railway. Two of them had been built by Chapman and Furneaux in 1898. They were numbered 820/1, and lightly 'Swindonised' in 1922 and 1926. They were sold to collieries in 1930 and 1932 and worked on until the 1940s.

The youngest, which had been built by Hunslets in 1903, was given no 819. It was upgraded with new smoke box, top feed and extended bunker in 1925, survived the war with the GWR and was scrapped in 1946.

Cardiff Railway
Parfitt and Jenkins 0-6-0STs

Builder	Parfitt and Jenkins
Dates Built	1869 - 1881
Number Built	13 (see notes)

Route Colour	uncoloured
Power Class	A
Tractive Effort	15,000lbs
Driving Wheel Size	4ft 0in
Cylinder Dimensions	15½in x 22in
Dates Withdrawn	1923-1926

The Cardiff railway once had thirteen of these very small 0-6-0Ts, which were built between 1869 and 1881. Four survived to be absorbed by the GWR. They were withdrawn with little if anything in the way of changes. Parfitt and Jenkins are understood to have been a local engineering firm who do not appear to have built locomotives for any other organisation.

Kitson 0-6-0Ts

Builder	Kitson
Dates Built	1889-1899
Number Built	7
Route Colour	Yellow
Power Class	B
Tractive Effort	20,000lbs
Driving Wheel Size	4ft 6in
Cylinder Dimensions	17½in x 26in
Dates Withdrawn	1925-1929

There were seven of these, purchased in pairs in 1889, 1895 and 1899, and one singleton in 1919. They were basically similar to the Kitson 0-6-2Ts purchased at the same time, but had no bunkers – indeed little significant coal capacity at all. All but the first two had very distinctive shaped side tanks which came right to the front of the smokebox and sloped downwards considerably from about level with the dome to improve visibility. There were also fairly large cut-outs in the tanks to give access to the motion. After they were withdrawn, five of them went to various collieries, where most lasted until the 1950s.

Hudswell Clarke 0-6-0STs

Builder	Hudswell-Clarke
Line	Cardiff Railway

Dates Built	1920
Number Built	4
Route Colour	Blue/Yellow
Power Class	C
Tractive Effort	22,000lbs
Driving Wheel Size	4ft 1½in
Cylinder Dimensions	18in x 24in
Boiler Class	Standard 11 (after rebuild)
Dates Withdrawn	1953-1955

Four substantial 0-6-0ST delivered in 1920. They were a typical contemporary heavy industrial type with inside cylinders. Between 1926 and 1939 all were given the full Great Western treatment, with Standard 11 boilers and fittings, pannier tanks and a GWR bunker. The original cabs were retained, but the cabside door and cut-out were very similar to the typical Collett profile anyway. They were somewhat lighter after the rebuild, increasing to Yellow route availability.

Cleobury Mortimer & Ditton Priors Light Railway
Manning Wardle 0-6-0ST

Builder	Manning Wardle
Line	Cleobury, Mortimer and Ditton Priors Light Railway
Dates Built	1908
Number Built	2
Route Colour	Yellow
Power Class	A
Tractive Effort	18,000lbs
Driving Wheel Size	3ft 6in
Cylinder Dimensions	16in x 22in
Dates Withdrawn	1953/4

This tiny line, which started in 1908, only ever owned two locomotives. These were typical Manning Wardle 0-6-0 saddle tanks, inside frames and slightly inclined outside cylinders. The saddle tanks were high pitched and short, leaving both firebox and smokebox exposed.

The GWR numbered them 28 and 29. They were given the Swindon treatment in 1924 and 1931 respectively, gaining domed boilers and complete GWR pannier tank cabs and bunkers. In this form, they were a very pretty

CMDPLR Manning Wardle 0-6-0ST *before Swindon*

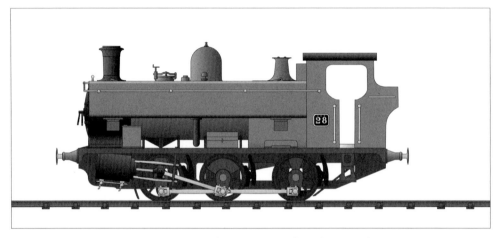

Ex CMDPLR Manning Wardle 0-6-0PT *after the Swindon treatment.*

pair of locomotives, very like the 1366 class and a considerable contrast to the original appearance.

They were withdrawn in 1953 and 1954.

Gwendraeth Valley Railway
Hudswell Clarke 0-6-0ST

Builder	Hudswell-Clarke
Dates Built	1905
Number Built	1
Driving Wheel Size	3ft 7in or 3ft 3½in (sources vary)

Cylinder Dimensions	14in x 20in
Dates Withdrawn	Sold 1927

The line owned two locomotives at the time of the grouping, but one (see 1378 above) had been sold. The locomotive the GWR acquired was a 1905 built Hudswell Clarke 0-6-0ST. No diagram was ever issued, but it was given the number 26. In 1928 the locomotive was sold into industry, and probably ended up in South America.

Llanelly and Mynydd Mawr Railway
Avonside 0-6-0T

Builder	Avonside Engine Co
Dates Built	1902
Number Built	1
Route Colour	Uncoloured
Power Class	B
Tractive Effort	19,500lbs
Driving Wheel Size	4ft 0in
Cylinder Dimensions	17in x 24in
Dates Withdrawn	Sold 1929

It was given number 944, a new chimney, safety valves and a slightly enlarged bunker in its time with the GWR. Sold off in 1929, it had a long career in the coal industry and was eventually scrapped in 1968.

Andrew Barclay 0-6-0T

Builder	Andrew Barclay
Dates Built	1907
Number Built	1
Route Colour	Blue
Power Class	A
Tractive Effort	18,500lbs
Driving Wheel Size	4ft 6in
Cylinder Dimensions	17½in x 24in
Dates Withdrawn	Sold 1935

This engine was numbered 312. Shortly after the grouping it was sent to Swindon and spent four years there, probably mainly in dark corners. When it emerged, it had a virtually new boiler and other westernisation. Sold into industry in 1935, it was not scrapped until 1961.

Hudswell Clarke 0-6-0Ts

Builder	Hudswell Clarke
Dates Built	1911-1917
Number Built	4
Dates Withdrawn	1923-1954

The LMM had a number of Hudswell Clarke 0-6-0T of varying design and size. 803, built in 1911, was given a substantial GWR overhaul/upgrade. It survived to BR and was scrapped in 1951. 937, built in 1912, was scrapped on sight by Swindon in 1923 and never carried the GWR number.

339, of 1913, was identical to 937. It was given a substantial GWR overhaul/upgrade and worked until 1943. 359, built 1917, was given a repair rather than an upgrade, although it did receive GWR safety valves and an enlarged bunker. Unlike the others, it was a saddle tank. It survived until 1954 working in Swansea Docks.

Manning Wardle 0-6-0T

Builder	Manning Wardle
Dates Built	1920
Number Built	1
Route Colour	Uncoloured
Power Class	A
Tractive Effort	17,500lbs
Driving Wheel Size	4ft 0in
Cylinder Dimensions	16in x 24in
Dates Withdrawn	1943

This side tank was fairly new at the grouping. It received safety valves, buffers and the number 704 but was otherwise unchanged. It was cut up in 1943.

Fox Walker 0-6-0T

There was also an elderly Fox Walker 0-6-0ST, built in 1875. Although it was allocated the number 969 it was never carried. It went to Swindon in 1923 and was dismantled for repair or upgrade, but when it reached the top of the queue in 1925 it was scrapped instead.

MSWJR
Dubs 0-6-0T

Builder	Dubs
Dates Built	1894
Number Built	2
Route Colour	Uncoloured
Power Class	Ungrouped
Tractive Effort	15,000lbs
Driving Wheel Size	4ft 7in
Cylinder Dimensions	17in x 24in
Dates Withdrawn	1926

These two small 1894 side tanks were numbered 825 and 843. They were withdrawn, unchanged, in 1926.

Neath and Brecon Railway
As noted in appendix D the GWR had been carrying out heavy repairs on the Neath and Brecon's locomotives since 1908.

Avonside 0-6-0STs

Builder	Avonside
Dates Built	1872/4
Number Built	6 (see notes)
Route Colour	Uncoloured/Yellow
Power Class	A
Tractive Effort	16,000lbs
Driving Wheel Size	4ft 7in
Cylinder Dimensions	17in x 24in
Boiler Class	Sir Daniel (on one)
Dates Withdrawn	1931/2

Originally the line had six of these, two delivered in 1873 and four in 1874. Two were sold to the Brecon & Merthyr in 1877, one was scrapped in 1910, and another was sold in 1916 so only two of these double framed saddle tanks reached the GWR. One, 2199, was given a major overhaul and Swindonisation at Swindon, emerging in 1924. It worked on until 1931 and was then sold into industry, where it worked until scrapped in the middle 1950s. The other had received the Swindon treatment before the grouping, acquiring various ex 1016 class components second-hand, and was allocated 2189. It was withdrawn and scrapped in 1932. The two sold to the Brecon & Merthyr were out of use by the grouping, and never became GWR stock. These locomotives were built with the same beam compensated suspension arrangement on the leading driving wheels as some of the B&M double framed saddle tanks, but it was removed by the end of their lives.

Nasmyth, Wilson 0-6-0ST

Builder	Nasmyth Wilson & Co
Dates Built	1898
Number Built	2
Route Colour	Yellow
Power Class	A
Tractive Effort	17,000lbs
Driving Wheel Size	4ft 7in
Cylinder Dimensions	17in x 24in
Dates Withdrawn	1927, 1933

A pair of inside framed locomotives delivered in 1899. Already featuring Swindon modifications when they came into GWR stock, they were numbered 2174/5. One went in 1927 and the other in 1933 after which it spent its last days as a Swindon works pilot.

Port Talbot Railway
Stephenson's 0-6-0ST

Builder	R. Stephenson & Co
Dates Built	1897/8
Number Built	3
Route Colour	Uncoloured
Power Class	A
Tractive Effort	15,000lbs

Driving Wheel Size	4ft 0in
Cylinder Dimensions	16in x 24in
Dates Withdrawn	1929/30

These two small tank engines, fairly standard of the period, were supplied in 1897 and one in 1898. One was condemned in 1911, but the other two were formally absorbed and given numbers 815/6. They received various standard GW components over the years and were sold into industry in 1929/30.

Hudswell-Clarke 0-6-0ST

Builder	Hudswell-Clarke
Dates Built	1900/1
Number Built	6
Route Colour	Yellow
Power Class	A
Tractive Effort	17,500lbs
Driving Wheel Size	4ft 0½in
Cylinder Dimensions	16in x 24in
Dates Withdrawn	1926 – 1934

These six were delivered in 1900/1. They were very similar to the Stephenson's locos listed above, being inside cylinder locos with 4ft 0½in driving wheels of moderate power. When fully absorbed into GWR stock, they were numbered 808-814. They were never given major rebuilds, but received the usual mild westernisation with the combined dome/safety valve cover seen on many smaller absorbed saddle tanks. Withdrawal came between 1928 and 1934, but three were sold into industry. One was scrapped in 1950, but the other two lasted in service until the 1960s. 813 was sold for and has run in preservation.

Rhondda and Swansea Bay Railway
Major repairs on the R&SB locomotives were always done by the GWR.

Beyer Peacock 0-6-0T

Builder	Beyer, Peacock
Dates Built	1884-1889
Number Built	5

Route Colour	Yellow
Power Class	A
Tractive Effort	16,000-18,000lbs
Driving Wheel Size	4ft 6in
Cylinder Dimensions	17in x 24in
Dates Withdrawn	1927-1940

A class of five, built between 1884 and 1889. The GWR reboilered them in the 1907-10 timeframe. In 1922, they were numbered 799, 801/2 and 805/6. Two were sold into industry in the 1930s, and survived until the 1950s. The last on the GWR was taken out of revenue service in 1940, after which it spent some time as a Swindon works shunter before being scrapped in 1943.

Rhymney Railway
H and I class 0-6-0ST

Builder	Nasmyth, Wilson & Co
Dates Built	1874
Number Built	22 (see notes)
Driving Wheel Size	4ft 7in
Cylinder Dimensions	16in x 24in
Dates Withdrawn	1925

These were originally a class of twenty-two locomotives. The first ten came from Sharp Stewart in 1872, six more from Nasmyth, Wilson & Co in 187 and finally six from Robert Stephenson & Co in 1878. They went through a number of rebuildings, and at one stage were divided into two classes. They started to go for scrap from 1914 and, after a pause caused by the First World War, the vast majority went in 1920 and 1921. Only two, both from Nasmyth Wilson, survived to become GWR locomotives. They were scrapped in 1925.

J class 0-6-0ST

Builder	Sharp, Stewart & Co
Dates Built	1884
Number Built	12 (see notes)
Route Colour	Blue
Power Class	A

Tractive Effort	17,000lbs
Driving Wheel Size	4ft 7in
Cylinder Dimensions	17½in x 24in
Dates Withdrawn	1925-1927

This 1884 class of 12 0-6-0ST had rather distinctive outside frames. They were just beginning to go for scrap at the grouping, and nine passed to the GWR. At one stage, there was a proposal that they should be reboiled with Standard Goods boilers and pannier tanks, but this never happened. All were withdrawn between 1925 and 1927, with only one going to a new career with a colliery.

B class Former Railmotor 0-6-0T.

Builder	Hudswell Clarke, Rebuilt Rhymney Railway
Dates Built	1907
Number Built	2
Route Colour	Uncoloured
Power Class	Ungrouped
Tractive Effort	7,000lbs
Driving Wheel Size	3ft 6in
Cylinder Dimensions	12in x 16in
Dates Withdrawn	1925

These two locomotives had started life as 0-4-0 power sections of railmotors. As railmotors, they had had no water tanks, the water being carried under the coach unit, and small coal bunkers in front of the cab, with the rear of the cab forming the front of the coach section. They were converted into 0-4-2 configuration almost immediately. In 1910 and 1919, they lost their coach sections and were converted to 0-6-0T of distinctly odd configuration. The frames had been extended several feet beyond the cab, a third set of driving wheels added, plus a very large bunker, the greater part of which was in fact the water tank. The GWR numbered them 661 and 662, and used them as works shunters and other similar duties. They were withdrawn in 1925.

S class 0-6-0T

Builder	Hudswell Clarke
Dates Built	1908

Number Built	4
Route Colour	Red
Power Class	C
Tractive Effort	24,000lbs
Driving Wheel Size	4ft 4½in
Cylinder Dimensions	18in x 26in
Wheelbase	7ft 3in + 8ft 0 in
Boiler Class	Own, Standard 10
Dates Withdrawn	1953/4

The S class were four shunting engines, delivered by Hudswell Clarke in 1908. They bore a definite family resemblance to the R class 0-6-2T, with the same coupled wheelbase but a shorter boiler and firebox and smaller driving wheels. They joined the GWR as 608-611.

In 1930, all were rebuilt with superheated Standard 10 tapered boilers and new GWR style larger bunkers. They were renumbered 93-96 in the 1946 renumbering and all survived to British Railways to be withdrawn in 1953/4.

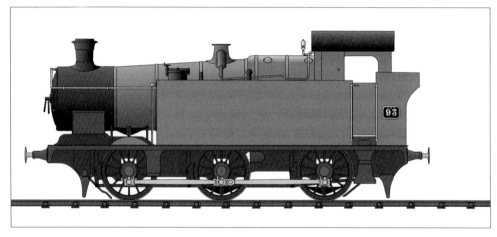

93 Class *ex Rhymney Railway S Class based on diagram B57, with amendments based on a post war photograph.*

S1 class 0-6-0T

Builder	Hudswell Clarke
Dates Built	1920
Number Built	3
Route Colour	Red

Power Class	C
Tractive Effort	24,000lbs
Driving Wheel Size	4ft 4½in
Cylinder Dimensions	18in x 26in
Dates Withdrawn	1953/4

These were essentially updates of the S class, but based on A1 class 0-6-2T components and with slightly larger bunkers. They also had a slightly larger boiler with a Belpaire firebox. They were delivered in 1920 by Hudswell Clarke. They were numbered 604-606. Plans to reboiler them with Standard 10 boilers were never acted on, although one did receive an enlarged GWR style bunker. They were renumbered 90-92 in the 1946 renumbering and were all withdrawn in 1954.

Swansea Harbour Trust
Pecketts class X2 0-6-0ST.

Builder	Peckett & Sons
Dates Built	1912-1915
Number Built	3 (see notes)
Route Colour	Uncoloured
Power Class	A
Tractive Effort	16,500lbs
Driving Wheel Size	3ft 10in
Cylinder Dimensions	16in x 22in
Dates Withdrawn	1926, 1951

These were three standard industrial saddle tanks. Two had significant repairs in 1926, without any very significant changes, but the third was scrapped that year. The other two survived into the 1950s. They were originally numbered 1085/6 and renumbered 1146/7 in the 1946 scheme although the new numbers were not actually carried until BR days. They were scrapped in 1951.

Taff Vale Railway
H class 0-6-0Ts.

Builder	Kitson & Co
Dates Built	1884
Number Built	3

Route Colour	Yellow
Power Class	A
Tractive Effort	15,000lbs
Driving Wheel Size	5ft 3in
Cylinder Dimensions	17½in x 26in
Dates Withdrawn	1951-1953

These were three specialised locomotives for working on the cable assisted Pwllyrhebog incline, part of which is as steep as 1:19. They had very exaggerated tapered boilers to ensure the firebox crown remained covered in water. They were withdrawn in 1951/2 when the incline was closed. Two were sold to the NCB and the last not scrapped until 1960.

V class 0-6-0ST.

Builder	Kitson & Co
Dates Built	1899
Number Built	6
Route Colour	Blue
Power Class	A
Tractive Effort	18,500lbs
Driving Wheel Size	4ft 6½in
Cylinder Dimensions	17½in x 26in
Dates Withdrawn	1926-1930

This was a class of six, built by Kitsons. All were out of GWR service by 1930, but five of the six were sold to industry, one lasting until 1963.

CHAPTER 7

Eight Wheeled Tank Engines

Four Coupled Classes
GWR Classes
No. 1490 4-4-0T

Builders	GWR/Swindon
Date built	1898
Number Built	1
Tractive Effort	16,000lbs
Driving Wheel Size	4ft 7½in
Cylinder Dimensions	15½in x 26in
Dates Withdrawn	Sold 1907

This odd experimental locomotive is arguably significant only as having the first set of pannier tanks. It had outside frames and, initially, a very unconventional firebox featuring water tubes inside the firebox. Apparently, it was unsuccessful in its designed role as a passenger engine and was relegated to shunting duties before being sold, firstly to the Brecon & Merthyr, and then to a Northumberland Colliery who scrapped it in 1929.

Swindon 3600 class 2-4-2T

Builders	GWR/Swindon
Dates Built	1900-1903
Number Built	31
Route Colour	Blue
Power Class	A,B

Tractive Effort	17,000-18,500lbs
Driving Wheel Size	5ft 2in
Cylinder Dimensions	17in x 24in
Wheelbase	7ft 9in + 8ft 6in + 7ft 9in
Boiler Class	Standard 3
Dates Withdrawn	1930-1934

The first of the class was built in 1900 – a time that has been described as Churchward's regency – and they had a something of the look of the Churchward standard classes. They had many of the features that were to become characteristic of the standard classes, combined with others in common with the Aberdares and other classes from the end of the Dean era. The 56XX 0-6-2 tanks, built under Collett, had quite a resemblance to the 36XX.

A prototype, then numbered 11, was built in 1900 and thoroughly evaluated. Thirty production locomotives, numbered from 3601, followed in 1902/3. The driving wheels were the Dean Goods size. The prototype and the first production lot had parallel Standard 3 boilers, but those from 3621 were built with tapered Standard 3s. The prototype had a 3ft 6in rear overhang, the first twenty 4ft, giving increased water capacity, and the last ten 4ft 1in, giving a further small increase in water capacity, there being a water tank under the coal in the bunker as with most of the large Churchward tank engines.

They had water pick up apparatus, causing what must have been an entertaining incident with the prototype when it picked up water far faster than the air vents in the tank could cope with and split the side tanks open! Consequently much larger air vents were fitted.

No. 11 was renumbered 3600 in the 1912 renumbering. All those built with parallel boilers had taper boilers by 1915. The detail design of the boilers changed over the years as Churchward optimised the standard boiler designs.

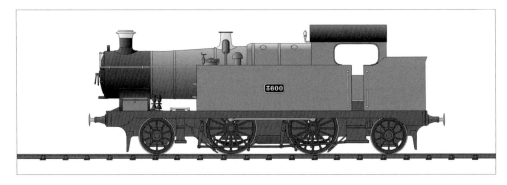

3600 class. *Diagram H. This is the final configuration of the second batch with long cone superheated boiler.*

They gained superheating between 1912 and 1927. The earlier ones received larger (deeper) bunkers in time, but never the overhanging rear extension seen on most other classes. They were withdrawn between 1930 and 1934, having been made redundant by the standard large 2-6-2 tanks on their normal suburban passenger work.

Absorbed Classes at the Grouping
Barry Railway
Class C 2-4-0/2-4-2T (also Port Talbot Railway)

Builders	Sharp, Stewart & Co
Dates Built	1889/90
Number Built	4
Route Colour	Blue
Power Class	Ungrouped/A
Tractive Effort	14,000-15,500lbs
Driving Wheel Size	5ft 3in
Cylinder Dimensions	17in x 24in
Boiler Class	Own/T
Dates Withdrawn	1926-1931 (2 sold to Port Talbot in 1898)

Built by Sharp Stewart, the class C was originally a 2-4-0T, without the standard boiler used by most Barry Railway classes. At the grouping, the two remaining with the Barry had been converted to 2-4-2T. They were numbered 1322/3. Both were gone by 1928, even though one received a major rebuild with a Metro boiler. The other two had been sold to the Port Talbot Railway and came under GWR control in 1908 when the Port Talbot was taken over by the GWR. One remained as a 2-4-0T and was given a Metro boiler (diagram N) in 1915 and numbered 1189 at the grouping. The other had been converted to 2-4-2T. Numbered 1326, it received the Metro boiler treatment and diagram S in 1925. Both were gone by 1931.

Class G 0-4-4T

Builders	Vulcan Foundry, Sharp Stewart & Co
Dates Built	1892, 1895
Number Built	4
Route Colour	Red
Power Class	A

Tractive Effort	16,000lbs
Driving Wheel Size	5ft ¾in
Cylinder Dimensions	17½in x 26in
Boiler Class	Own
Dates Withdrawn	1925-9

This was a passenger class, using the Barry standard boiler and cylinders. Four were built, but did not survive long with the GWR, the last scrapped in 1929. They were given numbers 2, 3, 4 and 9.

Class J 2-4-2T.

Builders	Hudswell, Clarke, Sharp, Stewart & Co
Dates Built	1897-9
Number Built	11
Route Colour	Red/Blue
Power Class	A
Tractive Effort	15,000-16,000lbs
Driving Wheel Size	5ft 7½in
Cylinder Dimensions	17½in x 26in
Boiler Class	Own/Standard 9
Dates Withdrawn	1926-30

This was the last essay at a passenger loco using the Barry standard cylinders and boiler. They had wheels and other components in common with the G class. They were numbered 1311-1321. Four were given minor rebuilds in 1924 with new smokeboxes and bunkers and later one was rebuilt with a Standard 9 boiler. The unrebuilt locomotives went in 1926 and the rest had all gone by 1930.

Cambrian Railway
Bogie Side Tank class 0-4-4

Builders	Nasmyth, Wilson & Co
Dates Built	1895, 1899
Number Built	6
Route Colour	Yellow
Power Class	A
Tractive Effort	15,000lbs

Driving Wheel Size	5ft 3in
Cylinder Dimensions	17in x 24in
Boiler Class	Own
Dates Withdrawn	1922-1932

A class of six 0-4-4 tank engines from Nasmyth, Wilson and Co, three built in 1895 and three in 1899. They were allocated numbers 10, 11, 15, 19-21 and diagram E, but the GWR scrapped three on sight without carrying the new numbers. Of the others, one received little more than GWR safety valves and was scrapped in 1928, whilst the other two received GWR smoke boxes and bunkers, plus some boiler work, and were given diagram H, lasting until 1932.

Ex Metropolitan Railway 4-4-0T class

Builders	Beyer Peacock for Metropolitan Railway
Dates Built	1864-70, purchased 1905
Number Built	6 (see Notes)
Route Colour	Blue
Power Class	Ungrouped
Tractive Effort	13,500lbs
Driving Wheel Size	5ft 10in
Cylinder Dimensions	17½in x 24in
Boiler Class	own
Dates Withdrawn	1922/3

The Cambrian had bought 6 of these Beyer Peacock locomotives, rendered redundant by electrification, very cheaply. By the time they reached the GWR, two had been converted to 4-4-0 tender configuration. The tender engines were allocated 1113/14, the tank engines 1129-1132. They were scrapped very quickly by the GWR; only one (of the tank locomotives) lasted into 1923 and long enough to carry its GWR number.

Midland and South Western Junction Railway
Beyer Peacock 0-4-4T

Builders	Beyer., Peacock & Co
Dates Built	1895
Number Built	1

Route Colour	Yellow
Power Class	Ungrouped
Tractive Effort	13,500lbs
Driving Wheel Size	5ft 2in
Cylinder Dimensions	17in x 24in
Boiler Class	Own/Standard 11
Dates Withdrawn	1930

An 1895 locomotive, absorbed as No. 23, and rebuilt in 1925 with a Standard 11 boiler. Withdrawn in 1930.

Sharp Stewart 4-4-4T

Builders	Sharp, Stewart & Co
Dates Built	1897
Number Built	2
Route Colour	Yellow
Power Class	Ungrouped
Tractive Effort	14,000lbs
Driving Wheel Size	5ft 3in
Cylinder Dimensions	17in x 24in
Boiler Class	Own/Standard 10
Dates Withdrawn	1927/9

There were two of these, built in 1897. They had inside frames and cylinders and flush round top fireboxes. They were the only 4-4-4s the GWR ever owned and were numbered 25 and 27. One was withdrawn in 1927 and the other, rebuilt that year with a Standard 10 boiler, lasted until 1929.

Neath and Brecon
Yorkshire Engine Co 4-4-0T

Builders	Yorkshire Engine Co
Dates Built	1871
Number Built	1
Route Colour	Blue
Power Class	Ungrouped

Tractive Effort	14,000lbs
Driving Wheel Size	5ft 0in
Cylinder Dimensions	17in x 24in
Boiler Class	own
Dates Withdrawn	1926

Built in 1871, this locomotive was the N&B's main passenger engine. By the grouping, it already had GWR safety valves and other fittings and was allocated number 1392. It worked on until 1926.

Rhondda and Swansea Bay Railway
Kitson 2-4-2T

Builders	Kitson & Co
Dates Built	1895
Number Built	3
Route Colour	Uncoloured
Power Class	A
Tractive Effort	19,000lbs
Driving Wheel Size	5ft 3in
Cylinder Dimensions	18in x 26in
Boiler Class	Own/Standard 5
Dates Withdrawn	1926/8

These were delivered in 1895 and had 5ft 3in driving wheels. They were numbered 1307, 1309 and 1310. In 1921/2, one was rebuilt with a Standard 5 (45xx) boiler. The unrebuilts went in 1926, while the reboilered one lingered on until 1928.

Rhymney Railway
L class 2-4-2ST

Builders	Vulcan Foundry
Dates Built	1890
Number Built	5 (2 to GWR)
Route Colour	Blue
Power Class	A

Tractive Effort	15,500lbs
Driving Wheel Size	5ft 0in
Cylinder Dimensions	17½in x 24in
Boiler Class	Own
Dates Withdrawn	1928

These were saddle tanks with double frames. Five were built in 1891 by the Vulcan Foundry. By GWR days, one had been withdrawn and two more converted to 0-6-2ST. The two remaining 2-4-2s were numbered 1324/5 and acquired GWR safety valves (and cover) and other minor features. They were scrapped in 1928.

Taff Vale Railway
I class 4-4-0T

Builders	TVR/Cardiff
Dates Built	1884/5
Number Built	3
Route Colour	Blue
Power Class	Ungrouped
Tractive Effort	12,500lbs
Driving Wheel Size	5ft 3in
Cylinder Dimensions	16in x 24in
Boiler Class	Own
Dates Withdrawn	1925

A class of three outside cylinder side tank engines, built by the Taff Vale for passenger traffic in 1884/5. By the time of the grouping, they were fitted with the Taff Vale's idiosyncratic autotrain equipment – a system of wires and pulleys at roof height of locomotives and coaches. They were originally allocated 1133, 1184 and 1186, but it was then realised that GWR 1186 was still running, so 999 was substituted. They were withdrawn in December 1925.

0-6-2T Classes
Boilers

Class	Name	Barrel length	Barrel diameter	Firebox Length
B	Standard 2	11ft 0in	5ft 0in tapering to 4ft 5in	7ft 0in
C	Standard 3	10ft 3in	5ft 0in tapering to 4ft 5in	7ft 0in

Class	Name	Barrel length	Barrel diameter	Firebox Length
D	Standard 4	11ft 0in	5ft 6in tapering to 4ft 11in	7ft 0in
E	Standard 5	10ft 6in	4ft 9in tapering to 4ft 2in	5ft 0in
J	Standard 9	10ft 3in	4ft 5in	6ft 6in
K	Standard 10	10ft 3in	5ft 0in tapering to 4ft 5in	6ft 0in
L	Standard 11	10ft 6in	4ft 3in	5ft 6in

GWR Class
5600 class

Builder	GWR/Swindon, Armstrong Whitworth
Dates Built	1924-1928
Number Built	200
Route Colour	Red
Power Class	D
Tractive Effort	26,000lbs
Driving Wheel Size	4ft 8½in
Cylinder Dimensions	18in x 26in
Wheelbase	7ft 3in + 8ft 0in + 8ft 6in
Boiler Class	Standard 2
Dates Withdrawn	1962-5

The Welsh valleys traffic had some unusual aspects. Much of it was coal traffic. The wagons were privately owned, indifferently maintained, and fitted only with hand brakes. Once loaded they had to be hauled out of the yards and started down the hills, after which the main problem was stopping them. The empty wagons then had to be dragged up the hills again. The lines tended to have restricted clearances and relatively tight curves, which precluded the use of large outside cylinders.

What was produced, without the usual prototype, was a locomotive with the Standard 2 boiler, freight size wheels, piston valves and inside cylinders. Much of the motion design was new, with a three-bar crosshead setup. The wheel spacing was the same as the Rhymney Railway M and R classes, which surely influenced the general concept.

Swindon built 150 in four lots from 1924 to 1928. Armstrong Whitworth built fifty, delivered in 1928. There were no major differences between the batches, but the suspension arrangements changed, probably with the 6600 series.

There were some problems experienced with wheel balancing and driving wheel bearings, so different wheel balancing schemes were tried to compromise between loads on the bearings and the various forces generated by the reciprocating and rotating weights. Cabside sliding shutters were installed from 1930-39; this was a feature found on some of the absorbed Welsh locomotives, which was fitted across the larger tank engine classes. The bunker tops were altered to accept a recessed lamp between 1934 and 1956. There was only ever a single diagram for the 56xx.

They all lasted until the 1960s, two being withdrawn in 1960 and no more until 1962. The majority went in 1964 and 1965. Nine have survived into preservation and of these, at the time of writing, six are running or have run in preservation, one is under active restoration and two are effectively still in scrapyard condition.

5600 class. *Based on diagram A30 but with changes to reflect a post 1934 configuration.*

Absorbed Classes at the Grouping
Alexandra (Newport and South Wales) Docks and Railway
ADR Andrew Barclay 0-6-2STs

Builders	Andrew Barclay & Co
Dates Built	1908
Number Built	3
Route Colour	Blue
Power Class	C
Tractive Effort	21,000lbs
Driving Wheel Size	4ft 3in
Cylinder Dimensions	18in x 26in
Boiler Class	Own
Dates Withdrawn	1934-1948

Three Andrew Barclay 0-6-2STs, built to a standard Barclay design. These were bought new, in 1908, and had outside cylinders with full length saddle tanks. They were numbered 190-192 on absorption. In 1925, they were given shorter saddle tanks to reduce the weight and the combined dome/safety valve cover arrangement used on most of the smaller absorbed saddle tanks. In this form one was withdrawn in 1934 and the other two survived the war, the last spending its last few months under British Railways ownership.

Barry Railway
Barry Railway B (and original B1) class 0-6-2T

Builders	Sharp, Stewart & Co,
Dates Built	1888-1890
Number Built	15 (B class) 10 (original B1 class)
Route Colour	Blue/Yellow
Power Class	B
Tractive Effort	21,000lbs
Driving Wheel Size	4ft 3in
Cylinder Dimensions	17½in x 26in
Boiler Class	Barry Standard/Standard 9
Dates Withdrawn	1922, 1931-1949

The class B was based on the A class 0-6-0T, but was an 0-6-2 tank with a bigger bunker. The original B1 class was a variation on the B class with an uprated version of the Barry standard boiler. By the time they reached the GWR the B class had received uprated boilers and the B and original B1 classes had been merged. The fifteen original locomotives retained a much shorter front overhang. On the grouping the enlarged B class were numbered 198-201, 203/4, 206-214 and 223-232. About half of them received the Standard 9 boiler, which was the replacement for the standard Barry boiler. All those with GWR boilers, plus a few without, were given Swindon style bunkers. One was scrapped in 1922, but otherwise they started to be withdrawn in the 1930s, with, as one would expect, those still carrying Barry boilers going first. Almost all retained the distinctive Barry cab, even with enlarged bunkers and GWR boilers.

Four survived to British Railways, but none beyond 1949. One that had been sold in 1934 survived with a colliery company until 1960.

Barry Railway B1 (originally B2) class 0-6-2T

Builders	Sharp, Stewart & Co, Vulcan Foundry S. A. Franco-Belge
Dates Built	1890-1900
Number Built	42
Route Colour	Yellow/Uncoloured
Power Class	B
Tractive Effort	21,000lbs
Dates Built	4ft 3in
Cylinder Dimensions	18/17½in x 26in
Boiler Class	Barry Standard/Standard 9
Dates Withdrawn	1932, 1936-1953

The original B2 class had greater water capacity, but was otherwise very similar to the B class. It was renamed B1 class when the B and original B1 classes were merged.

Twenty-seven were built by Sharp Stewart, ten came from the Vulcan Foundry and another five from a Belgian concern, the Société Anonyme Franco-Belge.

On the grouping, the B1s were given numbers between 233 and 277. About half of them received the Standard 9 boiler, which was the replacement for the standard Barry boiler. These were mostly, but not invariably, superheated. The B class started to be withdrawn in the 1930s, with, as one would expect, those still carrying Barry boilers going first. Two received a large GWR style cab, but otherwise they retained the distinctive Barry cab, even with enlarged bunkers and GWR boilers.

Eighteen survived to British Railways, the last leaving revenue service in 1951. That was not quite the end of them, as several were used as works shunters in Swindon works, the last surviving until 1953. Two were sold into industry in the 1930s, and also lasted until the 1950s.

Barry Railway K class 0-6-2T

Builders	Cooke Loco and Machine Co
Dates Built	1899
Number Built	5
Route Colour	Red
Power Class	B/C
Tractive Effort	20,000-22,000lbs

Driving Wheel Size	4ft 3in
Cylinder Dimensions	18in x 26in
Boiler Class	Barry Standard/Standard 3
Dates Withdrawn	1927-1932

In 1899, the Barry railway desperately needed some new locomotives, but all British builders were at full capacity. To resolve this, the five locomotives of the K class was ordered from Cooke Loco and Machine Co in the USA. It seems the Barry railway really wanted something as close as possible to the B1 class and the Americans wanted to build something as close as possible to their standard product. The result was a decidedly odd hybrid, with the back half and boiler largely complying with Barry standards, whilst the cylinders and the frames for the coupled wheels were pure US – bar frames, outside cylinders and all. The combination does not appear to have been a happy one, and yet when the GWR got their hands on them they elected to rebuild two in the best GWR style with Standard 3 taper boiler and full GWR side tanks, cab and bunkers. They were numbered 193-197. The rebuilds do not seem to have been significantly more satisfactory and all were scrapped between 1927 and 1932, no industrial user having elected to purchase one.

Brecon & Merthyr Railway
Vulcan Foundry 0-6-2ST.

Builders	Vulcan Foundry
Dates Built	1894
Number Built	4
Route Colour	Uncoloured
Power Class	A
Tractive Effort	16,000lbs
Driving Wheel Size	4ft 7½in
Cylinder Dimensions	17in x 24in
Boiler Class	Own
Dates Withdrawn	1922-1928

A class of four inside framed locomotives, two built in 1894, and two in 1905. They were odd looking machines, with 6ft 11½in + 5ft 2½in + 7ft 2in wheelbase, so the middle and trailing driving wheels were close together and ahead of the firebox. They did not last long with the GWR; one was scrapped on sight and the last went in 1928.

Modified Rhymney R class

Builders	R Stephenson & Co
Dates Built	1909/10, 1913
Number Built	8
Route Colour	Red/Blue
Power Class	D
Tractive Effort	24,500lbs
Driving Wheel Size	4ft 6in
Cylinder Dimensions	18½in x 26in
Boiler Class	Own/Standard 2
Dates Withdrawn	1947-1951

In 1909, the B&M ordered four new 0-6-2Ts from Stephenson's, based on the RR R class, but with flush round top rather than Belpaire fireboxes. Four more, with some slight detail changes, followed in 1913. The numbers used were 11, 21, 332, 504, 698, 888, 1084 and 1113. Two received Standard 2 boilers, in 1924, another in 1929 and one in 1941. The reboilered engines were lighter and had Blue route availability. Three more received ex-Rhymney R class boilers during their lives. In the 1946 renumbering, they were all due to be renumbered between 421 and 428, but in the event only 422, 425 426 and 428 were actually carried. One was scrapped in 1947, but the others all reached British Railways and were scrapped between Jan 1948 and 1951.

Modified Rhymney P class

Builders	R Stephenson & Co
Dates Built	1915, 1921
Number Built	6
Route Colour	Blue
Power Class	B
Tractive Effort	21,000lbs
Driving Wheel Size	5ft 0in
Cylinder Dimensions	18in x 26in
Boiler Class	Own/Standard 10
Dates Withdrawn	1951-1954

Three of these were built by Stephenson's in 1915, and three more in 1921. As with the previous class listed, they had round top fireboxes, not Belpaire. They were numbered 1372-1375, 1668 and 1670 by the GWR. Between 1926 and 1936, five received Standard 10 boilers, whilst the odd one out received a RR A1 class boiler. They received the usual GWR fittings, and often GW tanks and bunkers, but all retained their original cabs. In 1946, they were renumbered 431-436. They were scrapped between 1951 and 1954, with one spending some months as a Swindon works shunter.

Cardiff Railway
Kitson 0-6-2Ts

Builders	Kitson & Co
Dates Built	1869-1898
Number Built	6
Route Colour	Uncoloured
Power Class	A, B
Tractive Effort	19,000-21,000lbs
Driving Wheel Size	4ft 6in
Cylinder Dimensions	17½in x 26in
Boiler Class	0wn
Dates Withdrawn	1928-1932

The Cardiff Railway bought 13 0-6-2Ts of varying design from Kitsons over the years, all of which were absorbed by the GWR. The first six were similar enough to be treated together.

1869 – One locomotive. It received a GWR smokebox and boiler fittings before being withdrawn in 1932.

1887/94 – Three locomotives. They had a larger firebox and increased boiler pressure compared to their predecessor. They did not receive much attention from the GWR. Two were sold in 1931 and survived in industrial service until the 1960s, the third was withdrawn in 1932.

1898 – Two locomotives. These two had a bigger bunker and increased spacing to the trailing wheels. One received a GWR smokebox and boiler fittings, and was withdrawn in 1928, while the other, which received an overhaul from Kitsons after the grouping, lasted until 1932.

Builders	Kitson & Co
Dates Built	1905, 1919

Number Built	4
Route Colour	Blue/Yellow
Power Class	B,C
Tractive Effort	22,500lbs
Driving Wheel Size	4ft 6in
Cylinder Dimensions	18in x 26in
Boiler Class	own
Dates Withdrawn	1929-1936

Two locomotives of this design were purchased in 1905 and two more the same in 1919. Although largely similar to the 1898 batch, these four looked quite different as they had very distinctive shaped side tanks; they came right to the front of the smokebox and sloped downwards considerably from alongside the dome to improve visibility. There were also large cut-outs in the tanks to give access to the motion.

One of them received a GWR built boiler, but not a standard type, but otherwise they were little altered beyond safety valves. One of the 1919 locos lasted until 1936, but the others went in 1929/30.

Builders	Kitson & Co
Dates Built	1908
Number Built	3
Route Colour	Red
Power Class	C
Tractive Effort	23,000lbs
Driving Wheel Size	4ft 6in½in
Cylinder Dimensions	18in x 26in
Boiler Class	Own/Standard 3
Dates Withdrawn	1929-1936

These were the last 0-6-2Ts bought by the Cardiff railway. They were rather larger and more powerful than their predecessors, but still retained the long sloping tanks. With the exception of tanks and bunker they were very similar to the Taff Vale O4 class. At one stage the GWR planned to rebuild all three with Standard 3 boilers, but in the end only one was given the treatment. This locomotive survived to British Railways and lasted until 1953. The other two were withdrawn in 1930 and 1934 respectively, and one of these was sold to a colliery and worked on until 1960.

Port Talbot Railway, Neath and Brecon Railway, Rhonnda and Swansea Bay Railway

The Port Talbot and R&SB locomotives were managed by the GWR from before the First World War, but were treated as separate locomotive studs.

Port Talbot Stephenson's 0-6-2T.

Builders	R Stephenson & Co
Dates Built	1897/8
Number Built	11
Route Colour	Yellow
Power Class	C
Tractive Effort	21,000lbs
Driving Wheel Size	4ft 6in
Cylinder Dimensions	18in x 26in
Boiler Class	Own/Standard 10
Dates Withdrawn	1928-1948

Five of these were supplied in 1897, and a further six in 1898. Within a very few years, the line had bought some powerful 0-8-2 tanks and four of the 0-6-2Ts were sold off, two to the Rhondda & Swansea Bay, and two to the Neath and Brecon.

At the grouping, the R&SB locomotives were numbered 180 and 182, and the PTR engines were numbered 183-9. The N&B locos were numbered 1327 & 1371.

The R&SBs were never significantly altered and were withdrawn in 1928/9. Three of the PTR engines went, unmodified, in 1929/30. Two more, 186/7, with GWR bunkers added, were withdrawn in 1934/5. 1371, 184 and 188 were rebuilt with Standard 10 boilers and GWR cabs. 1327 & 1371 were withdrawn in Oct 1929. 184 & 188 lasted until 1947/8.

Neath and Brecon Modified Rhymney M class

Builders	R Stephenson & Co
Dates Built	1909/10, 1913
Number Built	3
Route Colour	Blue
Power Class	C
Tractive Effort	23,000lbs

Driving Wheel Size	4ft 6in
Cylinder Dimensions	18½in x 26in
Dates Withdrawn	1929/30

The N&B purchased three of these from Stephenson's in 1904. As on the RR the original boilers were unsatisfactory, and were altered. They were numbered 1114, 1117 and 1277. They were withdrawn in 1929/30 after boiler repairs under GWR auspices, but it seems curious that they were not given Standard 2 boilers like their sisters.

Rhondda & Swansea Bay Railway Kitson 0-6-2Ts

Builders	Kitson & Co
Dates Built	1886
Number Built	1
Route Colour	Yellow
Power Class	B
Driving Wheel Size	4ft 6in
Cylinder Dimensions	17½in x 24in
Dates Withdrawn	1929

One odd engine, very similar to a Taff Vale M class, was purchased in 1886. It was numbered 181 at the grouping and scrapped in 1929.

Builders	Kitson & Co
Dates Built	1889-1895, 1899
Number Built	12
Route Colour	Yellow
Power Class	C
Tractive Effort	20,000-22,000lbs
Driving Wheel Size	4ft 6in
Cylinder Dimensions	18in x 26in
Dates Withdrawn	1926-1936

The R&SB bought these rather larger Kitson 0-6-2Ts between 1889 and 1899. The GWR numbered them 168-179 at the grouping, by which time they had GWR built boilers, but not one of the standard types. They received bunker extensions, but few other changes until they were withdrawn.

Builders	Kitson & Co
Dates Built	1902, 1904
Number Built	4
Route Colour	Blue
Power Class	B
Tractive Effort	22,500lbs
Driving Wheel Size	4ft 9in
Cylinder Dimensions	19in x 26in
Dates Withdrawn	1927-1936

The last of the Kitson 0-6-2Ts came in 1902 and 1904: two each year. These were rather bigger than their predecessors. They were numbered 164-167 when absorbed. There was a proposal to fit Standard 5 boilers, but it was not implemented and they were withdrawn in 1927-1936.

Rhymney Railway
K class 0-6-2ST

Builders	Vulcan Foundry, Sharp, Stewart & Co Hudswell, Clarke & Co, Neilson, Reid & Co
Dates Built	1090-1900
Number Built	47 (46 to GWR)
Route Colour	Blue
Power Class	A
Tractive Effort	17,000lbs
Driving Wheel Size	4ft 7in
Cylinder Dimensions	17½in x 24in
Dates Withdrawn	1925-1934

This was a substantial class of forty-seven locomotives, built in seven batches by the Vulcan Foundry (1890, 1891) Sharp Stewart (1894, 1897), Hudswell Clarke (1899, 1900) and Neilson Reid (1900). 46 (one having been destroyed in a boiler explosion) passed to the GWR.

In most respects, they were similar to the RR J class 0-6-0ST with much the same style of outside frames, but they had a good sized coal bunker and a trailing wheel to carry the weight. As with the J class, there was a plan to give them Standard Goods boilers and pannier tanks, but in the end they kept their own boilers. There was some rebuilding: seven received revised boilers and pannier tanks, (perhaps the only 0-6-2PT) but not necessarily at the same time or in that order. Withdrawals had started in 1925 and many of the unconverted locomotives went in 1927 and 1928. The last unconverted K class went in 1929, whilst the pannier tanks went in 1932 and 1934, scrapping for at least one being postponed by a spell as Swindon Works shunter.

L1 class 0-6-2ST

Builders	Vulcan Foundry, rebuilt RR
Dates Built	1890 rebuilt as 0-6-2T 1908-11
Number Built	2 (conversions)
Route Colour	Blue
Power Class	A
Tractive Effort	15,500lbs
Driving Wheel Size	5ft 0in
Cylinder Dimensions	17½in x 24in
Dates Withdrawn	1922/3

The L1 class were built as L class 2-4-2 saddle tanks with double frames. By GWR days these two had been converted to 0-6-2T, given new design boilers, and called class L1. The rebuilds presented an odd appearance, since the 2-4-2s had a small rise in the footplate over each crank on the drivers, but this was not repeated over the new leading driving wheel. The 0-6-2s, allocated diagram J, were scrapped in 1922 and 1923, and never carried their allocated GWR numbers, 1324 and 1325.

M class and R class 0-6-2T

Builders	R. Stephenson & Co, Hudswell, Clark & Co, Beyer, Peacock & Co
Dates Built	1904-1921
Number Built	6, 15
Route Colour	Red/Blue (M Class with Standard 2 boiler)
Power Class	D
Tractive Effort	24,500lbs
Driving Wheel Size	4ft 6in
Cylinder Dimensions	18.5in x 26in

Boiler Class	Own/Standard 2
Dates Withdrawn	1935-1957

The M class, a much more modern design than their predecessors, were a class of 6 built by Stephenson's in 1904. Their 7ft 3in + 8ft 0in + 6ft 0in wheelbase was repeated on all subsequent Rhymney Railway 0-6-2s, some very similar classes built for other lines and even the GWR's own 5600 class. The original boilers were considered unsatisfactory, and by the grouping all were running boilers of the design used by the R class.

Stephenson's built the first three locomotives of the R class in 1907. Although based on the design of the Ms, they had quite different boilers and cylinders. Two more followed in 1909. In 1921, another ten, slightly different in detail, were added to the R class, four from Hudswell Clark and six Beyer Peacock.

At the absorption, the GWR tended to treat them all as one class, albeit with subclasses represented with different diagrams. They were numbered 30-44 and 47-51, with 33 and 47-51 being the M class.

The Ms received R class cylinders in the 1930s. One was rebuilt with a Standard 2 boiler and GWR style cab, but otherwise they had few changes beyond safety valves and larger bunkers. Two Ms were withdrawn in the 1930s, but the rest survived the war, three getting to British Railways and the last going in 1951.

Five of the Rs eventually received Standard 2 boilers, the last actually under British Railways ownership. The rest kept Rhymney boilers to the end. All the class reached British Railways and they were withdrawn between 1949 and 1957, and were the last Welsh class in main line service. None have survived.

P, P1 & AP classes 0-6-2Ts

Builders	R Stephenson & Co, Hudswell, Clarke & Co
Dates Built	1909, 1917, 1921
Number Built	3 P Class (2 to GWR), 1 P1 (2 to GWR), 4 AP class
Route Colour	Blue/Red
Power Class	B/C
Tractive Effort	21,000-22,000lbs
Driving Wheel Size	5ft 0in
Cylinder Dimensions	18½in x 26in
Boiler Class	Own/Standard 10
Dates Withdrawn	1950-1953

Like the R and M classes, these were closely related classes that the GWR treated as a single class. They were intended as passenger locomotives, and had larger driving wheels. In other respects, notably wheelbase, they were similar to their cousins.

Three P class were delivered by Stephenson's in 1909. One more, classified P1, followed in 1917, from Hudswell Clarke. One of the earlier locomotives was altered to P1 specification, which included a Hudswell Clarke-built boiler.

Four more locos, classified AP, were built by Hudswell Clarke and delivered in 1921. They were a little longer than their predecessors and carried a little more coal and water.

At the grouping they were renumbered 76-83, 76/7 being the remaining P class, 78-81 being the AP class locomotives and 82/3 the P1s. The entire class received Standard 10 boilers, but the work was spread out between 1926 and 1949. There were also suspension changes. One was withdrawn in 1950, the rest going between 1953 and 1955.

A and A1 class 0-6-2Ts

Builders	R Stephenson & Co, Hudswell, Clarke & Co
Dates Built	1910-1918
Number Built	A Class 16 (10 to GWR), A1 Class 8 (14 to GWR)
Route Colour	Red
Power Class	C
Tractive Effort	24,000lbs
Driving Wheel Size	4ft 4½in
Cylinder Dimensions	18in x 26in
Boiler Class	Own/Standard 10
Dates Withdrawn	1948-1955

The A class could be considered an enlarged S class 0-6-0T, but then the S class could be considered a smaller R class 0-6-2T. They had 4ft 4½in driving wheels like the S class, the Rs having 4ft 6in. Stephenson's delivered 10 Rs in 1910, and Hudswell Clarke 6 more in 1911. The A1s were essentially the same as the As except for having Belpaire fireboxes. Three came from Hudswell Clarke in 1914, two more in 1916, and three from Stephenson's in 1918.

Several of the A class were given A1 boilers, which put them in the A1 class. By the time of the grouping the A class was reduced to ten and the A1 class increased to fourteen. They were allocated numbers 52-75. The sub class complications continued under the GWR and some A1s received

A boilers and vice versa as boiler swaps occurred. From 1929 standard 10 boilers were introduced and these were fitted to about half the class. GWR bunkers appeared on most, and GWR cabs on some. Withdrawals started in 1948 with some of the earlier locomotives, and the majority went between 1953 and 1955.

Taff Vale Railway
Taff Vale M1 class 0-6-2T

Builders	Kitson & Co, TVR/Cardiff
Dates Built	1884-1892
Route Colour	Yellow
Number Built	41
Power Class	A
Tractive Effort	17,500-18,500lbs
Driving Wheel Size	4ft 6½in
Cylinder Dimensions	17½in x 26in
Boiler Class	Own/Standard 11
Dates Withdrawn	1925-1934

These were (just) the first of the Welsh 0-6-2T classes and were used as mixed traffic locomotives. Forty-one were built between 1884 and 1892, almost all by Kitsons. They became the M1 class as a result of a rebuild with new design boilers around the turn of the century. The Taff Vale were considering scrapping the earliest ones at the time of the grouping. Numbers allocated by the GWR were between 442 and 586.

Fifteen were scrapped in 1925, but 8 were given a significant rebuild. The other seventeen unrebuilt locomotives went by 1930. The rebuilds included a Standard 11 boiler, GWR tanks and bunker and the GWR design of autofitting. These lasted until 1932/4, when they were replaced by the new 6400 class.

Taff Vale N class 0-6-2T

Builders	Kitson & Co
Dates Built	1891
Number Built	10
Route Colour	Yellow
Power Class	A
Tractive Effort	17,500-18,500lbs

Driving Wheel Size	4ft 6½in
Cylinder Dimensions	17½in x 26in
Dates Withdrawn	1928-34

A class of ten built by Kitsons in 1891. They were essentially similar to the M class, but with larger boilers. They were mainly used for mineral traffic and shunting, although the Taff Vale had autofitted one. The GWR gave them numbers between 485 and 502. The majority were withdrawn from 1928-30, but one, fitted with cable gear for work on the Pwllyrhebog incline, survived until 1934.

Taff Vale O class 0-6-2T

Builders	TVR/Cardiff
Dates Built	1894/5
Number Built	6
Route Colour	Yellow
Power Class	A
Driving Wheel Size	4ft 6in
Cylinder Dimensions	17½in x 26in
Dates Withdrawn	1925-30

This class of six was built by the Taff Vale, and was very similar to the N class. They were mainly used on goods and shunting work. On absorption, they were numbered 446-448, 452, 453 and 581. 581 was so removed in the sequence from the others because it was operating at reduced boiler pressure. Apart from the fitting of GWR safety valves they were little altered and all had been withdrawn by 1930. Two were sold into industrial use, one lasting until the 1950s and the other the 1960s.

Taff Vale O1 class 0-6-2T.

Builders	Kitson & Co, TVR/Cardiff
Dates Built	1894, 1897
Number Built	22
Route Colour	Yellow
Power Class	A
Driving Wheel Size	4ft 6in

Cylinder Dimensions	17½in x 26in
Dates Withdrawn	1925-1931

Fourteen were built by Kitsons and eight by the Taff Vale, virtually the last locomotives to be built by the TVR. They were almost identical to the O class, but had a longer front overhang and so were slightly heavier. They were mainly used on coal traffic with some relief or weekend passenger work.

They were numbered between 449 and 480. All were withdrawn between 1925 and 1928 except for one, which lasted until 1931. One of the TV-built locomotives was sold to the Longmoor Military Railway where it worked until 1947, when it was sold to a Welsh colliery. In 1960, it became redundant and was eventually preserved. Taff Vale 28, ex GWR 450, is therefore the last South Wales built 0-6-2T left, is now part of the National Collection, and has run in preservation.

Taff Vale U/U1 class 0-6-2T

Builders	Vulcan Foundry
Dates Built	1895/6
Number Built	8, 7
Route Colour	Blue
Power Class	A
Tractive Effort	16,000-19,000lbs
Driving Wheel Size	5ft 3in
Cylinder Dimensions	17½in x 26in
Boiler Class	Own/Standard 10
Dates Withdrawn	1927-1931

The U and U1 classes were intended for passenger work, and had larger driving wheels than the pure freight classes. They were built by the Vulcan Foundry in 1895 and 1896 respectively. The only significant difference between the two was the size of the trailing wheels. By the time of the grouping they had been relegated to coal traffic. The GWR numbered them between 587 and 603.

One U and one U1 were given significant rebuilds by the GWR with a Standard 10 boiler and GWR style tanks, cab and bunker. The others were withdrawn by 1930, and the rebuilt locomotives followed in 1931. One was sold into industrial use, and lasted until 1954.

Taff Vale O2 class 0-6-2T

Builders	Neilson, Reid and Co
Dates Built	1899
Number Built	9
Route Colour	Blue
Power Class	B
Tractive Effort	20,000lbs
Driving Wheel Size	4ft 6½in
Cylinder Dimensions	17½in x 26in
Dates Withdrawn	1926-1928

The nine O2s were very similar to the O and O1, with one or two features from the U1 class, notably the trailing wheel diameter. They were built by Neilson, Reid and Co in 1899/1900.

On joining the GWR they were numbered from 412 to 4266. They received little attention from the GWR other than new safety valves and all were withdrawn by 1928, made redundant by the new 56xx. One was sold into industrial use, and remained with a colliery at Philadelphia, County Durham until the 1960s. This one, ex Taff Vale 85, was preserved and has run in preservation.

Taff Vale O3 class 0-6-2T

Builders	Kitson & Co, Hudswell, Clarke & Co, Vulcan Foundry
Dates Built	1902, 1904, 1905
Number Built	15
Route Colour	Blue
Power Class	B
Tractive Effort	20,000lbs
Driving Wheel Size	4ft 6½in
Cylinder Dimensions	17½in x 26in
Dates Withdrawn	1928-34, 1948

There were fifteen of these, with batches built by three manufacturers, Kitsons (1902), Hudswell Clarke (1904) and the Vulcan Foundry (1905). They were substantially similar to their predecessors but had different motion arrangements and larger cabs and fireboxes. As with their close cousins they were built as mixed traffic locomotives.

The GWR numbered them between 410 and 437. They received a little more attention from the GWR than their predecessors – quite a few were fitted with GWR bunkers and two received GWR tanks, cabs and bunkers. In some cases, the cabs were shortened to give a larger bunker. Although the majority were withdrawn between 1928 and 1934, two of them survived longer – until early 1948 – so just coming into British Railways ownership. Surprisingly, although put up for sale, none was sold into industrial use and none survive.

Taff Vale O4 class 0-6-2T

Builders	Manning, Wardle & Co, Beyer, Peacock & Co, Vulcan Foundry
Dates Built	1907-1910
Number Built	41
Route Colour	Red/Blue
Power Class	C
Tractive Effort	22,000lbs
Driving Wheel Size	4ft 6½in
Cylinder Dimensions	17½in x 26in
Boiler Class	Own/Standard 3
Dates Withdrawn	1948-1955

There were no less than forty-one of these, also intended for mixed traffic. They were divided in two groups, the later group with a longer rear overhang and larger cab than the earlier ones. Other differences from the earlier O classes were a wheelbase, a longer boiler and a slightly raised round top firebox. The first group comprised seven engines from Manning Wardle in 1907 and fourteen from Beyer Peacock in 1908. The second group, delivered in 1910, consisted of ten from Beyer Peacock and ten from the Vulcan Foundry.

Unlike their predecessors, the O4s had a substantial life with the GWR. They were numbered between 236 and 420. Nearly all were rebuilt with Standard 3 boilers to diagram A26, starting in 1924 and the last as late as 1946. The cabs were shortened, in most cases twice, in order to make room for larger coal bunkers.

In the 1946 renumbering, the eighteen of the class with numbers above 300 were renumbered 200-211, 215-220. They all survived to British Railways, although scrapping started in 1948, those few without Standard 3 boilers being amongst the earliest – some indeed so soon that they never got to carry the new numbers allocated in 1946. A handful survived in service until 1955 and one, albeit as a stationary boiler, until 1958. After official withdrawal, at least one served a term as a Swindon works shutter. None have been preserved.

Taff Vale A class 0-6-2T

Builders	Hawthorn Leslie & Co, North British Locomotive Co, Vulcan Foundry, Nasmyth Wilson & Co
Dates Built	1915-1921
Number Built	58
Route Colour	Red
Power Class	C
Tractive Effort	19,000-21,000lbs
Driving Wheel Size	5ft 3in
Cylinder Dimensions	18½in x 26in
Boiler Class	Own/Standard 10
Dates Withdrawn	1953-1957

These were the last and largest class of Taff Vale 0-6-2Ts. They were significantly different from their predecessors with a new style boiler, which had a Belpaire firebox. They were intended as passenger engines and had the 5ft 3in wheels of the passenger U class and the longer wheelbase of the O4 class. The design was completed in 1912, with orders placed with a number of builders – one was Hannoversche Maschinenbau-Action-Gesellschaft, and for obvious reasons this order was cancelled in 1914. Deliveries were from Hawthorn Leslie in 1914, North British in 1915, Vulcan Foundry in 1916, Nasmyth Wilson in 1919, Hawthorn Leslie in 1920/1 and Vulcan Foundry in 1921 resulting in a class of fifty-eight.

In Taff Vale condition, they were given diagram A4. The numbers allocated were between 335 and 441. Such a large class of new locomotives were always going to be retained by the GWR, but they seemed to take some time to decide exactly what to do with them. A number had major repairs with outside companies.

A few received larger GWR style bunkers in 1923 and one was more extensively rebuilt with a Standard 10 boiler. Between 1926 and 1932 all the rest were rebuilt with Standard 10 boilers. A majority received GWR tanks with the rebuilds, but most retained the original cabs. A few years later, the cabs were shortened by a few inches to increase the bunker size. Further modifications by the GWR included reducing the cylinder size to 17½in with a concurrent increase in boiler pressure to 200psi.

Ten were renumbered in the 1946 scheme, those between 401 and 441 becoming 303-309, 312, 316 and 322. All survived to British Railways, but from 1953 they were withdrawn from passenger services and at the same time scrapping started. The last were withdrawn from revenue service by September 1957, although a few stayed on a bit longer as Swindon works shunters and one was in use as a stationary boiler until 1959. None have been preserved.

CHAPTER 8

Ten Wheeled Tank Engines

Boilers

Excluding the 2ft gauge VOR locomotives and absorbed classes, the GWR-built 2-6-2T and 4-4-2T classes used only Standard 2, 4 and 5 boilers. However, there were still a lot of variations and some thirty boiler variations are recorded by RCTS. The leading dimensions of the major classes were approximately as follows.

Class	Name	Barrel length	Barrel diameter	Firebox Length
B	Standard 2	11ft 0in	5ft 0in tapering to 4ft 5in	7ft 0in
D	Standard 4	11ft 0in	5ft 6in tapering to 4ft 11in	7ft 0in
E	Standard 5	10ft 6in	4ft 9in tapering to 4ft 2in	5ft 0in

4 Coupled Classes
GWR classes
2221 (County Tank) class.

Builders	GWR Swindon
Dates Built	1905-1912
Number Built	30
Route Colour	Red
Power Class	C
Tractive Effort	20,000-20,500lbs
Driving Wheel Size	6ft 8½in
Cylinder Dimensions	18in x 30in
Wheelbase	7ft 0in + 8ft 6in + 8ft 6in + 8ft 0in
Front Overhang	2ft 6in

Rear Overhang	3ft 2in
Boiler Class	Standard 2
Dates Withdrawn	1931-1935

Roughly speaking a 4-4-2T version of the large prairie tanks with a Standard 2 boiler. They had the full express sized 6ft 8½in wheels, the same as the Saints and Stars, the largest ever used on tank engines on the GWR narrow gauge – maybe even on any standard gauge tank engines, at least in the twentieth century.

The rear of the bunker was essentially vertical and the bunker contained a water tank. Like several of the larger tank engine classes, they started life with bi-directional water pickup apparatus.

The first of the class differed from all the others in having the cab sides flush with the tanks. The rest all had the cab narrower than the tanks and bunker, a feature common enough on older classes, but the only other example of a Churchward standard tank built like that was No. 99, the first large prairie. The first two batches, 2221-30 in 1905/6 and 2231-40 in 1908/9 were unsuperheated and had straight front end framing. The last lot, 2241-50 in 1912, had curved frames, top feed and were superheated right from the start.

Curiously these engines were not renumbered in 1912, but left in a Dean series sharing the 22xx range with a small class of 2-4-0 tender engines.

A single engine was built with the larger Standard 4 boiler. This was found to be too heavy and it was removed within a year. The two lots of unsuperheated locos were superheated between 1912 and 1914 and gained top feed about the same time. They also gained extended smokeboxes. This brought them to largely the same specification as the final batch. There were two changes to bunkers – first a fender was added as an upward extension to the centre

2221 (County Tank) class. *Diagram A. The first batch of the class as built with short smokebox and no superheater.*

of the bunker around 1920, then the usual bunker extensions were added in 1922/26. The fender later gained a recess to house the upper lamp. There were the usual variations in superheating arrangements.

They were all withdrawn between 1931 and 1934, at the same time that the large wheeled 4-4-0s came out of service. They were replaced by large prairies.

4600

Builders	GWR Swindon
Dates Built	1913
Number Built	1
Route Colour	Blue
Power Class	A
Tractive Effort	17,000lbs
Driving Wheel Size	5ft 8in
Cylinder Dimensions	17in x 24in
Boiler Class	Standard 5
Dates Withdrawn	1925

This was a 4-4-2 version of the 44/4500 2-6-2 tanks, intended for faster work on lighter grades. It had the same boiler and cylinders as the 4500s. Only one, no 4600 was built.

4600 had the bogie moved forward in 1915 to improve weight distribution and was superheated in 1918. With the 4500s proving well capable of reaching 60 mph in service there must have been no point in repeating the design, and the locomotive was withdrawn in 1925.

4600. *The sole representative of a small 4-4-2T class.*

Absorbed Classes at the Grouping
Taff Vale Railway
C class 4-4-2T.

Builders	Vulcan Foundry
Dates Built	1888/91
Number Built	6
Route Colour	Yellow
Power Class	A
Tractive Effort	16,000-17,000lbs
Driving Wheel Size	5ft 3in
Cylinder Dimensions	17½in x 26in
Boiler Class	Own
Dates Withdrawn	1925/6

A class of six, built in 1888 and 1891 for passenger work by the Vulcan Foundry. By the time of the grouping, they were auto-fitted with the Taff Vale system. They were given diagram H and numbered 1301-6. They were withdrawn in 1925/26 when the Taff Vale coaches were converted to the GWR autotrain system.

6100 class *6106 out of service in the shed at Didcot Railway Centre. (Photo: Jim Champ)*

Six Coupled Classes
GWR classes
Odd men out – the 3901 class

Builder	GWR/Swindon
Dates Rebuilt	1907/10
Number Built	20
Route Colour	Blue
Power Class	A, B
Tractive Effort	16,500-21,000lbs
Driving Wheel Size	5ft 2in
Cylinder Dimensions	17½in x 24in
Wheelbase	7ft 0in + 7ft 0in + 7ft 0in + 7ft 0in
Front Overhang	2ft 9in
Rear Overhang	2ft 9in
Boiler Class	Standard 5
Dates Withdrawn	1930-34

In the early 1900s additional powerful tank engines were urgently needed for the Birmingham suburban traffic. There were bottlenecks in the works, notably with machine shop capacity and there were plenty of 0-6-0 tender engines available. In the best style of major GWR rebuilds, an entire batch of Dean Goods were withdrawn to provide components for a new class. The conversion was dramatic. The wheels, cylinders and motion components were retained, but other major components were discarded. The new engines had a Standard 5 (44/45xx boiler) and new frames, cabs and tanks. They were built from 1907-10 in pairs as the donor engines came into the works for overhaul, so at the same time as the earlier lots of 4500s but after the

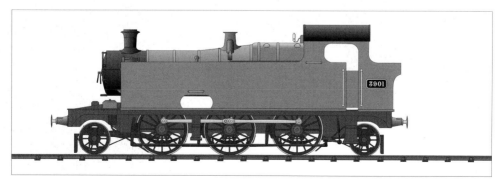

3901 class. *Diagram A8. Towards the end of their lives with top feed and superheating.*

4400s. In most respects, they were roughly intermediate in size between the small and large prairies.

They received superheating between 1914 and 1917, with a slight lengthening of the smokebox, and most, if not all, received enlarged coal bunkers in the 1920s. There were also variations in boiler tube arrangement and pressure, the boilers having been built at 200psi, but later changed to 165 or 180 psi.

Large prairies replaced them on the Birmingham traffic in 1929, and were all withdrawn between 1930 and 1934. There were three diagrams, concerned with superheating variations.

Small Prairies
4400 (ex 3101) class

Builder	GWR/Swindon/Wolverhampton
Dates Built	1904-1906
Number Built	11
Route Colour	Uncoloured
Power Class	B,C
Tractive Effort	18,500 – 21,500lbs
Driving Wheel Size	4ft 1½in
Cylinder Dimensions	16½/17in x 24in
Wheelbase	8ft 0in + 6ft 0in + 5ft 6in + 7ft 0in.
Front Overhang	2ft 3¾in
Rear Overhang	3ft 2¾in (later 3ft 11¾in)
Boiler Class	Standard 5
Dates Withdrawn	1949, 1951-1955

One of the earliest Churchward standard engines was 115, built in 1904, which had 16½in x 24in cylinders and 4ft 1½in driving wheels. This was the size used on the small Wolverhampton 0-6-0Ts, the 850s and 2021s, and indeed the production batch of ten – the first of the standard classes to be ordered, were constructed at Wolverhampton from 1905-6. The leading and trailing wheels were both on pony trucks, unlike their bigger sisters, which had radial rear axles.

The ten production engines were numbered 3101- 3110. As built they were unsuperheated and had a short smokebox and a small bunker, no higher than the side tanks. The tanks were level topped and of 1,000 gallons capacity. They had square front framing and no struts from the smokebox. There was only a very shallow rise from the buffer beam to the main footplate height.

4400 class. *Diagram C. This was the configuration when the class was built.*

4400 class. *Diagram A4. This was the final condition, superheated and with a rather larger bunker,*

As with other early standard classes the cylinder centre line was offset above the centreline of the wheels.

In the 1912 renumbering, 115 was renumbered 4400, and the rest followed on to 4410.

The first change was an increase in the height of the bunker for more coal capacity, usually with bracing struts added at the front end. They started to acquire a slightly (6in) extended smokebox a little later, but superheating followed soon after. Most acquired both at the same time, between 1915 and 1927, and all but three were done between Dec 1920 and Dec 1924. With superheating came an increase from 165psi to 180psi boiler pressure.

From 1924, they received new and rather bigger bunkers, with a 9in extension at the back. This extension was done with a fabricated extension to the drag box. The last change to the bunker area was a recess to protect the upper lamp position, but probably not all received this. Cab shutters were fitted to all the class between 1934 and 1936.

Five acquired new cylinders with outside steam pipes, between 1932 and 1948. At least some of these were 17in diameter, which took the locomotives to power class C. In all but one case they received a new curved frame front end at the same time as the cylinders.

There were three diagrams: as built, superheated with the taller bunker and superheated with the rearward bunker extension.

They all survived to British Railways, but withdrawals started from 1949, when 4402 was damaged in an accident, and then from 1951. The last two went in 1955. None were preserved, which is a pity for they would have been ideal locomotives for 25mph limited preserved lines.

4500 (ex 2161) class

Builder	GWR/Wolverhampton/Swindon
Dates Built	1906-1924
Number Built	75
Route Colour	Yellow
Power Class	C
Tractive Effort	19,000-21,000lbs
Driving Wheel Size	4ft 7½in
Cylinder Dimensions	17in x 24in
Wheelbase	8ft 4in + 5ft 6in + 6ft 0in + 7ft 0in.
Front Overhang	2ft 5¾in
Rear Overhang	2ft 9¾in (later 3ft 6¾)
Boiler Class	Standard 5
Dates Withdrawn	1950-1964

These were very similar to the 4400s, but with larger driving wheels, larger cylinders, and an adjusted wheelbase and thus weight distribution. The larger wheels were successfully intended to give them a greater speed capability – many sources claim they frequently reached 60mph in normal service. The first twenty were built at Wolverhampton, but were the last locomotives to be built there, the works there being really too cramped for building the larger locomotives of the twentieth century.

The result of the changed wheelbase was that the leading and trailing driving wheels were effectively moved back six inches relative to the boiler and cylinders. The leading pony truck was two inches further back relative to the cylinders, and the front overhang two inches longer so the net result was the buffer beam was the same distance from the boiler and cylinders on both classes. At the rear the trailing pony truck had moved back six inches, and the rear of the locomotive had been lengthened by one inch.

4500 class. *Diagram D. The early locomotives as built with small bunker, straight frames and no front end struts.*

4500 class. *Diagram A2. This was the last diagram for the 4500s.*

As with the 4400s, they retained the offset between cylinder and wheel centres for all their lives. The earlier batches of 4500s were significantly different to the later ones, but they tended to be updated over time and received the later features.

2161 to 2180 were built at Wolverhampton 1906 to 1908. Like the 44s, they were built with 165 psi boilers, short smokeboxes, straight frames, small bunkers level with the tanks and no struts at the front end.

2181-90 followed at Swindon in 1909/10. They were built with the intermediate sized (taller) bunker, longer smokeboxes and with the front end struts. They also had slightly different boilers pressed to 200psi.

The next lot were 4530-4539, built in 1913 after the renumbering with curved front end framing but without superheaters. 4540-4554 followed in 1914/15 and were superheated and had top feed from new.

4555 – 4574 followed in 1924 and therefore under the Collett regime. These had outside steam pipes, curved drop ends and a 3ft 6¾ rear overhang from new.

2161-2190 were renumbered 4500-4529 in the 1912 renumbering.

The early 4500s received modifications as listed for the 4400s. Superheating started from 1913, but was not complete until 1926. The earlier engines received the 9in rear extension and the full size bunkers from about 1924. Like the 4400s, this was a fabricated extension, and modellers should note that this came in two arrangements, so there were at least three variations of the framing under the bunker on 4500s with the full size bunker.

New cylinders with outside steam pipes started to be fitted from the earlier engines from 1929 and continued to be fitted as late as the 1950s, but a fair number never received them. Usually curved front end framing was fitted at the same time, but some retained the straight frames to the end of their lives. All combinations of inside and outside steam pipes and straight and curved frames were visible on the class until withdrawal. Cab shutters were fitted en masse from 1931 to about 1937, the majority also receiving the bunker recess for the upper rear lamp at this time.

There were four diagrams for the 4500s, one showing the first forty as built while the other three covered configurations with top feed, extended bunker and superheater (or lack of) variations.

The early lots started to go from 1950 and were withdrawn fairly steadily through that decade. Only a few of the 1915 or earlier locomotives were still in service in 1960 and none of them have survived. On the other hand, none of the 1924 batch were withdrawn until 1958 and most were withdrawn in the early 1960s. Three have survived, and they have all run in preservation.

4575 class

Builder	GWR/Swindon
Dates Built	1927-1929
Number Built	100
Route Colour	Yellow
Power Class	C
Tractive Effort	21,000lbs
Driving Wheel Size	4ft 7½in
Cylinder Dimensions	17in x 24in
Wheelbase	8ft 4in-5ft 6in-6ft 0in-7ft 0in.
Front Overhang	2ft 5¾in
Rear Overhang	3ft 6¾in
Boiler Class	Standard 5
Dates Withdrawn	1957-1964

The 4575s, based on the 4500 class, were built in four lots from 1927 to 1929. They were a significant upgrade as the new engines had appreciably larger sloping topped tanks, holding 1,300 gallons of water. Like most Collett (and the later Churchward) classes they had the later style small flanged motion brackets rather than the larger ones of earlier designs. Other than those changes, they were the same as the 4555 series, so had outside steam pipes, curved ends and the longer rear overhang from new.

These were, as noted, built with most of the updates that the earlier 4500s received during their lives. Like the 4500s they received cab shutters and lamp recesses in the 1930s. In 1953, an improved timetable in the Cardiff valleys saw fifteen 4575s given auto gear to take push pull passenger services.

Only a single diagram was ever released for the 4575s.

The 4575s started to go from 1957, with a fair number scrapped in 1958 when the Cardiff Valley services went to DMUs. The rest went steadily during the 1960s, the last being withdrawn at the end of 1964. Eleven avoided scrapping in the 1960s, but only eight have run in preservation. Of the others, as of 2012 one is under active restoration, one has been reduced to spare parts and one is still in scrapyard condition.

4575 class. *Diagram A5. This was the only diagram for the 4575 series.*

Large Prairies

The large prairie classes comprised a confusing group of closely related designs, made even more complicated by renumbering and locomotives built out of numerical sequence. They divide into Standard 2 and Standard 4 boiler variants, with a subdivision into 200psi and 225psi boilers. In the Collett era, there were also variations in wheel size, which are reckoned to have been as much for the accountants' benefit as anything else.

The specific meaning of renewal for the railway company is discussed in the introduction. By the late 1930s the early large prairies of the 5100 (ex 3100) and 3150 classes were thirty years old, and getting towards the mileage where new cylinders and front end extension frames were going to be required. Cook and Collett wanted to use renewal fund money for this work rather than book it against revenue. Using the renewal fund would mean the repaired locomotives would be classified as renewed, and they decided this would not be permissible. What Collett elected to do was to design new variations of the classes with significantly increased power; the intention being to use them for roles where the increased power would be valuable. So, a new version of the Standard 2 boiler was designed, uprated to 225 psi, but with no increase in weight due to the use of high tensile nickel alloy steel for use on the 5100 type. 225 psi Standard 4 boilers, but without the use of nickel steel, were constructed for the larger boiler variation. Smaller, non-standard wheels of two different sizes were used to further increase tractive effort. The result was the new 3100, 6100 and 8100 classes.

All the large 2-6-2T had spring compensation between the leading pony truck and the leading driving wheels, but they never had compensation between the driving wheels, unlike the Saints and Stars. There was spring compensation between the trailing driving wheels and the rear radial truck on the Churchward large prairies which was absent from Collett-build locos and the major rebuilds. This was retained when the 3111 series had springing arrangements and weight distribution altered in the 1930s and they were renumbered in the 5100 series, even though compensation was removed from 4-6-0s at this time.

3100 (1903) 3111 (1905), 5100 class

Builder	GWR/Swindon
Dates Built	1903, 1905/6
Number Built	40
Route Colour	Red/Blue
Power Class	D
Tractive Effort	24,000lbs
Driving Wheel Size	5ft 8in
Cylinder Dimensions	18in x 30in
Wheelbase	8ft 9in +7ft 0in + 7ft 9in + 8ft 3in.
Front Overhang	2ft 5in
Rear Overhang	3ft 2in
Boiler Class	Standard 2 (200psi)
Dates Withdrawn	1937-9 (rebuilds to 8100), 1947-1959

In 1903, No. 99 was one of Churchward's first three standard prototypes, alongside the 4-6-0 and 2-8-0. No. 99 had quite small and short flat topped side tanks and 1,380 gallons water capacity, some of it in a tank in the bunker. It had a short cone Standard 2 boiler running at 195 psi. Like all the other early

No. 99. *Diagram A. The first large prairie as built.*

3111 class. *Diagram B. This was the first production lot of large prairies.*

5100 (ex 3111) class. *Diagram A7.*

standard locomotives there was a 2½in offset between cylinder centreline and wheel centreline and, unlike the 4-6-0s, this was retained on all classes, even the late Collett rebuilds. There was spring compensation between the leading pony truck and the leading driving wheels and between the trailing driving wheels and the rear radial truck.

3111-3149 were built in three lots in 1905/6. These production engines had long cone Standard 2 boilers and larger and longer tanks with sloping tops for a total of 2,000 gallon water capacity. At least some of the first locomotives were fitted with water pick up apparatus. The brake rigging on at least the earlier locomotives varied. Photographs suggest that no. 99 and at least some of the 3111 were built with the brake pull rods inside the driving wheels, but, by the time they were rebuilt as 5100s, the brake rodding was outside the driving wheels in a discontinuous run. The brake shoes were set very low down on the wheels and frames.

With a little over 18tons on the driving wheels, they were red route engines as built, but well within the limit. Tractive effort was nominally 23,690 when new.

No. 99 was renumbered 3100 in the 1912 renumbering. 3101-3110 were left unused rather than renumber 3111-3149 to 3101-3139. The characteristic front end struts of the 2 cylinder classes were fitted from 1909. The extension frames were especially vulnerable when used for banking. Superheating came from 1910-1915, most by 1912, and several arrangements were tried in the early days. Boilers were uprated to 200psi from about 1912, which increased the nominal TE to 24,300.

Coal bunkers were extended at the top in 1919-22 and rear fenders added at much the same time. This increased the weight, but the addition came mainly on the trailing axle and did not affect route availability. No. 99 received normal sized tanks in 1929.

About 1927, some 31s were run with reduced weight, mainly as a result of limiting tank capacity. The tanks were then altered back to the full capacity and the weight distribution altered for all the class, bringing more weight on the carrying wheels and bringing them within the blue route limit, but reducing the adhesive weight available for acceleration and braking. Diagram T, which gives the weights for before the changes, but with extended bunker etc. shows the weight on each wheel set to be respectively 9 tons 0cwt, 17tons 13cwt, 18tons 4cwt, 18tons 4cwt, 12tons 9 cwt. The revised weights, shown on diagram A7, were 10 tons 5 cwt, 17 tons 5 cwt, 17 tons 2 cwt, 16 tons 18 cwt, 14 tons 0 cwt; 75 tons 10cwt in total. All were renumbered in the 51xx series, keeping the same last two digits, after this change was made, making the class 5100 and 5111-5149. So during the conversion period 31xx had red route and 51xx blue route availability.

Most received lower cab roofs with a shallower radius between 1931 and 1939, but some may have kept the originals until they were scrapped. Sliding shutters for the cab sides were added between 1933 and 1939. They also received some variations on the recessed fender/bunker top theme and one or two received steps on the bunker on the fireman's side after 1943.

Ten, including no. 5100 ex no. 3100 ex no. 99, were converted to 8100 class by the time the war started, but there were no further conversions. Outside steam pipes and curved front ends appeared on some locomotives from 1943 after the conversion programme was abandoned – presumably before then those requiring new cylinders were put on the conversion programme. Although one more was scrapped in 1947 the remainder survived to British Railways, but were withdrawn steadily from 1948 on, the last surviving until 1959.

There were no less than ten diagrams. Three of those were for no. 99, which had diagrams to itself until it became 5100, and two were to do with the weight distribution changes and the 5100 conversion. The rest were all superheating variations.

3150 class

Builder	GWR/Swindon
Dates Built	1906-8
Number Built	41
Route Colour	Red
Power Class	D
Tractive Effort	25,500lbs
Driving Wheel Size	5ft 8in
Cylinder Dimensions	18½in x 30in
Boiler Class	Standard 4 (200psi)
Wheelbase	8ft 9in + 7ft 0in + 7ft 9in + 8ft 3in.
Front Overhang	2ft 5in
Rear Overhang	3ft 2in
Dates Withdrawn	1938-9 (rebuilds to 3100), 1947-1958

3150 class. *Diagram Q. The large boiler variant of the large prairies.*

The 3150s were the second variation on the large prairie theme, having the larger Standard 4 boilers. The 'prototype' 3150 came out in 1906 and was built alongside a batch of the 3100 class. It had 18in x 30in cylinders. Forty production locomotives followed in 1908/9 and had 18½in cylinders. Four were built with water pickup apparatus. They were, of course, quite a bit heavier than the 3111s at 78 tons 16cwt when new (increasing to 81 tons 12cwt later) and theoretically a little more powerful with the larger cylinders giving 25,670 TE.

Like the 3111s, there seem to have been variations in the brake rigging. Photographs of 3170 and 3171, in very early, if not as-built configuration, seem to show them with pull rods outside the leading two pairs of driving wheels and inside the last pair. The brake shoes look to have been set a little higher on the frames than the 3100s, but this sort of change was regularly made in the course of producing batches of locomotives.

They received most of the developments that their Standard 2 boilered sisters received in the same sorts of date ranges. There is no evidence that changes to the weight distribution were considered in the 1930s. The front end struts appeared first on this class about 1907, but later became universal on all the 2 cylinder classes.

Later photographs suggest they were all fitted with the brake rigging inside the wheels, unlike the 3111/5111 series. Outside steam pipes and curved front end frames started to be fitted from 1934; a few had outside steam pipes but retained the straight framed front end.

Five were withdrawn before the war for reconstruction as the new smaller wheeled Collett 3100 class (see below). Scrapping started from 1947; thirty-three lasted to British Railways and the last went in 1958. None survive into preservation.

There were six diagrams. One concerned the water pick up apparatus, but all the other diagrams were superheating variations.

5101 class

Builder	GWR/Swindon
Dates Built	1929-1949
Number Built	140
Route Colour	Blue
Power Class	D
Tractive Effort	24,500lbs
Driving Wheel Size	5ft 8in
Cylinder Dimensions	18in x 30in

Wheelbase	8ft 9in + 7ft 0in + 7ft 9in + 8ft 3in.
Front Overhang	2ft 5in
Rear Overhang	3ft 2in
Boiler Class	Standard 2 (200psi)
Dates Withdrawn	1958-1964

The 5101s were effectively more batches of the original 3100 class, but built with the various design improvements that had been made in the meantime. 5101-10 were built in 1929, filling in the gap in the number sequence of the Churchward 3100 class (now numbered in the 51xx series) followed by 5150-5189 in 1930/31. 5190-5199 and 4100-4139 came between 1934 and 1939 and finally 4140-4179 from 1946 to 1949, the last leaving the works as British Railways locomotives.

The overall weight was 78tons 9cwt, and the tractive effort 24,300. They had similar weight distribution to the altered Churchward engines, but they had no compensation on the radial trailing wheels. This resulted in less weight on those and more on the last set of drivers, but they still came within the blue weight restriction.

They had 200psi Standard 2 boilers, curved front end frames, outside steam pipes, the later style small flanged motion plates and a new cab design with roof and sides integrated. They had prominent external sandboxes under the cab, unlike the Churchward batches. 5190 on were built with sliding cab shutters. The brake rigging was significantly different to the earlier locomotives with the brake shoes set much higher on the frames and the rodding all running inside the driving wheels.

Sliding cab shutters were fitted as new equipment from 5190 on and were fitted to the earlier locomotives from 1933. Bunker steps were added in the 1950s. All survived to (or were built by) British Railways. Withdrawals started in 1956, but the vast majority survived well into the 1960s.

5101 class. *Diagram A9, but shown in post 1952 condition with cab shutters and bunker steps.*

Ten survived into preservation. Of these one has been converted into a 2-6-0 tender engine – a sort of lightweight version of a 43xx with a Standard 2 boiler. Another is being reduced to spares as a donor towards GWS rebuilds of extinct classes. Of the remaining eight, five have or are running in preservation, whilst the others are under restoration to a greater or lesser extent, all with a lot of work left to do.

6100 class

Builder	GWR/Swindon
Dates Built	1931-1935
Number Built	70
Route Colour	Blue
Power Class	D
Tractive Effort	27,000lbs
Driving Wheel Size	5ft 8in (one altered to have 5ft 3in wheels)
Cylinder Dimensions	18in x 30in
Wheelbase	8ft 9in + 7ft 0in + 7ft 9in + 8ft 3in.
Front Overhang	2ft 5in
Rear Overhang	3ft 2in
Boiler Class	Standard 2 (225psi)
Dates Withdrawn	1958-1964

These were effectively a 5101 development, using the nickel steel 225psi version of the Standard 2 boiler but maintaining the standard size wheels. This made for a more powerful locomotive with a tractive effort of 27,340. The intention was faster acceleration. They were intended and used for London suburban services, and were fitted with trip cock apparatus for working over London Transport Lines. Sixty were built between 1931 and 1933, and then another ten in 1935. The overall weight was 78tons 0cwt.

The first ten received sliding cab shutters in the 1930s, the rest having been built with them. 6116 was rebuilt with smaller wheels in 1932, serving as a prototype for the 8100 rebuilds, and retained these for the rest of its life. The only visible change made to the class was steps on the fireman's side of the bunker from 1952-1955.

The first went in 1958, as suburban work started to go to DMUs. The majority lasted until 1964/5, with no less than a dozen withdrawn in December 1965. 6106 survives with the Great Western Society at Didcot and has run in preservation.

6100 class. *Diagram A10. Shown before cab shutters and bunker steps were fitted. There are no obvious external differences between the 5101 and 6100, but this sketch shows the pre-war hand rail arrangement.*

8100 class

Builder	GWR/Swindon
Dates Built	1938/9
Number Built	10
Route Colour	Blue
Power Class	D
Tractive Effort	28,000lbs
Driving Wheel Size	5ft 6in
Cylinder Dimensions	18in x 30in
Wheelbase	8ft 9in + 7ft 0in + 7ft 9in + 8ft 3in.
Front Overhang	2ft 5in
Rear Overhang	3ft 2in
Boiler Class	Standard 2 (225psi)
Dates Withdrawn	1957-1964

This was one of the renewal fund classes. The 8100s were 3111/5100 rebuilt with 225 psi Standard 2 boilers and 5ft 6in wheels. This brought the nominal tractive effort to 28,165, and the weight to 76tons 11cwt, but they were still within the blue route availability limit. They could be regarded as a smaller wheeled version of the 6100s.

At one stage, there was a plan to rebuild all the original 3111s as 8100, and probably 5101-10 too, but the war put an end to it. The first 8100 was turned out in 1938. Withdrawn 5100s were taken into the factory and all good parts were reused. They were given new cylinders, extension frames and new curved frame front ends. RCTS states positively that the main frames were retained,

8100 class. *Diagram A12. This was the final configuration of No 99 at the start of this section.*

but unlike their parents they had no spring compensation on the rear carrying wheels and an external sandbox by the cab steps, so at the least the frames must have been significantly altered.

The concept was that the smaller wheels and increased tractive effort would give increased acceleration for suburban services: as noted a 6100 had been rebuilt with 5ft 3in wheels. 8100, rebuilt in September 1938 and surviving until 1962, was in theory the original no. 99 from 1903, but one may question whether very much of the original had survived two significant rebuilds and all the normal maintenance. It was – nominally at least – the last survivor of the Churchward prototypes.

The only visible change was steps on the fireman's side of the bunker from 1954. The first went in 1957 and the last in 1964. None have survived.

3100 (1938) class

Builder	GWR/Swindon
Dates rebuilt	1938/9
Number Built	5
Route Colour	Red
Power Class	D
Tractive Effort	31,000lbs
Driving Wheel Size	5ft 3in
Cylinder Dimensions	18½in x 30in
Wheelbase	8ft 9in + 7ft 0in + 7ft 9in + 8ft 3in.
Front Overhang	2ft 5in
Rear Overhang	3ft 2in
Boiler Class	Standard 4 (225psi)
Dates Withdrawn	1957-1960

3100 class. *Diagram A13*

The other Collett renewal class, intended to be principally banking locomotives. They were reconstructions of the 3150 class and, in the same way that the 8100s were 3111/5100s upgraded with smaller wheels and a higher pressure boiler, these were upgrades of the 3150s. Withdrawn 3150s were given smaller wheels, new curved frame front ends and new Standard 4 boilers set to 225psi. Thus, they were much the most powerful of the large prairies with a tractive effort of 31,170. They were also the heaviest at over 81 tons. It is believed that the intention was to rebuild the whole 3150 class, but only five had been built/ rebuilt by the time the Second World War interrupted the programme.

There were few modifications in their life. The majority were withdrawn in 1957 and the last in 1960. None have survived.

Vale of Rheidol
7, 8 (GWR VOR class)

Builders	GWR/Swindon
Dates Built	1923
Number Built	2 or 3 (see notes)
Tractive Effort	10,500lbs
Driving Wheel Size	2ft 6in
Cylinder Dimensions	11½in x 17in
Dates Withdrawn	Still in service.

The GWR absorbed the 1ft 11½in gauge Vale of Rheidol line with the Cambrian railway. They built two new engines for the line in 1923 to a very similar design to the line's existing Davies and Metcalfe Locomotives, but with Walschaerts valve gear, using components originally designed for the GWR rail motors. A third was constructed, but considered a reconstruction or possibly a renewal of one of the existing locomotives. These three survived to British

Railways, then survived the end of steam to be the last steam locomotives operated by British Rail – even being repainted in Rail Blue and carrying the double arrow logo. They then survived British Rail to be privatised in 1989 and are still running. Arguably then, with the Snowdon Mountain Railway, these are the only unpreserved operational steam locomotives in Britain.

Absorbed Classes at the Grouping
Alexandra (Newport and South Wales) Docks and Railway
ADR Beyer Peacock 0-6-4Ts

Builders	Beyer, Peacock & Co
Dates Built	1885, purchased ADR 1903
Number Built	3 (see notes)
Route Colour	Red
Power Class	D
Tractive Effort	30,000lbs
Driving Wheel Size	4ft 6in
Cylinder Dimensions	21½in x 26in
Boiler Class	Own
Dates Withdrawn	1923, 1927

These 0-6-4Ts, which had been built by Beyer Peacock in 1885 for the Mersey Railway, had outside frames and 4ft driving wheels and the odd wheel spacing of 7ft 3in + 4ft 10in + 9ft 3 + 5ft rear bogie. They were bought by the ADR in 1903. At the grouping, they were numbered 1334-1346. They had a short life on the GWR, who scrapped two in 1923 and, having tried a reconditioned boiler, the last in 1928.

Alexandra Docks and Railway Co
Beyer Peacock ex Mersey Railway 2-6-2T

Builders	Beyer, Peacock & Co
Dates Built	1887
Number Built	6
Route Colour	Yellow
Power Class	C/D
Tractive Effort	23,000-24,500lbs
Driving Wheel Size	4ft 6in

Cylinder Dimensions	19½in x 26in
Boiler Class	Own/Standard 3
Dates Withdrawn	1929-1932

The Alexandra Dock and Railway had six Beyer Peacock outside cylinder 2-6-2 tanks, bought from the Mersey Railway when it was electrified. They had 4ft 7in driving wheels, inside frames, outside cylinders, inside valve gear and were somewhat intermediate in size between 45xx and 51xx classes. They had partially enclosed cabs with short roofs that did not reach the spectacle plate on the rear bunker. They were numbered 1201, 1204, 1207-9 and 1211. Most went in 1929, including 1204, which had been rebuilt with a Standard 3 boiler and a more weatherproof cab. One survivor made it until 1932.

Kitson 2-6-2T

Builders	Kitson & Co
Dates Built	1892
Number Built	1
Route Colour	Uncoloured
Power Class	D
Tractive Effort	25,000lbs
Driving Wheel Size	4ft 7½in
Cylinder Dimensions	19½in x 26in
Dates Withdrawn	1931

The ADR also acquired a Kitson built 2-6-2T of substantially similar design. This was renumbered 1199 at the grouping and scrapped in 1931.

Hawthorn Leslie 2-6-2T

Builders	Hawthorn, Leslie & Co
Dates Built	1920
Number Built	2
Route Colour	Yellow
Power Class	C
Tractive Effort	23,000lbs
Driving Wheel Size	4ft 7in

Cylinder Dimensions	19in x 26in
Dates Withdrawn	1951,1956

The last two absorbed 2-6-2Ts, also from the ADR, were two Hawthorn Leslie & Co locomotives, again of fairly similar design to the Beyers, but with longer tanks and a proper enclosed cab. Built new for the ADR, they had gone into service in 1920. Numbered 1205 and 1206, they experienced few changes other than GWR safety valves and covers. They survived to British Railways, being scrapped in 1951 and 1956.

Barry Railway
Barry Railway L class 0-6-4T

Builders	Hawthorn, Leslie & Co
Dates Built	1914
Number Built	10
Route Colour	Red
Power Class	D
Tractive Effort	25,000lbs
Driving Wheel Size	4ft 7in
Cylinder Dimensions	18½in x 26in
Boiler Class	Own/Standard 4
Dates Withdrawn	1926

These ten locos, built in 1914, discarded the old Barry standards and were a bigger loco overall with a much bigger boiler and a very large bunker. They were generally considered successful with the exception of a serious and strange flaw. When running forwards the rear coupled wheels had a tendency to switch points as they passed through them, sending the trailing bogie down the other branch. In reverse, they were fine. Naturally this resulted in an immediate derailment, and this was usually coupled with a fracture of a main water distribution pipe. This lost all the water, meaning the fire had to be immediately thrown out.

On absorption, they were numbered 1347-1355 and 1357 and given diagram B. Four were rebuilt in 1922 with Standard 4 boilers, the first Welsh class to receive such a major change. This was allocated diagram C. In 1926, with the loss in traffic resulting from the General Strike, it appears the GWR lost patience with their reluctance to stay on the track and all were scrapped in short order.

Cambrian/Vale of Rheidol
Davies & Metcalfe 2-6-2Ts

Builders	Davies & Metcalfe
Dates Built	1902
Number Built	2
Tractive Effort	10,500lbs
Driving Wheel Size	2ft 6in
Cylinder Dimensions	11.5in x 17in
Dates Withdrawn	1932, Still in service

The VOR locomotive fleet included two 2-6-2T, built in 1902 by Davies and Metcalfe, and rather substantial locomotives by Welsh narrow gauge standards. They had outside frames, outside cylinders and Stephenson valve gear. One of the Davies and Metcalfe locos was reconstructed by the GWR about 1923 to the same specification as the GWR built locomotives, and the other one was considered surplus to requirements and scrapped in 1932. The reconstruction probably included few or no original parts.

8 Coupled Classes

These comprise a surprisingly incestuous and complicated group of sub classes by twentieth century GWR standards, especially when looked at alongside the much simpler history of the 2800 class tender engines. They all had the same boiler type, the Standard 4.

GWR classes

Builder	GWR/Swindon
Dates Built	1910, 1912-1923
Number Built	105
Route Colour	Red
Power Class	E
Tractive Effort	31,500 - 33,000lbs
Driving Wheel Size	4ft 7½in
Cylinder Dimensions	19in x 30in
Wheelbase	8ft 9in+ 7ft + 6ft+7ft
Front Overhang	2ft 6in

Rear Overhang	5ft 5in (later 5ft 11in)
Boiler Class	Standard 4
Dates Withdrawn	1937-1939 (rebuilds to 7200) 1959-1965

RCTS states that originally a straight tank version of a 28xx with a 2-8-2 wheel arrangement was considered, frames extended at the rear for a bunker and a radial axle added, keeping the Standard 1 boiler. This was probably considered too long, and most likely would also have been excessively heavy.

What was eventually built, in 1910, was 4201, a 2-8-0 tank with a very different wheel spacing to that of the 2800s. The connecting rods ran to the second pair of driving wheels, not the third. The boiler used was the Standard 4, without top feed at this date. The standard front end with 18½ inch cylinders was used.

Preserved 5205 5239 *on the Paignton and Dartmouth Railway. It was not, of course, named and lined out when it was a freight locomotive. (Photo: Jim Champ)*

4200 class. *Diagram D. The shorter bunker of the original batch.*

The loco had all the features of the early standards with straight frames, but something a little unusual was a raised cover plate over the cylinders above the line of the footplate, the running plate being a few inches lower than that of the 2800. The bunker had the normal vertical back of the early Churchward tank engines, containing 3 tons of coal with a water tank underneath.

To help the loco negotiate sharp radius curves, required by its intended use on mineral traffic, the trailing drivers had extra side play, accommodated by a spherical joint in the coupling rods to give three dimensional movement.

4202-4261 followed in three lots between 1912 and 1917. They had top feed and a bunker extension at the top for additional coal capacity giving the classic GWR appearance. As was normal at this time, there were variations in the superheating arrangements. The next batch, 4262-85 in 1919/20, had 6-inch extensions to the frames and thus a 5ft 11in rear overhang for additional coal capacity. The water tank was lowered slightly to maintain the same volume.

4286-5204 (and 4200!) followed in 1921/23. They all had the 5ft 11in rear overhang but some of them were built with the original length frames and frame extensions and some with full length frames.

5205 class

Builder	GWR/Swindon
Dates Built	1923-1926
Number Built	60
Route Colour	Red
Power Class	E
Tractive Effort	33,000lbs
Driving Wheel Size	4ft 7½in
Cylinder Dimensions	19in x 30in

Wheelbase	8ft 9in+ 7ft + 6ft+7ft
Front Overhang	2ft 6in
Rear Overhang	5ft 11in
Boiler Class	Standard 4
Dates Withdrawn	1934-1936 (rebuilds to 7200) 1961-1965

5205-5214, in 1923, were treated as a separate sub class. They had outside steam pipes and cylinders taken out to 19in diameter from new. The framing was still, at this late date, straight, with the cover over the cylinders. Sources vary on whether these had the full length frames. 5215-74, which followed in two lots from 1924 to 1926, certainly did have full length frames with no extension for the bunker. They still retained the large unflanged motion bracket.

5275 class

Builder	GWR/Swindon
Dates Built	1930, 1940
Number Built	30 (see notes)
Route Colour	Red
Power Class	E
Tractive Effort	33,000lbs
Driving Wheel Size	4ft 7½in
Cylinder Dimensions	19in x 30in
Wheelbase	8ft 9in+ 7ft + 6ft+7ft
Front Overhang	2ft 6in
Rear Overhang	5ft 11in
Boiler Class	Standard 4
Dates Withdrawn	1934 (rebuilds to 7200) 1964-1965

In 1930, there was another small design change with 5275-94. A curved front end finally appeared, together with a raised section of footplate replacing the old cover plate. They also had the new style, smaller flanged motion bracket and sliding shutters over the cab windows – a feature apparently introduced from absorbed Welsh classes. They also had from new a recess in the top of the

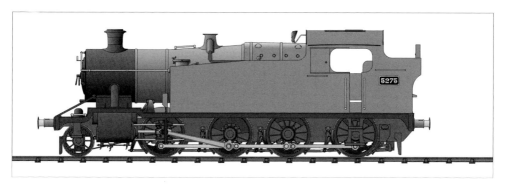

4200 (5275) class. *Diagram F. The 5275 and the second 5255 series were built to this configuration.*

bunker for the lamp. These engines ran only test mileage and were put straight in store from new, the depression having resulted in a dramatic reduction in minerals traffic in Wales. 5255-5294 were later converted to 7200s.

Finally, a new 5255-5264 were constructed in 1940 to the 5275 design: these were the only 2-8-0Ts built with curved frames to enter service.

The 42s were unaffected by any renumbering exercises per se, but the series 5255-5264 was used twice, once in 1926 for locomotives in the 5205 subclass, which were rebuilt as 7200 in 1935, and again for engines to the 5275 design in 1940.

Around 1919 the early engines started receiving the six inch bunker extensions that later engines were built with. Sliding cab shutters appeared on existing locomotives from 1931/6. A recess in the bunker for the lamp appeared slowly from the mid-1930s to about 1947.

From 1930 until 1943 earlier locomotives, when requiring new cylinders, received the 5205 type front ends with outside steam pipes and retained the straight framing. After 1940, at least some earlier engines received the 5275 curved frame front ends with new cylinders, including a few of the 5205s.

There were six diagrams, four concerned with superheating variations and one each for 5205 and 5275 specification.

As noted above, the original 5255-5294 were all withdrawn and converted to 7200s between 1934 and 1936. Fourteen locos between 4202 and 4245, not in any particular pattern or sequence, were withdrawn and converted to 7200 between 1937 and 1939. The rest all survived to British Railways.

Scrapping started in 1959, and the majority went in 1963 and 1964. Five 4200 have survived. Three of these have run in preservation, one is currently under restoration and the last is unrestored but conserved at Swindon Steam as an 'under maintenance' exhibit.

Three 5205 survived into preservation. Two have run, one each with curved and straight frames, whilst the last is acting as a spares donor to the GWS 4700 project, with current plans including conserving the major structure as an example of a 'Barry wreck'. None of the 5275 or 5255 series have survived as 2-8-0Ts, but two 5275s have survived as 7200s.

7200 class

Builder	GWR/Swindon
Dates rebuilt	1934 -1939
Number Built	54
Route Colour	Red
Power Class	E
Tractive Effort	33,000lbs
Driving Wheel Size	4ft 7½in
Cylinder Dimensions	19in x 30in
Wheelbase	8ft 9in+ 7ft + 6ft+7ft + 6ft 6in
Front Overhang	2ft 6in
Rear Overhang	3ft 6in
Boiler Class	Standard 4
Dates Withdrawn	1962-1965

As noted above, the 7200s were conversions of 4200 class locomotives. As a result, like the 4200s, there were three main sub groups.

The first twenty, 7200-19, were built in 1934 from new 5275s (5275-5294). Thus, they had curved front ends, raised footplate over the cylinders and small flanged motion brackets. An extension was bolted to the frames and a trailing radial axle added. The trailing axle was 6ft 6in behind the trailing driving

7200 class. *Diagram A. This is the first batch of 7200s, converted from the 5275 series.*

wheel, and there was a 3ft 6in overhang beyond this, so the bunker extension was 4ft 1in. This gave an extra 2 tons of coal and 700 gallons of water. The resulting 2,500 gallon capacity was enough to give them a reasonable range on the main lines and they were used to replace the old outside framed Aberdare 2-6-0 class.

7220-7239 followed in 1935/6. They were rebuilt from 5255-5274 of the 5205 sub class, which had been put in store when coal traffic declined. They retained the straight frames and large motion bracket of the 5205 series, but were otherwise similar to the first batch.

Finally, 7240-7253 were rebuilt from older 4200s. They received new 5275 style cylinders and curved front ends, but retained the large motion brackets. Although the bunkers were externally similar the capacities were adjusted and they carried 1 ton less coal and an extra 200 gallons of water. This selection of locomotives for rebuilds leads to the paradox that the first batch of 7200s built were the newest engines, and the last built were the oldest!

Modifications were few. Bunker recesses for the rear lamp were fitted to at least some and a few of the 7220 series received 5275 style front ends when new cylinders were required.

There were three diagrams, one for each of the three sub classes.

All survived to British Railways. The first couple went at the end of 1962, the majority in 1963/4 and a few in 1965.

Three have survived, but are yet to run in preservation. At the time of writing, two of the 7200 series are under active restoration and look likely to run in the foreseeable future, but the third, 7229, still with straight frames, is essentially in scrapyard condition.

Absorbed Classes at the Grouping
Vale of Neath 0-8-0T

Builders	Slaughter, Gruning & Co
Dates Built	1864
Number Built	2
Driving Wheel Size	4ft 6in
Dates Withdrawn	1871

Two outside cylinder 0-8-0T built by Slaughter, Gruning and Co in 1864, absorbed by the GW in 1865. They were possibly the first 8 coupled locomotives on a main line railway in the UK. They do not appear to have been very successful and were scrapped in 1871.

Barry class H 0-8-2T

Builders	Sharp, Stewart & Co
Dates Built	1896
Number Built	7
Route Colour	Blue
Power Class	D
Tractive Effort	27,000-28,000lbs
Driving Wheel Size	4ft 3in
Cylinder Dimensions	20in x 26in
Dates Withdrawn	1925-30

Seven 0-8-2 side tanks built by Sharp Stewart in 1896. The only recorded modifications in GWR hands were to safety valves and funnels. All were gone by 1930.

Port Talbot 0-8-2T

Builders	Cooke Locomotive Co
Dates Built	1899
Number Built	2
Route Colour	Red
Power Class	D
Tractive Effort	25,500-28,000lbs
Driving Wheel Size	4ft 4in
Cylinder Dimensions	19in x 24in
Dates Withdrawn	1928/9

Although not officially absorbed until 1922, the Port Talbot was taken over by the GW in 1908 and its locomotives added to GWR stock. These two 0-8-2 outside cylindered side tanks were built by the Cooke Locomotive Co in the USA in 1899. They had a taper boiler with the taper in front of the dome, much further forward and at a steeper angle than Churchward favoured, and bar frames as was normal in the USA. They were reboilered with custom designed boilers based on the Standard 4 in 1908. They lasted until 1928/9.

Port Talbot 0-8-2T

Builders	Sharp, Stewart & Co
Dates Built	1901
Number Built	3
Route Colour	Blue
Power Class	E
Tractive Effort	31,200
Driving Wheel Size	4ft 3in
Cylinder Dimensions	20in x 26in
Dates Withdrawn	1926, 1935, 1948

These Sharp Stewart engines were very similar to the Barry Railway H Class. They had various internal tweaks and smokebox doors before the grouping and received GWR style bunkers and smokeboxes. The three were withdrawn in 1926, 1935 and 1948 respectively.

Recreating the scene: *Preserved 8750 class pannier tank 3650 shunting below the coaling stage at Didcot Railway Centre.*

Appendix A – Factory Maintenance

This was an evolving process, and the way things were done in 1898 were very different to the methods of 1948. The cost of overhauls and the time out of service were very significant expenses for the railway. Collett, and his successive heads of Swindon Works R.A.G. Hannington and K.J. Cook, put great emphasis on both improving the efficiency of repairs and increasing the time between overhauls. In the nineteenth century a locomotive might spend three months in the works for a heavy general repair, but by 1947 it was down to a month.

A railway company factory was unusual in that it cared for its products from cradle to grave. The product did not simply go out of the door; it came back in again at regular intervals for repairs and major overhauls. Minor maintenance and repairs were done at the locomotive sheds; larger sheds had a lifting shop (as survives at Didcot), which had 35 or 50 ton hoists or overhead cranes to give them the ability to lift locomotives off their wheels for repairs. Scheduled maintenance ranged from boiler washing to examinations of the condition of boilers and pistons. Repairs would be anything the facilities permitted, sometimes fitting parts sent from the factory. The ideal was that the sheds would keep the locomotives running until sufficient wear and tear had accumulated for a major overhaul to be required. On the GWR, as well as the major factory at Swindon, there were factories at Wolverhampton and Caerphilly (ex Rhymney Railway) which would perform full repairs, but mostly on smaller locomotives and with some parts supplied from Swindon.

Most of the work undertaken at a works like Swindon was maintenance, not new building. By the late 1930s, a GWR standard locomotive was called in for a major (heavy general) overhaul approximately every 80,000 miles, and might be expected to run for as much as 2 million miles before it was eventually scrapped. A heavy general overhaul was a complete strip down to bare frames, and components were repaired or replaced to leave the locomotive in effectively as-new condition. The intention was that it should run another 80,000 miles without major attention. As maintenance and engineering practice improved Cook was able to introduce what was called an intermediate repair. This was one where an engine was in sufficiently good condition that attention to wearing components would enable it to run another 80,000 miles without completely stripping the locomotive down. A light overhaul was normally the resolution of a problem or failure that was too complex to be handled at the running shed, but did not involve significant scheduled maintenance of other components, and it was not reckoned to change the date of the next major repair. In addition to these there would also be locomotives undergoing repairs to accident damage.

The Chairman of the GWR Locomotive committee once commented that the head of the works must be an accountant and a statistician as well as an engineer, and certainly under Cook the shopping policy was very numerically based. When wars did not intervene, the policy was that as a loco approached the shopping interval, its condition was monitored and it was scheduled for a repair. As the manufacture of new cylinders or a major repair of a boiler would take much longer than the overhaul, the aim was that all large items that would be needed for a particular repair would be ready by the time they were needed, be it a refurbished boiler to exchange or new wheels or cylinders. The head of the works planned the shopping programme himself, using statistics gathered from the running sheds. The mileage run was the key statistic in estimating component wear, and the time since last overhaul the most useful figure for estimating boiler life.

Boiler condition was a key factor in overhauls. If all that was required was a new set of tubes, this could be done with the boiler in the frames, making it an intermediate overhaul. However, especially on tender engines, it was often quicker to simply install a refurbished boiler. By the end of the GWR, it is reckoned that they might have three boilers for every two locomotives over their life, although the actual number of spares held at any time was much lower.

The small 4700 class of nine locomotives, with a unique design of boiler, gives a good picture of how this was managed. The prototype was built with a Standard 1 boiler in 1919, then rebuilt with the new Standard 7 or class G boiler in 1921. Between 1921 and 1923, eight identical boilers were built, code GA. Two more GA boilers, of slightly differing superheater dimensions, were built in 1923/4. 4701-4705 were delivered January-April 1922, then 4706-4708 March-April 1923. So, there was a spare available from 1924 and the class then rotated the ten boilers around the nine class members. This required careful planning to make sure they did not end up without a refurbished spare when one was needed. In 1955, it was decided to build a new batch of boilers. Six more GA boilers were built from 1955-7, with another small change in superheater dimensions. The set of ten was completed with four more boilers, code GB, which had a distinctly different superheater design with fewer but larger elements.

Much work was done to improve the life of boilers. At one stage, boiler life had been reckoned at around 400,000 miles, but by 1939, with improvements resulting from top feed and the introduction of water softening plants where the water was most unsatisfactory, they were sometimes getting 400,000 miles between boiler lifts, and boilers running one million miles before replacement. In the case of the Standard 7 boilers above, boiler life was over thirty-three years – the last of the original boilers lasted until the early 1960s.

Appendix B - Boilers

Boiler Classes

The GWR boiler standardisation programme went beyond the numbered boilers of Churchward's standard classes, and enveloped earlier boiler designs. The number and variety of boiler types in use tended to reduce over the years and classes – both of boiler and locomotive – tended to merge. It's particularly evident in the 0-6-0 tank classes. Similarly, when the GWR inherited hundreds of locomotives at the grouping with hundreds of different boiler designs, they went through an exercise of reducing the number of designs in use. Paradoxically, this had the effect of greatly increasing the number of standard boiler designs. As has been noted above there were other occasions where there seems to have been no choice but to introduce a new boiler class.

There are two disparate boiler classification schemes that may be seen. In the RCTS volumes there is a system of two and three letter codes which covers firebox type, dome position and so on. This system is to be principally intended for discussing changes in the appearance of locomotives and is effective for this. By contrast the GWR classified boilers by major dimensions, and their scheme tells you rather less about what a boiler looked like, but much more about which locomotive classes it might potentially be fitted to. This system, originated under Churchward, used two letter codes for boilers. The first letter, as shown in the table, indicates the principle dimensions of the boiler. The second letter can be regarded as a subclass; in some cases there were twenty or more of these. Subclasses denoted significant design features like superheat (presence and degree), water feed location and firebox type as well as subtler things like minor variations in dimensions and the presence or absence of brackets to locate the boiler or water tanks. So, although all boilers of a specific class were nominally interchangeable, the subclass could influence exactly which locomotives a boiler could be fitted to without appreciable extra work. The boiler classes were given names as well as letters. The earlier names were usually that of the class the boiler was first used on, whereas the later ones were the well-known Standard 1, Standard 2 etc.

The Boiler Classes

Class	Name	Mainly Fitted to classes	Boiler Barrel				Firebox		Superheater	Total Heating Surface	Grate Area	Grate type	Smokebox Type	Notes
			Front Diameter	Rear Diameter	Length	Heating Surface	Length	Heating Surface	Heating Surface					
V	1393	1393, 1361, 1366	3ft 9in	3ft 10in	8ft 2in	816 sq ft	3ft 11in	75 sq ft	-	891 sq ft	10.7 sq ft	flat		
R	850	850	3ft 9in	3ft 10in	10ft 0in	905 sq ft	4ft 0in	76 sq ft	-	981 sq ft	11.1 sq ft	flat		1
S	517	517	3ft 9in	3ft 10in	10ft 0in	905 sq ft	4ft 6in	83 sq ft	-	988 sq ft	14.4 sq ft	flat		2
SS	4800	1400/5800	3ft 9in	3ft 10in	10ft 0in	870 sq ft	4ft 6in	83 sq ft	-	953 sq ft	12.8 sq ft	flat	drum	3
U	2021	2021, 3571, some 517	3ft 9in	3ft 10in	10ft 0in	905 sq ft	5ft 0in	90 sq ft	-	995 sq ft	14.7 sq ft	flat		4
Q	Standard 16	1600	3ft 9in	3ft 10in	10ft 1in	877 sq ft	5ft 0in	80 sq ft	-	957 sq ft	14.9 sq ft	sloping	drum	5
T	Metro	Metro, some 060T	4ft 2in	4ft 3in	10ft 6in	1125 sq ft	5ft 1in	101 sq ft	-	1226 sq ft	14.6 sq ft	flat		6
Q	Sir Daniel	Sir Daniel, River, some 060T	4ft 2in	4ft 3in	11ft 0in	1059 sq ft	5ft 4in	99 sq ft	-	1158 sq ft	15.6 sq ft	flat		7
L	Standard 11	various absorbed	4ft 2in	4ft 3in	10ft 6in	1008 sq ft	5ft 6in	82 sq ft	-	1090 sq ft	16.8 sq ft	sloping		8
F	Standard 21	54/64/74	4ft 2in	4ft 3in	10ft 6in	1004 sq ft	5ft 6in	82 sq ft	-	1086 sq ft	16.8 sq ft	sloping	drum	9
M	Bogie Single	30xx, 7,8,9,10	4ft 2in	4ft 3in	11ft 6in	1170 sq ft	6ft 4in	115 sq ft	-	1285 sq ft	20.8 sq ft	flat		10
E	Standard 5	4400, 4500, 3900, 4600	4ft 2in	4ft 9in	10ft 6in	993 sq ft	5ft 10in	94 sq ft	78 sq ft	1165 sq ft	16.6 sq ft	sloping	drum	
N	Duke	Duke, Barnum, Queen, Cobham, Dukedog 90xx	4ft 4in	4ft 5in	11ft 0in	1029 sq ft	5ft 10in	114 sq ft	81 sq ft	1224 sq ft	17.2 sq ft	flat		
P	2301	2301,3521, Large Pannier tank rebuilds	4ft 4in	4ft 5in	10ft 3in	961 sq ft	5ft 4in	106 sq ft	97 sq ft	1164 sq ft	15.5 sq ft	flat		11
P	2301	2301,3521, Large Pannier tank rebuilds, 57xx, 97xx	4ft 4in	4ft 5in	10ft 3in	1013 sq ft	5ft 4in	103 sq ft	-	1116 sq ft	15.3 sq ft	flat		12

Class	Name	Mainly Fitted to classes	Boiler Barrel				Firebox		Superheater	Total Heating Surface	Grate Area	Grate type	Smokebox Type	Notes
			Front Diameter	Rear Diameter	Length	Heating Surface	Length	Heating Surface	Heating Surface					
O	Standard Goods	Armstrong Goods, some Sir Daniel, some 060T	4ft 4in	4ft 5in	11ft 0in	1180 sq ft	5ft 4in	106 sq ft	-	1286 sq ft	15.5 sq ft	flat		13
W	Badminton	Badminton	4ft 4in	4ft 5in	11ft 0in	1175 sq ft	6ft 4in	122 sq ft	-	1297 sq ft	18.3 sq ft	flat		14
J	Standard 9	various absorbed	4ft 4in	4ft 5in	10ft 3in	961 sq ft	6ft 6in	104 sq ft	75 sq ft	1140 sq ft	19.7 sq ft	sloping		15
K	Standard 10	2251, 9400, 1500, numerous absorbed	4ft 5in	5ft 0in	10ft 3in	1070 sq ft	6ft 0in	102 sq ft	76 sq ft	1248 sq ft	17.4 sq ft	sloping	drum	16
B	Standard 2	Lighter 440s and 262T, 5600	4ft 5in	5ft 0in	11ft 0in	1145 sq ft	7ft 0in	122 sq ft	82 sq ft	1349 sq ft	20.4 sq ft	sloping	drum	
C	Standard 3	36xx, 3521, some absorbed	4ft 5in	5ft 0in	10ft 3in	1069 sq ft	7ft 0in	122 sq ft	76 sq ft	1267 sq ft	20.4 sq ft	sloping	drum	
Z	Standard 14	Manor	4ft 8in	5ft 3in	12ft 6in	1286 sq ft	8ft 8in	140 sq ft	190 sq ft	1616 sq ft	22.1 sq ft	sloping	drum	
D	Standard 4	Heavier 440s and 262T, 260s, 280T	4ft 11in	5ft 6in	11ft 0in	1349 sq ft	7ft 0 sq ft	129 sq ft	192 sq ft	1670 sq ft	20.6 sq ft	sloping	drum	
A	Standard 1	Most 8 wheel tender classes	4ft 11in	5ft 6in	14ft 10in	1687 sq ft	9ft 0in	155 sq ft	263 sq ft	2105 sq ft	27 sq ft	part sloping	drum	
O	Standard 15	County 4-6-0	5ft 0in	5ft 8in	12ft 7in	1545 sq ft	9ft 9in	169 sq ft	265 sq ft	1979 sq ft	28.8 sq ft	part sloping	drum	17
HA	Standard 8	4073 (Castle)	5ft 2in	5ft 9in	14ft 10in	1886 sq ft	10ft 0in	164 sq ft	263 sq ft	2313 sq ft	30.1 sq ft	part sloping	drum	18
HB	Standard 8	4073 (Castle)	5ft 2in	5ft 9in	14ft 10in	1856 sq ft	10ft 0in	163 sq ft	263 sq ft	2282 sq ft	29.4 sq ft	part sloping	drum	19
HC	Standard 8	4073 (Castle)	5ft 2in	5ft 9in	14ft 10in	1800 sq ft	10ft 0in	163 sq ft	313 sq ft	2276 sq ft	29.4 sq ft	part sloping	drum	20
HD	Standard 8	4073 (Castle)	5ft 2in	5ft 9in	14ft 10in	1670 sq ft	10ft 0in	163 sq ft	393 sq ft	2226 sq ft	29.4 sq ft	part sloping	drum	21
G	Standard 7	4700	5ft 6in	6ft 0in	14ft 10in	2062 sq ft	10ft 0in	170 sq ft	288 sq ft	2519 sq ft	30.3 sq ft	part sloping	drum	22

Class	Name	Mainly Fitted to classes	Boiler Barrel				Firebox		Superheater	Total Heating Surface	Grate Area	Grate type	Smokebox Type	Notes
			Front Diameter	Rear Diameter	Length	Heating Surface	Length	Heating Surface	Heating Surface					
W	Standard 12	King	5ft 6in	6ft 0in	16ft 0in	2008 sq ft	11ft 6in	194 sq ft	313 sq ft	2515 sq ft	34.3 sq ft	part sloping	drum	
F	Standard 6	Great Bear	5ft 6in	6ft 0in	23ft 0in	2597 sq ft	8ft 0in	159 sq ft	506 sq ft	3262 sq ft	41.8 sq ft	part sloping	drum	23

Notes

1 Extinct by end of 1950s.
2 Extinct by 1950s.
3 Modernised S class.
4 Extinct by end of 1950s.
5 Modernised U class. Code reused.
6 Extinct by 1950s
7 Somewhat interchangeable with O. Extinct by 1940s.
8 Modified T class for absorbed locos.
9 Modernised Standard 11.
10 Extinct by 1915.
11 Superheated.
12 Unsuperheated.
13 Extinct by 1940s. Somewhat interchangeable with the Q (Sir Daniel).
14 Extinct by 1913.
15 Modified P class.
16 Shortened Standard 3, originally for absorbed classes
17 Developed from LMS 8F boiler.
18 14 large tubes, 201 small tubes, 84 s/h elements in 2 rows (6 elements per large tube).
19 14 large tubes, 201 small tubes, 84 s/h elements in 2 rows.
20 21 large tubes, 170 small tubes, 84 s/h elements in 3 rows (4 elements per large tube).
21 28 large tubes, 138 small tubes, 112 elements (4 elements per large tube).
22 Used only on a class of 9 locomotives, but considered for use in several design proposals.
23 Extinct 1924.

This table needs to be read with *considerable* caution. In particular, the heating surfaces varied appreciably over the years. Boilers which were outwardly of the same dimensions and interchangeable were not all arranged in the same way internally. There were very great differences. Superheated boilers would have much lower heating surface area in the tubes than saturated boilers, because the superheater elements were installed in large tubes – flue tubes – each of which replaced a number of small tubes. There was a tendency for the size of superheaters to be reduced with shorter elements which reduced the heating surface of the superheater, but also reduced heat damage to the vulnerable ends of the elements.

To give an idea of this, the table includes the dimensions of the four main subtypes of the Standard 8, fitted only to the Castle class. Even within those there were variations; for all of them, superheater size was later varied.

The first batches of Castle boilers, HA, and HB were built with 84 elements in two rows of seven large tubes and a superheater heating surface of 262.62sq ft. The heating surface of these was later reduced to 253.38sq ft by reducing the length of the elements. HC was the three row increased superheat boiler, which came out from 1946, still, according to my edition of RCTS, with 84 elements, but distributed between twenty-one tubes, so four elements per tube. This design started off with 313sq ft. of surface, later reduced to 302 and then 295 by shortening the elements. Lastly, HD was the high superheat four row boiler, having 112 elements in twenty-eight large tubes. These started with 393.2sq ft, but were later reduced to 380.5sq ft.

Similarly, Standard 1 boilers were built first with 166 small tubes, fourteen large tubes (two rows) and eighty-four superheater elements (six per large tube), then 176 small tubes and eighty-four elements. Next were 176 small tubes and 112 element boilers, still with fourteen large tubes (eight elements per tube) and after building a substantial number of these they went back to six elements per tube. Finally, from 1944, three row Standard 1 boilers had twenty-one large tubes, only 145 small tubes, and eighty-four superheater elements (four per large tube).

Boiler Families
The standard boilers were not only standard in themselves, but there were also distinct families with various dimensions in common.

Taper boilers
Standard 1/2 Family
The Standard 1 was the boiler for Churchward's new 10 wheeled locomotives. The Standard 4 is a short version of the Standard 1, with both a shorter firebox and barrel. The Standard 2 has a very similar firebox to the Standard 4, but a smaller diameter barrel of the same length. The Standard 3 was a Standard 2 with a shorter barrel, but the same firebox dimensions, and finally the Standard 10 was based on the Standard 3, but with a shorter firebox.

Standard 6 Family
The Great Bear's 'Standard 6' boiler, although unique, was the foundation of another family of boilers – or at least the flanging blocks were. The Standard 7 (4700) had the same diameters as the Standard 6 (Great Bear), but with a conventional narrow firebox and much shorter barrel. The Standard 8 (Castle) was originally a Standard 7 with a

smaller diameter barrel although there were some changes to the firebox dimensions later. The Standard 12 (King) is effectively a Standard 7 with lengthened barrel and firebox.

The Standard 5, as used on the small prairies, had no derivatives, nor did the Standard 14 used on the Manors. As mentioned, the Standard 15 boiler on the Counties was a derivative of an LMS type.

Parallel boilers
Metro family
The T class was a moderately small boiler which originated on Metro tank engines. It was then used quite widely on lighter six wheeled classes. The Standard 11 was a T class boiler with a longer firebox, and a Standard 21 is a Standard 11 with a drum style smokebox.

Sir Daniel family
The Sir Daniel and Standard Goods boilers were similar enough that they were often used on the same classes; they also varied somewhat in diameter earlier in the nineteenth century. The Sir Daniel was a little smaller.

Dean Goods family
Class P boilers were normally domed parallel boilers and were used on larger pannier tank classes as well as the Dean Goods.

The N class boiler was the same diameter as the P with longer barrel and firebox. The Standard 9 was a P class boiler with a longer firebox. Class N boilers had round top fireboxes at first. Early Belpaire boilers had fireboxes raised a few inches above the barrel and a number of these were domeless. Otherwise, these boilers always carried large domes. The later boilers all had Belpaire boxes with the top of the barrel and the top of the firebox level. They started out at about 150psi, moving through 165 to 180psi at the end, and were later superheated.

U family
The Standard 16 is basically a U class boiler with a drum style smokebox. R, V and S class boilers were the same diameter as the U class but with different firebox and in the case of the V also different barrel lengths. The SS boiler is basically an S class boiler but with a drum style smokebox.

Others
The class W boiler used on Badmintons in their early years was a precursor of the Standard 2, of similar overall dimensions, but with a shorter firebox. They all had Belpaire fireboxes – the first to be used by the GWR – and came in both domed and domeless configurations. The Class M used on the Dean Singles was a special dictated by the requirements of the class.

Appendix C - Locomotive Numbering

The GWR locomotive numbering scheme in the twentieth century can be rather confusing. This summary is based mainly on the information in RCTS. At its peak in the 1930s, the GWR owned something over 3,600 locomotives, but of course had owned many more over the course of its history, and numbers were often reused, sometimes several times. No. 111, for instance, had been used on an 1863 built 2-4-0, *The Great Bear*, and then on the same locomotive rebuilt as a Castle, Viscount Churchill. This was not exceptional; 937 was held by three locomotives in 1923!

It is, I think, a mistake to think of each successive numbering scheme replacing the ones before, as with the wholesale renumberings which had to be done by some of the other grouping companies. The numbering is more like a palimpsest; where writing material has been reused, but the old is still visible underneath. Although locomotives and even classes were renumbered from time to time this tended to be avoided, so older locomotives still in existence were normally numbered according to the scheme in use when they were built.

Broad Gauge

GWR Locomotives built purely for the broad gauge did not have numbers. On the other hand, the 'convertibles' were given numbers from the standard gauge series and never names, although some of them, notably the Dean Singles, gained names once the Broad Gauge was gone and they were running on the narrower gauge.

Absorbed broad gauge engines were also treated slightly differently - they might keep their names, but they were numbered in the standard gauge series.

Narrow Gauge

All numbered GWR steam locomotives were numbered in the same series, whatever the gauge. Steam railmotors, diesel railcars and petrol and diesel engined locomotives were all numbered in different series. Narrow gauge in a nineteenth century GWR context includes standard gauge and the GWR standard gauge locomotives were numbered from the start. The limited number of sub 4ft gauge locomotives the GWR possessed on lines like the Corris and Vale of Rheidol were also numbered in the same series.

Three successive numbering schemes can be identified. These might be called:

- The sequential system, used for new and newly acquired locomotives from the early days up to about 1875.
- The Dean block system, used for new and absorbed locomotives between 1875 and 1912.
- The Churchward class system, used from 1912 on.

The Sequential System
This covered numbers from 1 to approximately 1300. Locomotives allocated numbers in this scheme continued in use right up until the 1930s and sometimes later. Once the Dean block system was in use, numbers within this range, especially those below 200, were often re-used for prototype and experimental locomotives. After the Churchward class system was adopted, this practice seems to have ceased. Numbers within this series were then reused for absorbed locomotives as covered below.

As the GWR started to acquire and build standard gauge locomotives from the 1850s, they were numbered sequentially, more or less in order. In general, when a locomotive was scrapped its replacement was given the same number. Although it suited the accountants, this was not the easiest of systems to manage, as soon became clear! Practicality dictated that the replacements had to be ordered and even built before the original was out of use and if number 110 had some worthwhile life left when its replacement was complete, the replacement was temporarily numbered 110A. There was also a fair bit of renumbering happening at that time, again, it seems, mainly to suit the needs of the accountants.

An example of the complexities this introduced is lot 26 of the Armstrong Goods (388) class 0-6-0s, constructed at Swindon in 1870/71. They were numbered, in order of construction, 657-676 (classified as expansion of the fleet), then 24, 31, 48, 51, 52, 116, 298, 300, 415 and 416 (classified as replacements for earlier locomotives).

The first change, around 1866, was that numbers above 1000 were allocated for replacement engines, but this soon became difficult to run too; it was even further complicated as the GWR was expanding its fleet with locomotives from the many smaller lines they were taking over in the 1860s and '70s.

The Dean Block System
The first block scheme was under Dean, and started around 1875. It was developed over the succeeding years and can be summarised as:

Under 1300	sequential system, prototypes and experimental
1301-1400	absorbed standard gauge
1401-1500	passenger tanks (e.g. 517, Metro)
1501-2000	0-6-0 tanks
2001-2200	absorbed broad gauge and 'convertibles' (vacated in 1892 of course)
2201-2300	passenger tender
2301-3000	goods tender (but 2701-2800 were later used for more 0-6-0 tanks)
3001-3200	singles
3201-3500	passenger 4 coupled

By the early years of the twentieth century this had expanded to include

2161-2200	2-6-2T
2901-3000	2 cylinder 4-6-0 (from the freight series)
3101-3200	small wheeled 2-6-2T (from the singles range)
3701-3900	more passenger 4 coupled
3901-4000	medium size 2-6-2T
4001-4100	4 cylinder 4-6-0
4101-4200	yet more passenger 4 coupled
4201-4300	heavy freight tanks
4301-4400	outside cylinder 2-6-0

Within these blocks, numbers were allocated as batches of locomotives were built; there was no any attempt to keep classes together. It looks as if the next available block of numbers was allocated when a batch (lot in GWR parlance) of locomotives were ordered from the works. Thus, for example, the later 4-4-0s were built and numbered in this order.

Numbers	Class	Lot	Date
3252-3253	Duke	97	1895
3254-3261	Duke	101	1895
3262-3272	Duke	102	1895
3272-3291	Duke	105	1896
3292-3311	Badminton	109	1897/9
3312-3331	Duke	113	1898/9
3332-3351	Bulldog	118	1899/1900
3352	Bulldog	120	1899
3353-3372	Bulldog	124	1900
3373-3392	Atbara	125	1900
3393-3412	Atbara	126	1901
3413-3432	Bulldog	137	1902/3
3433-3442	City	141	1903
3443-3452	Bulldog	142	1903
3453-3472	Bulldog	148	1904
3473-3482	County	149	1904
3701-3715	Bulldog	162	1906
3716-3730	Bulldog	163	1906
3801-3820	County	165	1906

4101-4120	Flower	176	1908
3731-3745	Bird	177	1909/10
3821-3030	County	184	1911/12

The 4-4-0 allocations became even more confusing because, during their lives, some individual locomotives were rebuilt with completely different designs of boilers, which effectively swapped them to a different class. Sometimes this was done with a block – 3400-3409 had a spell with No 4 boilers to make them equivalent to Cities for instance, but other times it was less logical. The twenty Dukes rebuilt as Bulldogs, for instance, were scattered at random through the Duke series. It's notable that classes usually started at xx01, rather than xx00.

The Churchward Class Scheme

There was a big renumbering involving 365 locomotives in 1912, which led to the familiar GWR system, where the second digit refers to class and/or wheel arrangement, with classes numbered from 00, not 01. Classes were kept in logical groups wherever possible and rarely split within 100 unit blocks. A new sub class, on the other hand, would be numbered consecutively, so the 4575 sub class followed on from the last 45xx, 4574. This leads to the interesting conclusion that, numbers wise, the Castles were considered as being simply further Stars, albeit a new sub class, rather than a new class.

Where Dean series allocations could be extended into the new scheme they were – the 2885 class being extended into the 3800 series when the 3800 4-4-0s were extinct is one example. Churchward classes starting at 4000 fitted both schemes, because numbers starting at 5000 were unused. Collett followed and built on the Churchward scheme as he did with many of Churchward's innovations; with the passing of the years, classes in the sequential and Dean series tended to become extinct or lost in minor renumberings so ranges below 4000 started to be re-used.

When locomotives were rebuilt and effectively changed class after 1912, the numbers were normally changed. Bulldogs from the 3300 and 3400 ranges were numbered from 3200 when converted to Dukedogs for instance, the low 3200s being vacant by then. Other examples include the 7200s and various varieties of large wheel 2-6-2T.

However, there was still a sequential element in the blocks allocated to new classes. We see that the 4400s and 4500s were allocated the next blocks after the 4300s in the 1923 renumbering, and 4600, which never became a class, was allocated the next block after that in 1913. In 1919, 4700 followed. Thereafter, though, allocating sequential series for new styles of locomotives became a bit more difficult. 4900 for the Halls in 1928 was probably an extension of the Saint series of 2900. 4800 was used for the new 0-4-2s in 1932. 5600 in 1924 seems odd. Presumably 5000 was reserved for future Castles. 5100 was free, but maybe more 2-6-2s were in hand, 5200 was used for 280T from 1923, and 5300 was already in use for 43s. By this time, it was surely clear that no more 44s were going to be built, but 5400 was not used until 1930. The 5600s did have a sort of family resemblance to the 3600 2-4-2T, so perhaps that was the thinking. 57s came along in 1929. From there the gaps were getting sparse, and the 68 slot for the Granges was probably a matter of running out of alternatives!

	Below 4000	Above 4000
x0xx	0-6-0T, Absorbed 2-8-0 etc.	4 Cylinder 4-6-0
x1xx	Absorbed various, Large Wheel 2-6-2T etc.	Large Wheel 2-6-2T
x2xx	2-4-0, 4-4-0, 4-4-0T, 0-6-0 etc.	8 Coupled Tanks
x3xx	6 Coupled Goods, 4-4-0 etc.	2-6-0 Mixed Traffic
x4xx	6 Coupled Goods, 4-4-0, 0-6-0PT etc.	Various 6 Coupled Passenger Tanks
x5xx	0-6-0T, 6 Coupled Goods etc.	Small Wheel 2-6-2T
x6xx	0-6-0T, 2-6-0 Goods, 2-4-2T etc.	6 Coupled Tanks
x7xx	4-4-0, 0-6-0PT etc.	8 Coupled MT, 6 Coupled Tanks
x8xx	0-6-0T, 8 Coupled Goods, 4-4-0 etc.	4 Coupled Tanks, 2 Cylinder 4-6-0 with 5'8 wheels
x9xx	0-6-0T, 2 Cylinder 4-6-0, 2-6-2T etc.	2 Cylinder 4-6-0

On the whole, this scheme is well enough understood not to need much elaboration here. These examples should suffice to show the scheme, its exceptions and the relationship with the Dean system.

x6xx – mainly 6 coupled tanks			
Range	Class	Date Range Allocated	Date Range Vacated
1600-1660	1076 class	1879	1946
1661-1699	1661 class	1886	1934
1600-1669	1600 class	1949	1966
2600-2699	Aberdare 2-6-0	1900	1949
3600-3630	3600 2-4-2T	1902	1934
3600-3699	8750 class	1938	1964
4600	4600 (one only)	1913	1925
4600-4699	8750 class	1941	1964
5600-5699	5600 0-6-2Ts	1924	1965
6600-6699	5600 0-6-2Ts	1927	1965
76xx and 86xx	Never used		
9600-9682	8750 class.	1945	1964

x7xx – mainly 0-6-0 Tanks			
Range	Class	Date Range Allocated	Date Range Vacated
1700-1799	1854 class	1891	1951
2701-2720	655 class	1896	1950
2721-2799	2721 class	1897	1950
3700-3719	City class 4-4-0s	1912 (renumbered)	1931
3700-3799	8750 class	1936	1964
4700-4799	Mixed Traffic 2-8-0	1919/23	1965
5700-5799	5700 class.	1929	1964
6700-6749	5700 steam brake only	1930	1964
6750-6779	8750 steam brake only	1947	1964
7700-7799	5700 class.	1930	1964
8700-8749	5700 class.	1930	1964
8750-8799	8750 class.	1933	1964
9700-9710	8750 with condensing gear.	1933	1964
9711-9799	8750 class.	1934	1964

x9xx - 2 Cylinder 4-6-0s			
Range	Class	Date Range Allocated	Date Range Vacated
1900-1999	1 x 1854 class (1900) 99 x 1901 class	1881	1958
2900-2998	Saint class.	1902	1953
3901- 3920	Dean Goods converted to 2-6-2Ts	1907	1934
3900-3904	Oil burning Halls from 49xx series	1947	1950
3950-3955	Oil burning Halls from 59xx and 69xx series	1946	1950
4900-4999	Hall class.	1928	1965
5900-5999	Hall class.	1931	1965
6900-6958	Hall class.	1940	1965

x9xx - 2 Cylinder 4-6-0s			
Range	Class	Date Range Allocated	Date Range Vacated
6959-6999	Modified Halls 1944/49	1944	1965
7900-7929	Modified Halls 1949/50	1949	1965
8900	Never used: presumably reserved for Hall replacements?		
9900	Originally planned for the County class		

The Absorbed Engines
The GWR acquired locomotives from companies it took over right through its life and there were blocks of numbers allocated for these, but at the grouping some seven hundred locomotives, few in uniform classes of any size, came into stock.

The grouping was not a single event. The major companies were theoretically absorbed on 1 January 1922, but their stock was not added to the GWR list until August. Three smaller lines were absorbed in August 1922, more in January and July 1923, and finally Powlesland and Mason in January 1924.

So, the first set of numbers were for the January 1922 stock and a numbering scheme was worked out for them between January and August. There was no attempt to put these into the Churchward scheme and there was insufficient room for all of them in the 1301-1400 series for absorbed engines, so they were fitted into spare numbers under 1390.

Locomotives from the lines absorbed in August 1922 were given numbers from those available under 2199. These included numbers that had previously been allocated to locomotives in the January batch and which had already been withdrawn. In the 1923 and 1924 absorptions the process of allocating spare numbers under 2199 was repeated, and many of these were newly spare as previous holders had been scrapped in the meantime. This meant that some numbers were allocated to several locomotives in quite short order – 937, for example, was allocated to three engines in 1923.

The basis of the numbering was that locomotives were sorted by wheel arrangement and then, by and large, and with exceptions, by company, but that the actual class was less important. From there they were mainly arranged by boiler pressure and then by original number.

The boiler pressure of an individual locomotive was an important factor in where in the series it was placed – more so than the class the builder had allocated. Boiler pressure has a major impact on the performance of the locomotive so this seems logical, until you consider that it is really something of a moveable feast. If an engine is given a new boiler, the working pressure may well change, most especially if it is given a completely new type of boiler, as happened with many of the absorbed classes. To make matters even more complicated, a small number of locomotives were numbered completely out of sequence from the rest of their class because they were running with a significantly lower pressure than their sisters. However in some cases this low working pressure was not because the boiler was constructed differently, but because it was not considered safe at its normal working pressure. The GWR never countenanced such practices and all such were repaired or reboilered at the first opportunity, rendering the place in the sequence quite meaningless. On the other hand, locomotive class was never as rigid a definition as might be expected. Older locomotives could have gone through several iterations of rebuilding and reboilering, with variations in cylinders, boiler size and boiler pressure, so in operational terms two locomotives of a different class might be more or less interchangeable in service, and two that were nominally the same class have rather different characteristics.

So the basics were –

0-4-4	under 30
0-6-2T	30-603
0-6-0T	604-843
0-6-0	844-1013
4-4-0	1014-1128
4-4-0T	1129-1184
2-4-0T	1189-1198
2-6-2T	1199-1213
4-4-2	1301-1306
2-4-2T	1307-1327
2-4-0	1328-1336
0-4-0T	1338-1343
0-6-4T	1344-1357
0-8-2T	1358-1386
0-8-0	1387-1390

But added to this were a fair number of later additions and one or two omissions which were shoehorned in where possible.

The 1946 renumbering
There was a significant renumbering in 1946, when some ranges previously used for older locomotives were vacated to make room for the abortive oil burning conversions and for blocks of new construction. The 48xx class 0-4-2T was renumbered into the 1400 series, which had, appropriately, previously been occupied by 517 and Metro class locomotives, now withdrawn, which they had replaced. The Dukedogs and the remaining Dukes were moved to the 90xx series, which cleared out the 32xx series for more 2251 class. At the same time, various surviving absorbed engines from the grouping were renumbered within the under 1300 range to bring similar classes together. As noted the original allocations were somewhat fragmented and the creeping program of reboilering with GWR boilers had effectively merged sub classes which had previously been considered separate.

British Railways
The two classes built solely under British Railways, the 1500 and 1600 pannier tank classes, reused ranges in the Dean scheme for 0-6-0 tanks, albeit as Churchward style ranges for each class: 1501 and 1601 had been Armstrong 0-6-0T classes which were by now extinct.

Appendix D - Diagrams and Lots

Locomotive Diagrams

Another of Churchward's innovations was to introduce a system of diagrams for locomotives. Each significant design change – new boiler, redesign or whatever, was recorded on a weights diagram with significant dimensions. Such drawings are the basis for many of the sketches in this volume. The description would contain details like:

- Cylinder size
- Boiler dimensions
- Firebox dimensions
- Number and size of boiler tubes
- Heating surface
- Firebox grate area
- Wheel sizes
- Water Capacity
- Boiler pressure
- Tractive effort
- Minimum curve radius

The coding scheme for locomotive diagrams had a separate series for each wheel arrangement, so all 4-4-0s were in one series, all 0-6-0Ts in another and so on. They started at A and continued, if necessary, to Z. Past Z the series started again at A1, and in the case of 0-6-0 tanks it was A1-A114, then B1-B81. The change from A114 to B1 was made when there was a big influx of 0-6-0 locomotives after the grouping. A selection of diagram lists is included below here to give a picture.

4-2-2	A-F	Dean Singles	Which gives an idea of the amount of change these went through in their short lifespan!
4-6-0	A-Z, A1-A26	Saints, Stars, Halls, Granges, Manors, Kings, 36, Kruger 2601	As an example of how these were issued there were 13 diagrams for 4-6-0 Saints, but of these 9 were for individual locomotives: 98, 171, 100 (twice), three early superheater installations, Saint Martin as a Hall, and Caynham Court's poppet valve installation.
4-6-2	A-C	*The Great Bear*	So three changes that were considered significant enough for a new diagram in the lifespan of this engine.
2-8-0	A-S	28xx, 47xx, RODs, WD and USA classes	But strangely there was no diagram for the batch of Stanier 8Fs built during the war.
0-6-0T	A-Z, A1-A114, B1-B81	Any number of classes and sub classes!	Endless variety of these - the 1076 Buffalo class had 9 diagrams over the years for example, and the 2021 class 11. But there were also a lot of small classes taken over at the grouping. Diagram B76, for example, was for the two ex WCPLR ex LBSCR Terriers.
0-6-2T	A-Z, A1-A44	Many absorbed classes, plus the 56xx	Only one diagram was ever issued for the 56xx: quite a contrast with the variations of the Dean singles for instance. The large number of diagrams gives an idea of the variety inherited at the grouping. Each absorbed class was allocated at least one diagram representing the condition of the class as absorbed. Then new diagrams were issued whenever there was a significant change – a rebuild with a GWR boilers being one of the most common.

Lot Numbers

Locomotives were typically ordered in batches which were called lots. A lot would normally consist of locomotives of the same class and built to the same detailed design, but there were exceptions. GWR official drawings usually listed the appropriate lot number(s), and the whole subject is covered in detail in the RCTS volumes. The detailed policy of how the lots were classified changed over the years, but it is worth mentioning that before Churchward renewed and purchased locomotives were generally not allocated to lots, but after Churchward they were. Swindon and Wolverhampton maintained different sequences of lot numbers.

Another thing to remember is that these locomotives were not mass produced. This was batch production, and the lots represented the batches. And even standardisation had its limits. Major parts were fundamentally interchangeable, and many small parts were completely standardised, but the precise location of fittings could and did change from lot to lot and even locomotive to locomotive.

Appendix E – Expansion and Absorption

Absorbed Lines and Locomotives

In the best modern style, the GWR expanded principally by acquisition, and in equally modern style some acquisitions were termed mergers.

The Foundation

The majority of GWR standard gauge locomotives existing before 1864 were built for the various standard gauge lines that were amalgamated into the GWR and formed the Northern division, which was to be run from Wolverhampton. These included the Shrewsbury and Chester; Shrewsbury and Birmingham; Birkenhead Railway; West Midland Railway; Oxford, Worcester and Wolverhampton; Newport, Abergavenny and Hereford; Shrewsbury and Hereford; and Leominster and Kington Lines.

The locomotives that came with these lines were of disparate design and sometimes dubious capability and there were few that could really be described as members of classes. A major part of Armstrong's work in the early days was maintaining and repairing and rebuilding these locomotives, standardising components where practical.

Nineteenth century Acquisitions

The first significant expansion was a set of Welsh lines, the Vale of Neath; Llanelly Railway and Dock Co; and the Llynvi and Ogmore. None of these had very large or significant locomotive fleets and had tended to buy their locomotives in twos and threes. The next group were mainly West of England lines, principally broad gauge. Among the more significant ones were:

Monmouthshire Railway

The Monmouthshire Railway and Canal Company was a sizable concern. The GWR worked their services from 1875, when they had fifty-three locomotives and took it over in 1880. Their locomotives had been very much bought in twos and threes and few survived very long with the GWR.

Bristol and Exeter Railway

The Bristol and Exeter was taken over in 1876. It was, of course, a very substantial concern, but was mainly a broad gauge line, which had twenty-eight standard gauge locomotives (and two of 3ft gauge).

South Devon Railway
The South Devon was entirely a broad gauge line.

Cornwall Minerals Railway
This line was unique amongst absorbed lines, maybe unique amongst British railway lines, in that it had a stud of eighteen almost identical locomotives and no others.

The Grouping
The engines absorbed in the grouping are a very complex subject in themselves. Being the stock of around a dozen different and often fiercely independent companies, there is even more variation than there was amongst the western stock. The small companies especially tended to order the stock in twos and threes and any class that made it into double figures was something of a rarity.

The Western did a lot of work on the absorbed stock. There was a significant cull and then a lot of changes. Swindon was in general not impressed with the way absorbed lines had maintained their stock (the Rhymney being a significant exception), and even after the initial winnowing out many of the remainder disappeared quickly, or were rebuilt with GWR standard boilers.

The really radical transformations Swindon had sometimes performed in the past were absent. Side tank locomotives kept side tanks, and wheel arrangements and motion were unchanged. Even saddle tank locomotives, especially the smaller ones, tended to keep saddle tanks until their demise and only a minority gained pannier tanks. The most universal change was GWR-style direct loaded safety valves in place of 'pop' or Ramsbottom types. Cabs were often replaced with a GWR style enclosed cab, quite a few receiving GWR style enlarged bunkers.

Some GWR built locomotives returned after being sold away, and were reintegrated with their sisters, gaining the usual updates and resuming their old numbers.

Alexandra (Newport and South Wales) Docks and Railway
Their locomotive policy could, with little unfairness, be caricatured as 'when you need a locomotive buy whatever's available on the second hand market'. They did, however, in 1905, standardise their whistles by buying twenty-nine new ones to the design used by the Caledonian Railway. One of the few times they achieved much standardisation beyond the whistle was when the Mersey line converted to electricity and they acquired 7 2-6-2T and three rather odd 0-6-4T.

Barry Railway
The Barry Railway was a very late line, not starting operations until 1889. Its first locomotive superintendent, J.H. Hosgood, must have been a man of vision and clear planning, because few other lines ever managed such wide ranging standardisation. Although there were a good number of classes of different locomotives for different roles, the vast majority used a common boiler and other features, although these did receive updates over time. The boiler especially received changes in construction and increases in working pressure over the years, which affected operation sufficiently for some classes to be divided into subclasses.

The Barry Railway locomotives do not seem to have been considered to be in good condition at the time of the grouping, and the line, which was particularly independently minded, was notoriously antagonistic to the amalgamation.

Brecon & Merthyr Tydfil Junction Railway

The B&M was a medium sized line as the Welsh railways went, with nearly fifty locomotives at the grouping. The company was a conglomerate of various small lines and at one stage had consisted of two unconnected halves. It included a seven-mile continuous bank. The line was entirely dependent on externally built locomotives, often using designs originated for other lines.

Burry Port and Gwendraeth Valley Railway.

The BPGVR was a small line with a fleet of fifteen miscellaneous 0-6-0 tanks, all with inclined outside cylinders. Very unusually for an absorbed line, all but one worked for over twenty years with the GWR.

Cambrian Railways

The Cambrian was quite a different system to the intensely worked Welsh valley lines with their heavy mineral trains worked over short distances. In terms of track mileage, it was much the largest of the Welsh lines, but had fewer locomotives than the Barry, Rhymney or Taff Vale lines. It was formed from at least a dozen earlier lines, and included two narrow gauge sections, which are still operational. The locomotive stud consisted mainly of tender engines, mostly 0-6-0 goods and 4-4-0 passenger.

Cardiff Railway

As one of the smaller lines, with just thirty-six locomotives, there were few large classes from the Cardiff Railway, but their policy was more consistent than some lines.

Cleobury Mortimer & Ditton Priors Light Railway

A short line in Shropshire which commenced operations in 1908. They only ever had two locomotives, a pair of standard industrial types.

Gwendraeth Valley Railway

Before the grouping, the GWR treated this small line more as a large industrial siding than a significant railway. They had two locomotives at the grouping, but only one really reached the GWR at that time, the other, which coincidentally had previously been owned by the GWR, had already been sold.

Llanelly and Mynydd Mawr Railway

Another short line with a long name, the L&MMR opened in 1883 on the track bed of an 1802 tramway which had been abandoned. The line never managed to get to a financial state where it could buy its own locomotives and it was worked by the contractors who built the line, John Waddell and Sons. They seem to have tended to use what locomotives were available, so there was never a rational locomotive policy. They had a fairly random collection of small industrial types. However, as often happened with small locomotives from backwater lines, some of them had long lives with the GWR and beyond.

Midland and South Western Junction Railway
The MSWJR was a long distance secondary line, effectively running from Cheltenham to Southampton. Quite different to the majority of Welsh lines, its main stock was in medium sized tender engines, and it had no 0-6-2Ts!

Neath and Brecon Railway
The Neath and Brecon was another of the South Wales lines. There were complications in their history related to the Swansea Vale railway, over which they operated through trains to Swansea from Brecon. That line was taken over by the Midland Railway and there were various arrangements by which the Midland worked the traffic all the way from Swansea to Brecon rather than the Neath & Brecon working those trains themselves. The ending or continuation of these arrangements at various dates had a big effect on how many locomotives the N&B needed, and on occasion they found themselves with too many or too few locomotives. By about 1908, most heavy maintenance on the line's locomotives was being done by the GWR at Swindon.

Port Talbot Railway
The Port Talbot Railway was incorporated in 1894 and taken over by the GWR in 1908, so only had a short life with its own locomotive policy. Its locomotives were added to the GWR books at the takeover, but they seem to have been treated as an independent group until 1922 – indeed few of the locos taken over worked away from the line. The locos were not renumbered until the grouping. The line had a variety of locomotives from various sources.

Rhondda and Swansea Bay Railway
Opened from 1885-90, this was another late line. Like the Port Talbot it was taken over by the GWR in 1906, and run as something of a separate concern until the grouping. GWR locomotives allocated to the R&SB had been renumbered. There were quite a number of these, mainly 633, 1813, 1854 and 1076 class 0-6-0ST and PT, but there were also some 45xx allocated for a few years before the First World War.

Rhymney Railway
Even though it only had fifty-one miles of route, the RR was a substantial company with 123 locomotives at the grouping. They had fairly recently (1901) built a fine new works at Caerphilly, where their locomotives were, as the GWR acknowledged, well maintained. This was to become a significant GWR repair works; enlarged in 1926, it was, with Swindon, Newton Abbot and Wolverhampton, one of the main GWR repair and rebuild centres after the grouping.

South Wales Mineral Railway
This was an early small line which had been built to the broad gauge, opened in 1861 and just under thirteen miles in length. It was leased to and run by the Glyncorrwg Coal Co. It included a steep incline which was cable worked, but which went out of use by 1910. Like the Port Talbot, it was taken over by the GWR in 1908, but treated as a nominally independent concern until 1922. After 1908, it was worked as if it were part of the Port Talbot system.

Swansea Harbour Trust & Powlesland and Mason
There had been various concerns providing dock shunters at Swansea Harbour in the nineteenth and early twentieth century, but by the time of the grouping all were owned by either the Swansea Harbour Trust or Powlesland and Mason. The SHT had a couple of inside cylinder 0-6-0ST, but otherwise the entire stock of both concerns consisted of small outside cylinder 0-4-0ST from a considerable variety of manufacturers.

Taff Vale Railway
The Taff Vale was the largest, oldest and normally the most prosperous of the South Wales lines with a number of significant classes, mostly 0-6-0T and 0-6-2T. Various sources suggest that in the immediate run up to the grouping the Taff Vale had ceased to maintain their locomotive stud as well as they might.

Locomotive Stock and Route Mileage at the Grouping

Company	Route Milage	Locomotive Stock
Great Western Railway	3,005	3148
Barry Railway	68	148
Cambrian Railways (Cambrian)	295	99
Cardiff Railway	12	36
Rhymney Railway	51	123
Taff Vale Railway	125	274
Alexandra (Newport and South Wales) Docks and Railway	11	39
Brecon and Merthyr Railway	60	47
Burry Port and Gwendraeth Valley Railway	21	15
Cleobury Mortimer and Ditton Priors Light Railway	12	2
Llanelly and Mynydd Mawr Railway	13	8
Midland and South Western Junction Railway	63	29
Neath and Brecon	40	15
Port Talbot Railway and Docks (PTR&D)	35	22
Rhondda and Swansea Bay Railway	29	37

Appendix F – Some Puzzles, Criticisms and Controversies

This appendix covers some topics which seem to justify a fuller treatment than is appropriate for the main body of the document, and for which the regular sources are contradictory or unclear.

Star Class Valve Gear

As has been noted, the prototype Star, no 40, had an ingenious valve gear system in which the movement ordinarily provided by eccentrics was instead obtained from the opposite valve gear. It did this with complex curved levers which permitted the cross connections to pass each other without contact. The way these overlapping levers crossed each other reminded the staff of a pair of scissors, and it was known as the scissors gear.

The gear was not repeated on the production Stars, and there are a number of published explanations for this design change.

The 'official' GWR explanation for the design change in the production Stars is that it was because a failure in the valve gear rendered the locomotive completely inoperable. With the later arrangement one side could be disabled so the engine could limp off the road with two cylinders. This explanation occurs in various documents from Swindon staff, and a special bracket was provided to make it easier to implement.

Another long standing one is that RM Deeley, Locomotive Superintendant of the Midland railway, claimed that the gear breached a patent of his.

A third story, for which '*Great Western Locomotive design – A Critical Appreciation.*' by the Rev J C Gibson isseems to be the only source, is that the gear was impractical to maintain because it took ten days or more to set the valves accurately.

Fourthly a contemporary student of valve gear, Don Ashton, considers that the final Walschaerts arrangement simply produced a better implementation.

Four cylinder locomotives on other lines did not have the 'limp home on 2 cylinders' bracket, instead requiring the crew to improvise an equivalent arrangement with wood packing and rope. It seems odd to include this arrangement for a relatively rare contingency. On the other hand, in a paper written by and read by W.H. Pearce, Churchward's valve gear specialist, '*Favourable Points in Four Cylinder Design*

Locomotives.', at the Swindon Engineering Society, Pearce puts some emphasis on this feature, and it also came up in the discussion after the paper was read, which does suggest it was a significant concern, and crews on all lines were instructed in how to deal with the need to disable the valve gear on one side of the locomotive.

Gibson claims that he was told by the Swindon valve setting chargeman, whilst working for him, that the scissors gear took days to set correctly. This tale of valve setting is to my knowledge unsubstantiated from any other sources, and Gibson has a number of these stories of Swindon design errors and cover-ups, some more credible than others.

The patent story seems unlikely: other cross connected valve gears had been created before Deeley's and the GWR design, by Pearce, was very different (and superior) in detail. In the discussion on Cook's Paper '*The late G.J. Churchward's locomotive development on the Great Western Railway*', K J Cook, Journal of the Institution of Locomotive Engineers, Journal 214 Cook said '*Regarding the Deeley gear, he thought the 'North Star' was first. Deeley published the gear shortly afterwards. There was correspondence between Swindon and Derby, with the result that acknowledgment was made that Swindon was entitled to use the gear.*'

On this page http://www.donashton.co.uk/html/more_cylinders.html the author, Don Ashton, a deep student of valve gear design, considers that it was not possible to achieve truly even valve timing with a scissors gear. I have corresponded with Mr Ashton, and he considers that valve setting on the scissors gear is likely to have been time consuming.

As for the truth: well, like much else it will remain shrouded in history, but none of these explanations are mutually exclusive: they may well have all been factors in the decision.

The more I study this topic the more uncertain I am about drawing conclusions. In the paper mentioned above Pearce mentions No 40, but has little to say on the differences between the valve gear and that used on the production engines other than the limp home feature. On the other hand Churchward set a high priority on even valve timing, and Ashton, with the benefit of modern computer simulation, considers Pearce's implementations of Stephenson's gear on the 2 cylinder locomotives to have been exceptional and his 4 cylinder Walschaerts' arrangement superior to the majority of other railway's designs. Holcroft, who had a keen interest in valve gear, doesn't mention valve timing in his books, but does mention that there was talk in the Swindon Office about Deeley writing to complain about the patent. The decision would have been made at about the time Holcroft joined the Swindon drawing office as a junior. It may be he never heard the reason for the design change or considered it too technical for his audience. When the time came to design the Kings, as Ashton relates, there were further improvements in the detail implementation of Pearce's design, so this was obviously a continuing pre-occupation in the Swindon drawing office.

The geometry – and thus design - of locomotive valve gear is an extremely complex topic: too much to cover here. Mr Ashton's web site is recommended for those interested. Much of the complication is a result of the subtleties of converting rotary motion to and from linear motion with cranks. A single example will suffice. Consider a piston, connecting rod and driving wheel. Start with the piston at front dead centre – when the piston is at the most forward point of its travel and a single straight line can be drawn between piston rod, connecting rod and axle. If you rotate the wheel through 90 degrees the piston will have travelled just a little more than half way through its travel. The amount of extra movement will depends on the proportions of the connecting rod and the wheel crank. This matters in a steam engine because steam is admitted on both sides of the piston and ideally the timing of the valve opening and closing would be identical on both sides. W.H. Pearce had a very deep understanding of this most technical of aspects of steam locomotive design, and produced quite exceptional work.

My thanks to Don Ashton for casting his expert eye over an early version of this note. Mistakes and misunderstandings are my own.

The Great Bear

The first mystery around No 111 is why it was built at all, and it seems likely this will never be satisfactorily resolved. Some writers claim that it was built chiefly at the board's behest as a status project, and Churchward didn't care for it much, others quite the reverse. There doesn't seem to be very much evidence to draw conclusions from.

Its perhaps more interesting to speculate on why the locomotive was not a great success. The problem is considered to have been that the boiler didn't steam satisfactorily when worked hard.

The basic boiler dimensions - unusually long tubes and a wide firebox - and later superheater design changes have been covered above. It has been stated that the 'Bear' had lower steam temperature than most other GWR standard classes, which suggests that by the time the exhaust reached the end of the very long boiler tubes the superheated steam was heating the exhaust rather than the reverse. So although the superheater had a large surface area - initially larger than that on the Gresley A1 Pacifics – it seems possible that much of the area was doing very little.

Holcroft, who was involved in designing the cylinders for '*The Great Bear*', states that much effort was put into the boiler design, but that Churchward vetoed any idea of a combustion chamber because so much trouble had been experienced with those on the Kruger class.

The 47XX boiler, the Standard 7, which was often regarded as one of the very best of the standard boilers, had diameters in common with the '*Bear's* boiler but was otherwise very different. The Standard 7 barrel was the same length as a Standard 1, 14ft 10in, and the 10ft firebox was a foot longer than the No1, so the relative proportions were more conventional. The King boiler, too was of the same external diameters, but with a yet larger firebox and a 16ft barrel. Again, with hindsight, it seems as if '*The Great Bear*' should have had a shorter - King sized - barrel and a combustion chamber added to the firebox. Take that and replace the Star front end with the larger King front end, and the result approximates to a Stanier Pacific. All in all the boiler seems wrong in proportion, and it's hard to avoid the conclusion that Collett's Castle conversion was the best thing to do with the locomotive.

Intermediate Tenders

There is a problem with understanding the production of what are generally called 'intermediate' tenders. Different writers have come to different conclusions, and the surviving records are fragmentary and contradictory. The intermediate label is applied to well tank tenders which have either or both the high sided type fenders and Lot A112 style scalloped frames.

The tender records file makes it clear that only Lot A112 was constructed with the scalloped frame type. However there is photographic evidence showing such frames on a 3,000 gallon tender. No 3,000 gallon tenders were built between 1903 and 1940, so these frames must be a factory replacement when repairing the tender. It is feasible that other sets of scalloped frames were constructed to repair other older tenders, so not all tenders with the scalloped type frames were from Lot A112. There is also photographic evidence of a different style of scalloped frame which was not fitted to any new tenders, so this too must have been a factory replacement.

The fitting of high tender sides is even more difficult to establish. There are notes on the tender records file that states that Lot A112 was built with high sides and that they were originally fitted to Stars and Castles. This note was clearly made some years after the tenders were produced. On the other hand the general arrangement drawing for Lot 112 shows low sides, and the one surviving tender from this lot is now fitted with low sides, which may well not be original. There is also photographic evidence from the 1920s and 1930s showing high sides on some tenders fitted with the earlier type frames.

In the writer's opinion, little can be said with certainty beyond noting that Swindon was building scalloped tender frames and turning out tenders with high sides in the early to mid 1920s. In spite of the drawings it seems probable that all tenders of lot A112 were built with high sides, but it also seems very likely that some earlier tenders were built with them. One would look especially at lot A111, which is noted as "For Lot 223 10 4cyl Engines". The high sided tender was aesthetically a better match for the 4 cylinder locomotive cabs than the low sided tenders, so one may speculate they were intended for Stars and Castles, but when the Castle class was equipped with new 4,000 gallon flush tank tenders the high sided 3,500 gallon tenders were cascaded around the rest of the locomotive fleet.

The 5600 Class – Design Issues?

The background to the 5600 class is straightforward. The GWR had acquired a lot of lines in Wales. The standard locomotive for those lines was the inside cylinder 0-6-2 tank. The GWR, profoundly unimpressed with many of the umpteen dozen different classes they had acquired – and probably even more unimpressed with the fact that there were umpteen dozen classes – decided to build some new ones, using as much standard hardware as possible. It sounds straightforward.

But there are a number of tales about the 5600 class. They seem to revolve around Collett's supposed incompetence as a locomotive designer. A senior executive like Collett would not have spent much time sitting at a drawing board, and his team would have been basically that formed by Churchward. It was some years after the great days of the main standard development, and, while some of Churchward's brightest young men had departed for pastures new, the drawing office staff must have been predominantly the people responsible for the Castle and the 47xx, two of the very best GWR locomotives. What might have been a factor was that the drawing office staff were working flat out. There was a big maintenance deficit dating back to the war and they had to deal with the grouping; hundreds of completely different locomotives with little common in design all requiring design work to standardise boilers and other equipment.

The first set of tales are about problems with the valve gear. In Cook's '*Swindon Steam 1921-1951*' Cook states that some of the early engines quickly developed an uneven beat, and had to have the valve gear reset, which he puts down to stresses working out in the cylinder castings. By contrast in 'Great Western Locomotive design – A Critical Appreciation', Gibson tells a much more dramatic story, claiming that when the first locomotive was steamed the valve gear failed completely because a crucial supporting structure had been completely missed from the design. The valve gear on the 5600 was a new design, incorporating some of the layout improvements introduced with the outside cylinder standard classes. It seems unlikely that Churchward's team would have missed something so basic so maybe the story, which Gibson had second hand, grew in the telling.

The other set of tales are about problems caused by the long wheelbase – the fixed wheelbase was greater than the Stars and Castles. This was published in the newsletter of the North London Society of Model Engineers by a Mr Peter Kearon, who was an apprentice in the 1940s at the GWR's Barry works, which had been the Barry Railway's main workshops before the grouping. He had the tale partly from his colleagues, and partly from Eric Mountford, the railway historian. To cut a considerable tale short, he reported that the 56s experienced great trouble with overheating axleboxes in their early days, and that the problem had to be resolved by considerably increasing the lateral movement available to the wheels. It's striking that many of the Rhymney engines had a horizontally pivoting joint in the coupling rods in addition to the usual one permitting vertical movement, which would allow for extra lateral movement, a feature only found on 8 coupled GWR designed locomotives and the 1813 class 0-6-0 tanks.

All these tales might have been exaggerated in the beginning and grown with the years. The staff of the Welsh lines probably didn't appreciate a new and distant management being imposed on them. In '*Master Builders of Steam*', H A V Bulleid wrote, '*Almost all the small railways in the Welsh valleys had stories about how their locos were replaced by G.W.R. locos which couldn't do the job, but these, progressively funnier as one travelled from Newport towards Swansea, were apocryphal.*'

The 9400 Class – why was it built?
There has been much criticism of the decision to build the 9400, and especially to order so many of them, even from GWR sources. According to Cook, the GWR General Manager Sir James Milne felt that the large domes on the 5700/8750 looked rather old fashioned. The writer believes that the large dome story is just an amusing anecdote that has been exaggerated, and that Cook used it as being a good tale to put in his book and that it was not a serious design input. To consider why a class was built, it is best to start by considering what it was intended to replace, and what else was being built at that time. When the external 9400 class orders were authorised in December 1947, there were enough 8750s and 7400s (all with domes!) on order to replace the last of the larger pre group GWR 0-6-0PTs; the 1600s (also with domes) would replace the smaller ones. The 57s themselves had many years of life left. Therefore the 94s cannot have been intended as an 8750 replacement/alternative so they must have been intended to replace other locomotives. The order for the class was officially described as 'in anticipation of future condemnations'. There were around 200 absorbed 0-6-0T and 0-6-2T tanks surviving at the end of the war, all of which were due to be withdrawn over the period that the 200 9400 class deliveries were scheduled.

Another point to consider is that, unlike the 5700s, the GWR-built 9400s were superheated, which had been abandoned for the pre-grouping 0-6-0Ts not many years before.

The GWR 'kit of parts', as it existed by the mid 1940s, included both parallel boilers, by now were all rather low pitched with large domes, and tapered boilers, higher pitched and without domes. There was no room in the loading gauge for a large dome on the taper boilers and the firebox corners were a quite satisfactory location for steam collection. If a larger boiler than the P class was required on a pannier tank, then the Standard 10 without dome was the only suitable existing design.

All these features suggest that passenger work was a big part of the intended role of the 9400s, whereas the wide cab and superheating made the class less well adapted for heavy shunting. This is confirmed by a statement in RCTS that the 9400s were originally intended to supersede the absorbed 0-6-2Ts. So the evidence strongly suggests that the 9400s were intended as a cheaper alternative to building more 5600s, as the bigger boiler and extra weight over the 5700s gave them steaming and braking capability close to the larger 0-6-2Ts and rather greater than the 5700s. Against this, though, are contemporary descriptions of the class as shunting locomotives.

Further Reading

Key Volumes
DAVIES, FK, WHITE, DE and others *The Locomotives of the Great Western Railway*, The Railway Travel and Correspondence Society, Long out of print, and much traded, this is an essential reference for the serious student of the subject.

Part 1 - Preliminary Survey, 1951
Part 2 - Broad Gauge, 1953
Part 3 - Absorbed Engines 1854-1921, 1956
Part 4 - Six-wheeled Tender Engines, 1956
Part 5 - Six coupled Tank Engines, 1958
Part 6 - Four coupled Tank Engines, 1959
Part 7 - Dean's Larger Tender Engines, 1954
Part 8 - Modern Passenger classes, 1953, 1960
Part 9 - Standard Two-cylinder classes, 1962
Part 10 - Absorbed Engines 1922-1947, 1966
Part 11 - Rail Motor Vehicles and Internal Combustion Locomotives, 1952, 1956
Part 12 - A Chronological and Statistical Survey, 1974
Part 13 – Preservation and Supplementary Information, 1983

RUSSELL, JH, *Pictorial Record of Great Western Engines*, Oxford Publishing Co, in 3 coffee table sized volumes, much more recently in print.
A Pictorial Record of Great Western Engines Vol. 1 Gooch Armstrong and Dean, 1999
A Pictorial Record of Great Western Engines Vol. 2 Churchward Collett and Hawksworth, 1999
A Pictorial Record of Great Western Absorbed Engines, 1978
COOK, KJ, *Swindon Steam 1921-1951*, Ian Allan Ltd, 1974, Ken Cook trained on the GWR and rose to be head of the works under Collett and Hawksworth. He was the man responsible for converting the designs to metal and keeping them running. Under British Railways he succeeded Hawksworth and occupied Churchward's chair as Mechanical and Electrical Engineer of the Western Region and later Gresley's chair as Mechanical and Electrical Engineer of the Eastern and North Eastern Regions.

HOLCROFT, H, *An Outline of Great Western Locomotive Practice*, Ian Allan Ltd, 1971, Harry Holcroft was one of Churchward's 'Bright young men' who converted Churchward's ideas – and his own – onto paper for the workshops to build. He was to go on to have senior roles at the Southern Railway under Maunsell and Bulleid.

Useful

AHRONS, EL, *The British Steam Railway Locomotive 1825-1925*, Ian Allan Ltd, 1969. A technical volume covering the development of British built locomotives both in Great Britain and abroad. Ernest L Ahrons was a former pupil of Dean at Swindon. He worked in the engineering industry until after the Great War when, in his 50s, he became a full time writer. His line drawings are widely reproduced, and have been vital as sources for the sketches of nineteenth century locomotives in this work.

COOK, KJ, *The Late G. J. Churchward's Locomotive Development on the Great Western Railway,* Journal of the Institution of Locomotive Engineers Paper 492, 1950. The original audience for this paper was other locomotive engineers. I'm quite sure it was studied by the authors of the RCTS series and numerous other writers: the contents are very often familiar. It has been reprinted, but is probably best read as part of the proceedings, as at least some of the reprints don't include the discussion after the paper, which includes comments from the likes of Holcroft, W H Stanier and E.S. Cox, which are valuable in themselves. The proceedings are available electronically as part of the Institute of Mechanical Engineers archive, but they are not cheap.

COPSEY, John et al, *The Great Western Railway Journal,* Wild Swan Publications, 1992 onwards. A very wide range of GWR topics. Some issues contain reproductions of GWR general arrangement drawings which were used as references for some of the sketches.

DURRANT, AE, *Swindon Apprentice,* Runpast Publishing, 1989, A E Durrant was a premium apprentice at Swindon, joining the GWR after WW2, and was employed in the Swindon Drawing Office during the 1950s. His book has much to say about the final developments of GWR design. He was a considerable steam locomotive enthusiast and the book contains much about off-duty travels around Britain and Europe locomotive spotting, and also much on the vast locomotives he believed that BR should have been building instead of the standard classes!

HOLCROFT, H, *The Armstrongs of the Great Western,* Railway World Ltd, 1953. An odd work in some respects, being a family biography than a technical work, but it's well written and contains useful material. In particular it contains a good number of E.L. Ahrons drawings which were used as references for some of the earlier classes.

NOCK, OS, *The GWR Stars Castles and Kings omnibus edition,* David and Charles, 1981 edition

Interesting

AHRONS, EL, *Locomotive and Train Working in the Latter Part of the 19th Century Volume Four,* W. Heffer and Sons, 1953, This book consists of articles written for the Railway Magazine, in the case of the GWR section in 1915/16. Insight into how the locomotives were used, but not much that is very relevant to this work. Ahrons was an excellent writer however, and the book contains a number of amusing anecdotes. The description of the Great Western Railway Bath Bun as 'met the specification of a close-grained chilled material, with an ultimate tensile strength of about 10 tons per square inch' stuck in my mind! That would, I think, be a contemporary specification for a good quality cast iron...

GIBBS, Ken, *Swindon Works Apprentice in Steam,* Oxford Publishing Co, 1986, Gibbs was an apprentice from 1944 to 1951. His book covers much the same ground as the first half of Durrant's, but stops at the end of his Works apprenticeship. There is much more detail on Swindon works working practices, but very little insight into design.

NOCK, OS, *The Great Western Railway in the 19th Century,* Ian Allan, 1971

NOCK, OS, *The Great Western Railway in the 20th Century,* Ian Allan, 1971, The very prolific Nock isn't always highly regarded, but these seem to be considered among his better volumes and are a worthwhile basic history.

NUTTY, EJ, *GWR Two Cylinder Piston Valve Steam Locomotives,* privately published, 1977, Another Swindon drawing office man, Ernie Nutty's volume is a strictly practical work intended for those maintaining and operating GWR locomotives in preservation.

POLE, Sir Felix, *His Book,* Town & Country Press Edition, 1968. As one would expect, primarily a book about the business, not the engineering.

SUMMERS, LA, *Swindon Steam – A New Light on GWR Loco development,* Amberley, 2013, Les Summers is a historian and teacher from a GWR family who is deeply involved in the Great Western Society and writes well. This volume is principally an assemblage of articles on disparate topics.

Treat with Caution

FREEZER, CJ, *Locomotives in Outline – GWR,* Peco Publications, 1977. Older model railway enthusiasts will need little introduction to Mr Freezer, who was a key figure in the hobby for many years. Both he and I were starting with the GWR weights diagrams, supplemented by additional detail. He's not immune from error and there are a number of drawings which seem to me to be less accurate than one might hope. As examples brake gear is sometimes at odds with contemporary photographs and his 9400 pannier tank drawing scales 10 inches too short according to my eyes. I hope I don't have too many similar errors: I caught some horrors at the proof stage.

GASSON, Harold, *Firing Days; Footplate Days; Nostalgic Days; Signalling Days,* OPC, 1973-1981, Gasson tells a good story, but as a Didcot fireman and signalman wasn't deeply involved in the engineering side. There's also evidence, not least in at least one of the book introductions, that not every tale that he tells in the first person actually happened to him. There's an interesting insight too in reading Gasson's books alongside Barlow's 'Didcot Engineman'. Both men came from Didcot families, and were contemporaries, but beyond senior men - foreman etc. - remarkably few names are mentioned in both books.

GIBSON AKC, The Rev JC, *Great Western Locomotive design – A Critical Appreciation.,* David and Charles, 1984, Gibson was an apprentice at the MSWJR and moved to Swindon after that railway was absorbed at the grouping. He was undoubtedly there and had the overalls. Nevertheless there are occasions where I consider the facts do not support his conclusions, and I suspect he has a bit of a weakness for a good controversial story.

TUPLIN, WA, *Great Western Power,* Allen & Unwin, 1975

TUPLIN, WA, *Great Western Steam,* Allen & Unwin, 1965, Tuplin was a professional engineer, who spent 30 years in industry with the notable company of David Brown of Huddersfield, and then finished his career in academia as professor of Applied Mechanics at Sheffield University. He was a great enthusiast for steam power, but was never a locomotive engineer. His theories and conclusions about the steam locomotive are sometimes highly controversial. In particular one may note his belief in the desirability of low boiler pressure. He also had theories, which he held were mathematically based, on the efficiencies of locomotives at different speeds. He went so far as to present a paper to the Institution of Locomotive Engineers, recorded in their Journal Volume 43 (1953). However some aspects of this paper were pretty sharply criticised by the likes of Holcroft and Ell. It seems wise to have a considerable pinch of salt available when reading Tuplin. See also an extended criticism at http://www.steamindex.com/library/tuplin.htm. There are those who suspect that some of his footplate tales owe as much to imagination as accurate reporting.

Armstrong Whitworth built 5600 Class *6697 at Didcot Railway Centre.*

Index of Illustrations

Index of Classes